Cultural Competence in Substance Abuse Prevention

Cultural Competence in Substance Abuse Prevention

Edited by Joanne Philleo
and Frances Larry Brisbane

Leonard G. Epstein, Managing Editor

NASW PRESS

National Association of Social Workers
Washington, DC

Jay J. Cayner, ACSW, LISW, *President*
Josephine Nieves, MSW, PhD, *Executive Director*

Linde Beebe, *Executive Editor*
Nancy A. Winchester, *Editorial Services Director*
Patricia D. Wolf, Wolf Publications, Inc., *Project Manager*
Marcia A. Metzgar, Wolf Publications, Inc., *Copyeditor*
Beth Gyorgy, Shenandoah Publications, Inc., *Proofreader*
Cynthia Hargett, Wolf Publications, Inc., *Proofreader*
Bernice Eisen, *Indexer*

Library of Congress Catalog Card Number
97-65987

Printed in the United States of America

Contents

v

Foreword

This publication is a product of the collaboration between the Center for Substance Abuse Prevention (CSAP) of the Substance Abuse and Mental Health Services Administration (SAMHSA), the National Association of Social Workers (NASW), the Council on Social Work Education (CSWE), the National Association of Deans and Directors (NADD), and the National Association of Baccalaureate Progam Directors (NABPD).

An objective of this collaboration was to broaden the substance abuse content in social work training to include issues of cultural diversity and cultural competency. Effective social workers acknowledge and incorporate the culture of the people they serve. Culture shapes how people experience their world, interpret their environment, live with their families, choose their lifestyle, work, play, and reside in their community. Culture is a vital factor in how people respond to social work services and preventive interventions. Social workers working in and serving culturally diverse communities must understand the cultures of the communities that they are serving and must design and manage culturally competent programs that reflect these cultures. Culturally competent social workers collaborate with culturally knowledgeable community members at every phase of program operation—design, implementation, and evaluation. Administrators, providers, staff, and clients work to enhance program integrity and clarify communication. The result is strong and sound interventions, leading to improved outcomes.

The original CSAP monograph fostered the prevention and intervention approaches to alcohol and other drug abuse within a culturally specific and multicultural context. Cultural competency comprises an essential set of skills for all social work students, practitioners, and educators to master and strengthen during the conclusion of this century and the beginning of the next. With this charge, the NASW Press is reissuing *Cultural Competence for Social Workers* as *Cultural Competence in Substance Abuse Prevention*.

As a result of a growing federal recognition of the importance of cultural competency, CSAP has joined with the Bureau of Primary Health Care (BPHC) of the Health Resources and Services Administration (HRSA) and the Office of Minority Health (OMH) of the Department of Health and Human Services (DHHS) to expand this publication series to include broader issues of health services and primary health care.

The NASW Press would like to acknowledge the editors, Joanne Philleo, MSW, a training and development consultant, and Frances Larry Brisbane, PhD, of the School of Social Welfare at SUNY–Stony Brook; managing editor of the Cultural Competence Series, Leonard G. Epstein, MSW, of the Bureau of Primary Health Care; and the editorial staff that made the original publication possible.

Jeanne C. Marsh
Dean
School of Social Service Administration
University of Chicago

Leonard G. Epstein
Senior Coordinator for Cultural Competency Initiatives
Health Resources and Services Administration
Bureau of Primary Health Care
Office of Minority and Women's Health
Bethesda, Maryland

Foreword to the Original Work

This fourth publication in CSAP's Cultural Competence Series presents the results of a highly productive partnership with the National Association of Social Workers (NASW), the Council on Social Work Education (CSWE), the National Association of Deans and Directors, and the National Association of Baccalaureate Program Directors. Without the strong commitment of these four partners, this monograph would never have attained the excellence that exemplifies the work of the social work professional.

This volume is one result of a CSAP–NASW–CSWE project that expands the substance abuse content in social work training, with particular emphasis on prevention and preventive services. This project brings new knowledge and insight to the preparation of social workers at both the bachelor's and master's levels, as well as to the continuing education of practitioners. The curriculum expands exposure to substance abuse prevention categories and also addresses the crucial issue of cultural diversity and cultural competency.

We believe that one of the important parts of the Social Work BSW/MSW Curriculum Enhancement Project is its recognition of the nature and complexity of social work and the need for additional information on the impact of culture on the prevention of alcohol and other drug abuse.

We commend the NASW Curriculum Enhancement Task Force, which demonstrated clarity of purpose and direction and created a forum for authors that allowed free expression while maintaining the highest academic standards.

We also acknowledge the authors of this historic curriculum. CSAP and NASW deeply appreciate their exceptional work and contributions. They reflect well on the profession's ability to anticipate and respond to the needs of the diverse populations we serve.

CSAP's Cultural Competence Series has as its primary goal the scientific advancement of practice and evaluation methodologies designed specifically for alcohol, tobacco, and other drug (ATOD) abuse problem prevention approaches within the multicultural context of U.S. community settings. The various multicultural communities that make up the United States comprise a rich and diverse ethnic heritage. The Cultural Competence Series is dedicated to exploring and understanding this heritage and its important role in the development of ATOD problem prevention programs.

CSAP, NASW, and CSWE are pleased to have participated in this creative collaboration.

Elaine M. Johnson, PhD, Director
Center for Substance Abuse Prevention

Introduction to the Original Work

As the 21st century approaches, cultural competence, like computer literacy, is a necessity. To be considered a competent professional, social workers must know more than the universal harm alcohol and other drugs (AOD) can exact on the human body. Unless prevention messages and treatment modalities are provided within a cultural context, professionals are unlikely to change attitudes or redirect behaviors.

With the new wave of immigrants and the growing assertion of cultural identity of second- and third-generation immigrant groups, a new communication edict of cultural dialogue is part of the professional mandate. Therefore, the ability to interact with people who are culturally different from the professional is a prerequisite to providing culturally competent services to these groups.

The authors of this book demonstrate that in the changing typology of American cultures, many languages, customs, rituals, beliefs, and values are constantly being added to the national landscape. At the same time, AOD problems call for cultural solutions with prevention and intervention approaches that are guided by cultural norms and individual uniqueness. Gaining the ability to do this is not easy, but professionals can learn from a growing body of knowledge. This book advances AOD professionals toward becoming culturally competent. It further demonstrates how to integrate cultural competency in the AOD abuse curriculum.

Five major cultural groups—American Indians, Hispanics/Latinos, African Americans, Asian Americans, and Pacific Islanders—have received thought-provoking, culturally sensitive treatment in this book, and the chapter on gay and lesbian people deals with sexual diversity in a cultural context.

With the concerted media focus on crack cocaine, cocaine, marijuana, heroin, and "designer" drugs, it is not unrealistic to believe alcohol use and abuse is a minor problem. Paling by comparison to the media and law enforcement preoccupation with other drugs, alcohol nonetheless continues to be the primary drug of abuse and is among the top in use and abuse among all the cultural groups. Because of alcohol prevalence among American Indians, the authors of the chapter on American Indians have confined their treatment of the subject to alcohol. They note that "although other drugs are plentiful among Indian people, alcohol remains the drug of choice." Likewise, Holmes and Hodge discuss the prominence of alcohol as a social lubricant for many gay and lesbian people. Gray discusses alcohol and other drugs among African Americans. Using the various social movements, she traces how drugs, particularly alcohol, were used in precolonial Africa during slavery and abolition and after emancipation and the civil rights movement.

To become competent to work with gay men and lesbians, Holmes and Hodge say we must recognize that no single homosexual community exists. Instead, gay communities are as diverse as the people found in any society. Gay men and lesbians come from different races, ethnic backgrounds, ages, economic and social classes, cultural identities, political persuasions, and religions.

In discussing the extent of the problem, the authors remind us that because of the pervasiveness of homophobia in our society, gay men and lesbians have not been exempt from having homophobic feelings. They describe this form of internalized homophobia as self-hatred, leading to the creation of alternative environments such as bars. Thus, the use and abuse of alcohol among these people bears some relationship to the prominence of bars in their social life.

Holmes and Hodge recommend prevention strategies that will address and hopefully eliminate religion-based homophobia and suggest ways current laws could be changed to enhance the acceptance of same-gender relationships. They believe that heterosexist attitudes and assumptions have produced research results about AOD abuse that have ignored or not been helpful to gay people. This, of course, needs to be changed. This chapter describes what the research should address in studying gay men and lesbians and AOD abuse.

Gray points to the importance of African Americans' belief in the supernatural, which most authors indicate is a belief among other groups. Religion is a protective factor against heavy drinking among some African American women who are frequent churchgoers.

Gray describes characteristics of African Americans such as their respect for "hunches" and the belief in spirit forces as ways to solve problems. She states that spontaneity is viewed as a strength because it indicates African Americans can quickly adapt to different situations.

Because of the history of racism and its affect on many African Americans, Gray suggests that primary prevention programs should include interventions that build racial consciousness and self-determination. She believes that racism has been experienced by every African American and this fact should help shape the response to AOD abuse among this population. AOD abuse curriculum in prevention, according to Gray, should include components that build self-esteem. The curriculum should connect individuals with their African origins, rather than beginning with slave origins in the United States. Gray advises that the way African Americans view alcohol use and abuse—often different from the indicators suggested by mainstream research data—will determine whether they seek treatment.

Delgado reminds us that God and other metaphysical forces, including spirits, tend to influence the Hispanic/Latino perception of problems. Their perception of abuse of alcohol and other drugs as a problem is closely linked to their religious and spiritual belief system. Hispanics/Latinos are most likely to seek help with their problems, Delgado points out, from their natural support systems. These systems include their families, botanical (herb) shops, and community grocers, where they receive assistance with crisis counseling, child care, and nutrition. Delgado believes that within the formal helping system, cultural competence can be more easily achieved when the workers and clients are from the same cultural background.

In citing sources in the literature, Delgado found the etiology of AOD abuse among Hispanics/Latinos attributable to stress, familial discord or disruption, and peer pressure. In addressing the causes of AOD abuse, Delgado reminds us that educational campaigns usually will not reach a universal Hispanic/Latino audience and should be targeted to specific Latino groups. He recommended four distinct groups to whom educational campaigns should be marketed. Also listed in the chapter are five questions to guide an evaluation of treatment outcomes for this cultural group.

In his discussion of Asian Americans, Kuramoto instructs us to include the immediate family in the treatment plan when working with Southeast Asian groups (Vietnamese, Cambodians, Lao) because the whole family accepts the shame and guilt that is incurred by individual family members. Kuramoto further explains the benefit of individual counseling over group counseling when working with at-risk Asian cultural groups. Among Koreans, men are considered high risk because they view drinking and smoking as a sign of masculinity. According to Kuramoto, it is often easier to help this group (and other Asian groups) in individual therapy. Korean culture emphasizes not "losing face," which would happen in group therapy or problem-focused group sessions.

A health focus—the health risks involved in abusive drinking and other drug use—is suggested when working with Japanese people because they are extremely health conscious. Approaches in prevention and treatment are suggested when working with other Asian and Pacific Islander populations. In every case, Kuramoto emphasizes the need to relate to these groups in their own language.

The Asian population in the United States comes from 20 countries, and Kuramoto explains that no single Asian culture exists. Similarly, Asians and Pacific Islanders are frequently linked together and under such a classification many groups are combined, although each group has a distinct culture. Therefore, Kuramoto limits the central discussion in his chapter to the largest Asian American populations: Chinese, Japanese, and Koreans. The states with the highest concentration of Asian and Pacific Islanders are California, New York, Illinois, and Texas.

One chapter is specifically devoted to Pacific Islanders who are described as a distinct people from Polynesia, Micronesia, and Melanesia. Hawaiians, Samoans, and Tongans are listed as the largest Polynesian groups. The largest population among the Micronesian groups are the Chamorro/Guamanians; the Fijuans are the largest population in the Melanesian group. Seventy-five percent of American Pacific Islanders live in Hawaii and California.

Mokuau's review of the literature suggests that the experience of immigration can create many situations leading to family conflicts and generational gaps with the potential for contributing to AOD abuse. This can be seen among the Samoans, who began migrating to the United States in 1950. She states that in moving from an agrarian culture to an industrialized culture, Samoans found it difficult to work as a communal unit and subsist on foods from the land and sea in a country that values individualism.

Pacific Islanders place great value on relationships and respect for and living in harmony with nature. They believe that spirits exist and play a central role in their lives. Mokuau points out that spirits, nature, and people are related and accepted as being one.

For each of the different cultural groups among Polynesian, Micronesian, and Melanesian people, Mokuau details the reasons they give for drinking (for example, Hawaiian youth get together to drink and *talk story*) and the health consequences among the populations for alcohol abuse. For example, many Hawaiian youth drink an excessive amount of beer, and the high incidence rate of esophageal cancer may be an outcome.

As other authors indicate in their chapters, Mokuau stresses the importance of having prevention messages and other services delivered by someone of the group's own culture. Other ways to enhance cultural responsiveness to prevention strategies, according to Mokuau, are to use youth when targeting messages to this population and to incorporate the value of relationships by having respected elders play a central role in AOD abuse prevention.

Moran and May think that reordering the prevention stages and approaches—beginning with tertiary, then secondary, and finally primary—has promise for American Indians. Based on this premise, they describe programs in each prevention area and give evaluative comments. In secondary prevention, for example, school-based programs emphasize information about the effects and consequences of AOD abuse. Citing the literature about school-based programs, Moran and May found that successful programs tried to build self-esteem, improve resistance to peer pressure, and increase awareness about the dangers associated with AOD abuse.

Moran and May state that the scientific data do not support the belief that Indians are genetically predisposed to alcohol. Evidence does suggest, however, that many Indians have internalized the stereotype of the "drunken Indian." In a similar manner this is consistent with Holmes's and Hodge's account of how some gay men and lesbians are as homophobic as some people in the heterosexual community. In both instances, it is important to direct prevention efforts to educating people within the cultural truth, thus destroying methods that frequently lock them into self-destructive behavior and low self-expectations.

The authors have made superb contributions to the social work curriculum about cultural competence in prevention and treatment of AOD abuse. Each author clearly demonstrates that cultural knowledge must form the foundation on which cultural competence is built. The lens through which cultural groups view their problems with AOD must reflect an understanding of the way different groups see and operate in their cultural world. NASW is to be commended for its leadership role in making this document possible.

Frances Larry Brisbane, PhD

American Indians 1

James R. Moran
Philip A. May

This chapter provides a guide to the literature dealing with the prevention of alcohol and other drug (AOD) abuse among American Indians. As a guide, rather than a critical review, the chapter provides an overview of potentially useful approaches. This strategy was chosen because the heterogeneity of the American Indian population requires that social work professionals explore many options and tailor their prevention approaches to specific communities. Thus, a broad review covering many approaches is more useful than an in-depth critical review of fewer strategies.

It should be noted that although this chapter focuses on preventing AOD abuse, most of the literature regarding American Indians primarily addresses alcohol. However, drugs other than alcohol also present problems in American Indian communities. Recent works by Beauvais (1992b); Mail and Johnson (1993); Okwumabua and Duryea (1987); and Swaim, Oetting, Edwards, and Beauvais (1989) provide good overviews of the range of drug and related problems experienced by American Indians. For example, inhalants are frequently abused by American Indian youths, especially by young adolescents before they gain access to alcohol (Beauvais, Oetting, & Edwards, 1985b; Wingert, 1982); use of marijuana is highly variable across different American Indian groups, but it appears to be higher among American Indian youths than among non-Indian youths (Mail & Johnson, 1993); heroin use is low among American Indian people (Bachman et al., 1991); and cocaine use is similar for American Indians and non-Indians (Beauvais et al., 1985b). After reviewing the evidence from several national studies, Mail and Johnson (1993) concluded that the availability and predictability of results have made and continue to make alcohol the drug of choice among American Indian people.

A consequence of alcohol being the preferred drug is that alcohol abuse represents a major problem for many American Indian communities. For example, as a group, American Indians and Alaska natives experience high rates of diseases of the heart, cancer, diabetes, and injuries or death as a result of accidents (Indian Health Service [IHS], 1991; May, 1995). An important observation is that alcohol abuse plays a significant role in these problems. Alcohol is a major factor in five of the 10 leading causes of mortality for American Indians (IHS, 1992). Morbidity data also indicate that alcohol abuse is a major factor contributing to health problems among this population. Both inpatient and outpatient data of the Indian Health Service (IHS) show alcohol-related trauma and diseases to be frequent reasons for health care and disability (Hisnanick & Erickson, 1993; IHS, 1993). More recently, Walker, Howard, Anderson, and Lambert (1994) found that among people newly discharged from Veterans Affairs hospitals, American Indian veterans had twice the rate (45 percent) of alcohol dependence that non-Indian veterans had. Because of the magnitude of the problems related to alcohol, most of the literature (and hence this chapter) focuses mainly on issues related to prevention programs that targeted alcohol abuse among American Indians.

This chapter begins with an overview of characteristics of the American Indian population that provides important background information for social workers planning to work with this population. Next, the extent of the problem of alcohol abuse is described, particularly as it is reflected in American Indian mortality data. This text also explores some of the common myths concerning American Indians and alcohol. Also included is a guide to the literature on preventing alcohol-related problems among the American Indian populations and a set of recommendations that can enhance the operation of prevention programs within American Indian communities.

The American Indian Population

The term *American Indian*, rather than *Native American*, is used throughout this chapter. The reason for this choice is that *Native American*, in addition to referring to indigenous peoples, can also refer to descendants of immigrants from other nations. Thus, the term *Indian* or *American Indian* is now more common in everyday usage and in literature addressing this population. Furthermore, for this chapter, the term *Indian* or *American Indian* is inclusive of Alaska natives.

The 1990 census counted 1,959,873 American Indians in the United States (U.S. Bureau of the Census, 1991). This group of people is characterized by its heterogeneity rather than its homogeneity. For example, as of 1993, there were 341 federally recognized tribes as well as another 111 tribal groups seeking federal recognition (Hirschfelder & Montano, 1993). Although some similarities exist across tribal groups, a great deal of cultural variation exists. For example, there are 17 distinct cultural areas (Manson, Shore, Barron, Ackerson, & Neligh, 1992) and more than 200 different American Indian languages currently spoken (Fleming, 1992).

In addition to tribal differences, American Indians differ greatly by degree of American Indian ancestry; this is important because American Indians are the only ethnic group in the United States that is legally defined by degree of ancestry. The degree of American Indian ancestry is referred to as blood quantum, with 25 percent American Indian blood being the most commonly accepted minimum threshold for tribal membership. Throughout the 20th century, mixed-blood American Indians have outnumbered full-blood American Indians (Wilson, 1992). This point draws attention to the social versus biological definition of who is an American Indian and calls the genetics-based explanations of American Indian drinking into question.

Geographically, American Indian populations tend to cluster in the western states, with 66 percent of all American Indians living in 10 states. Eight of these 10 are in the West or Midwest (Hodgkinson, Outtz, & Obarakpor, 1990; Snipp, 1989). Although American Indians are often thought of as living mainly on reservations, only about 35 percent actually do (U.S. Bureau of the Census, 1991). Finally, as a result of a birth rate that has consistently been twice that of the U.S. average, the American Indian population is young. The median age of the American Indian population was 24.2 years in 1990, compared with 34.4 years for U.S. whites (IHS, 1993).

Extent of the Problem

Alcohol takes a disproportionate toll among American Indians. An overall indicator of this toll is that American Indians have a higher rate of alcohol-related death than the general U.S. population (May, in press). This is especially true in the under-45 age group. For example, in the age group 25–34, American Indian men die 2.8 times more frequently than non-Indian men from motor vehicle crashes, 2.7 times more from other accidents, 2.0 times more from suicide, 1.9 times more from homicide, and 6.8 times more frequently from alcoholism (alcohol dependence syndrome, alcoholic psychosis, and chronic liver disease and alcoholic cirrhosis) (May, 1996).

More evidence of the problem is seen in the percentage of all American Indian deaths that involved alcohol. For 1986–1988, motor vehicle crashes, other accidents, suicide, homicide, and alcoholism caused a total of 5,781 American Indian deaths. On the basis of an approximation of alcohol involvement developed by May (1989a), a total of 3,656 of these deaths are estimated to have involved alcohol. This represents 16.7 percent of the 21,943 American Indian deaths from all causes in these years. The percentages of alcohol-involved deaths by gender were 26.5 percent for men and 13.2 percent for women (May 1989a, in press).

This difference in alcohol-involved deaths by gender is important. Although American Indian men have higher rates of death than American Indian women for all types of alcohol-involved causes and in all age groups, alcohol has major negative consequences for American Indian women. For example, American Indian women ages 25–34 die 1.4 to 12 times more frequently of alcohol-involved causes than non-Indian women (May, in press).

These data seem to support the common view that Leland (1976) described in her book, *Firewater Myths*. Leland said that many people believe that American Indians are inclined to develop an excessive craving for alcohol and to lose control of their behavior when they drink. Most often this view is couched in terms of a genetic predisposition to alcohol (Mail & McDonald, 1980). Of particular concern from a prevention perspective is that many American Indian people also accept the myth or stereotype of the "drunken Indian," that is, the idea that American Indians are somehow different from non-Indians in their susceptibility to alcohol. For example, most (63 percent) Navajo people believe that American Indians have a special physiological weakness to the effects of alcohol (May & Smith, 1988). Sage and Burns (1993) found that American Indian adolescents, particularly men, attributed American Indian drinking problems to being "in the blood." These adolescents tended to use the heredity or genetic explanation of American Indian drinking as an excuse for their own abuse of alcohol. Despite its common acceptance, many components of the myth are inaccurate (Leland, 1976; Westermeyer, 1974), and no major deficit in the rate of alcohol metabolism or any other particular physiological predisposition to alcohol abuse has been documented in the scientific literature (Mail & Johnson, 1993; May, 1989a; Reed, 1985; Schaefer, 1981).

However, from the mortality data presented earlier, it is evident that alcohol wreaks destruction among American Indians: American Indian men have a greater problem with alcohol-involved death than American Indian women; alcohol-involved mortality data are worse for both American Indian men and women than the overall U.S. averages; and the disparity between American Indians and the U.S. general population is greatest in the younger age groups (May 1986, 1989a).

Given that little scientific support exists for the belief that American Indians are genetically predisposed to alcohol, what explains the severe alcohol problems experienced by American Indian communities as reflected in the higher rates of mortality? The answer comes from understanding the variation in alcohol use among American Indians. Just as heterogeneity exists along other dimensions, a great deal of diversity is seen in the manner in which alcohol is used by American Indian people. One measure of this variation is presented by May (1982) in a report on studies that examined the prevalence of alcohol use in different American Indian communities. Compared with the overall U.S. prevalence of 67 percent to 68 percent (National Institute on Alcohol Abuse and Alcoholism, 1981), the Navajo of the Southwest had a rate of only 30 percent (Levy & Kunitz, 1974). The Standing Rock Sioux of South Dakota were at about the same as the U.S. figure, at 69 percent (Whittacker, 1962, 1982), whereas the Ute of Southern Colorado (Jessor, Graves, Hanson, & Jessor, 1968) and the Ojibwa of the Brokenhead Reserve in Canada (Longclaws, Barnes, Grieve, & Dumoff, 1980) were both higher at about 80 percent. From these studies, it is seen that not all American Indian people use alcohol; in fact, some groups such as the Navajo abstain from any alcohol use at twice the rate of the general U.S. population.

Perhaps more to the point regarding variation in alcohol use among American Indians is the literature that examines drinking styles (Levy & Kunitz, 1974; Weisner, Weibel-Orlando, & Long, 1984). The most frequently described styles are abstinence, recreational, anxiety, and moderated social drinking (Ferguson, 1968; May, 1982, 1989a). Of these four, only the recreational and the anxiety styles are linked to the problems outlined here. In other words, abstinence, common among many tribes (see May 1989a), particularly among middle-aged and older people, obviously causes no alcohol-related problems. Similarly, many American Indians tend to drink as do others in the strata of society to which they are attached (see Levy & Kunitz, 1974; Liban & Smart, 1982). Many American Indians, therefore, tend to practice a moderated or light social drinking style, which produces few or no problems related to morbidity, mortality, arrest, or other health or social problems.

However, Ferguson (1968) described the subgroups of recreational and anxiety drinkers that are also common among most American Indian communities. The recreational drinker is typically a young man who drinks with friends (predominantly men, but also in mixed groups) on weekends and for parties, special occasions, and other social events. As with other groups of young people, drinking and intoxication are important for social cohesion and are generally highly valued. Recreational drinking among American Indian groups of many tribes may be different from some other groups in the United States only in matters of degree and cultural meaning. As described by many authors, American Indian recreational drinking is more rapid and more forced, and the "bouts" are extended over long nights, weekends, and for other lengthy periods (Dozier, 1966; Hughes & Dodder, 1984; Lurie, 1971; Savard, 1968; Weisner et al., 1984). High blood alcohol concentrations are commonly found in American Indians who practice this style of drinking.

Anxiety drinkers tend to be older and they drink chronically, are more solitary, and are generally physically addicted to alcohol. They generally drink cheap wine and beer and supplement with hard liquor, but they will consume almost any alcoholic beverage available. They also use nonbeverage items that contain alcohol, such as hair spray, aftershave, and disinfectant. Anxiety drinkers are mostly unemployed, live in border towns and skid row areas, and are not usually associated with the mainstream society of their tribe or of Western society. Most anxiety drinkers are ostracized to a great degree, whereas the recreational drinkers may be in the mainstream of society and associated with abusive peer clusters only when drinking.

These two patterns, the recreational and anxiety drinking, represent the types of alcohol-abusing or alcohol problem–generating styles that account for most of the problems related to alcohol in American Indian communities. It is from these two groups that the stereotype of the "drunken

Indian" gains meaning. The people involved in these two styles of drinking do not include all American Indian people. However, the problems encountered by these drinkers are a significant issue (for example, higher mortality rates) for American Indian communities.

From these data, the need for programs for preventing alcohol-involved problems is evident. However, differences by tribal group, cultural orientation, degree of American Indian ancestry, and residency (that is, reservation versus urban) make it difficult to prescribe what prevention efforts should be. Considering this heterogeneity, what then does the literature tell us about alcohol abuse prevention among American Indians?

The Literature on Prevention

The criterion for inclusion of articles in this chapter was an assessment of their use for alcohol-related prevention activities. In some cases, the works are more concerned with etiology than application, and others describe specific strategies of prevention. Nevertheless, the basic insights in the articles reviewed hold promise for reducing alcohol-related problems. As stated previously, this chapter is a guide to the literature to help develop prevention efforts with this population, not a critical review of the research literature. It should also be stressed again that the heterogeneity of the American Indian population makes it difficult to generalize specific interventions.

This chapter should be useful to social workers pursuing applied programs of alcohol abuse prevention. An attempt has been made to focus on ideas and alcohol programs that are primarily prevention oriented, rather than treatment oriented. The emphasis is on tertiary, secondary, and primary prevention, including comprehensive programs that address more than one level. Because some programs have diverse elements that address multiple levels, categorization in this chapter is intended to reflect the predominant theme of the programs.

Overview Articles

Several articles identifying key issues related to the prevention of AOD abuse among American Indians have been published. Most of this literature focuses on young people. Alcohol, marijuana, and inhalants are the three drugs most commonly abused by American Indian youths. American Indian youths generally report they use alcohol as frequently or more frequently than other youths in the United States. For example, by the 12th grade, lifetime prevalence of alcohol use is quite high: 96 percent for American Indian men, and 92 percent for women (Oetting & Beauvais, 1989). However, the major difference between American Indian youth data and U.S. youth averages is found in measures dealing with age at first involvement and degree of involvement.

The age at first involvement with alcohol is younger for American Indian youths, the frequency and amount of drinking are greater, and the negative consequences are more common (Beauvais, Oetting, & Edwards, 1985a; Forslund & Cranston, 1975; Forslund & Meyers, 1974; Hughes & Dodder, 1984; Oetting, Beauvais, & Edwards, 1988). Oetting, Swaim, Edwards, and Beauvais (1989) have found that at all ages and grades, a greater percentage of American Indian youths are more heavily involved with alcohol than non-Indians are.

Several studies indicate that alcohol use is both encouraged and expected among many peer groups as the "Indian thing to do" (Winfree & Griffiths, 1983b). By 12th grade, 80 percent of American Indian youths are current drinkers, but variation exists from reservation to reservation (May, 1982). Severity measures show that American Indian youths who drink are more likely to report having been drunk and to have "blacked out" (Oetting & Beauvais, 1989).

The American Indian patterns are similar to general U.S. high school data, which show an increase in drinking and marijuana use through 1980 and subsequent declines after 1980. That is, American Indian youths have reported reduced AOD use in recent years (Oetting & Beauvais, 1989; Winfree & Griffiths, 1983a). However, the subgroup of American Indian youths who indicate heavy use has not declined but rather has remained steady at 17 percent to 20 percent (Beauvais, 1992b).

The youths most likely to abuse alcohol are those tied to AOD-abusing "peer clusters." Also, American Indian youths who do not do well in school, who do not strongly identify with American Indian culture, and who come from families who also abuse alcohol (Guyette, 1982) are more likely to abuse AOD. The findings of Oetting and Beauvais (1989) further characterize AOD abusers as having poor school adjustment, weak religious and spiritual foundations, poor family and peer group associations, and little hope for the future. However, American Indian youths with strong attachments to families in which culture and school are valued and abusive drinking is neither common nor positively valued tend to be less likely to get seriously involved with AOD.

Low self-esteem, depression, anxiety, and other negative emotional states—taken independently—are not highly influential or discriminating in alcohol abuse among American Indian youths (Oetting & Beauvais, 1989; Oetting et al., 1988). Biculturalism (the ability to function well in both tribal, American Indian society and the modern, Western world) tends to have a low association with AOD abuse or other predisposing variables (Moran, Fleming, Somervell, & Manson, in press; Oetting & Beauvais, 1990–1991). In their most recent works, Swaim, Oetting, Thurman, Beauvais, and Edwards (1993) emphasize resocialization (the learning or relearning of modes of adjustment to life that are AOD free) in the family, schools, peer groups, and religious institutions as preventive of AOD abuse among American Indian youths (Beauvais, 1992a; Swaim et al., 1993).

With these overview articles as background, this chapter now turns to specific prevention approaches. May, Miller, and Wallerstein (1993) describe seven steps that are useful in developing appropriate community-based prevention programs: (1) listen; (2) develop a relationship and rapport; (3) promote dialogue; (4) avoid polarization; (5) maintain ongoing dialogue and roll with any resistance; (6) provide a menu of options; and (7) help the community initiate options on its own. The following text covers tertiary, secondary, and primary programs because this order represents a progression from a more traditional and somewhat limited view of prevention to broader approaches that hold more promise for American Indian communities.

Tertiary Prevention Programs

Tertiary prevention consists of measures taken to reduce existing impairments and disabilities and to minimize suffering caused by severe alcohol abuse or alcohol dependence (Last, 1983). Programs that emphasize tertiary strategies with American Indian alcohol abuse are listed in Table 1-1. The first three listings, Shore and Von Fumetti (1972), Wilson and Shore (1975), and Weibel-Orlando (1989) described the typical methods used in American Indian alcohol treatment programs and also the tertiary prevention issues that are important to consider with adult American Indians who abuse alcohol.

For example, Weibel-Orlando (1989) reports on a survey of 26 federally funded rural and urban treatment programs. She compared them across factors such as ethnicity of staff, strength of Alcoholics Anonymous (AA) affiliation, cooperation with tribal healers, and treatment effectiveness. Most programs were staffed mostly by American Indian people, and this was positive because non-Indian counselors often faced reactions from overt hostility to sullen resistance. Most programs had a strong AA affiliation, which was seen as related to the AA background of most of the counselors.

Most programs were accommodating to cultural practices—at least to a limited extent—through display of American Indian posters and handicrafts. Several programs included such practices as sweats and praying with a sacred pipe. However, traditional American Indian healers played only a minor role in the 26 programs. Weibel-Orlando stated that several medicine men whom she interviewed expressed doubt that traditional healing practices are appropriate in typical treatment settings. Furthermore, they indicated that most traditional healing is tribe specific and not available to outsiders. Documenting treatment effectiveness proved elusive in this study. Program directors could provide only anecdotal accounts of posttreatment abstinence from drinking. In effect, no program had evaluated its outcomes. She concludes by calling for both more local focus on treatment programs to enable increased cultural involvement and more systematic evaluation to document treatment outcomes.

Table 1-1. Tertiary Level Prevention

Author	Topic and Target Groups
Shore and Von Fumetti (1972)	Three adult alcohol treatment programs; Northwest Indians
Wilson and Shore (1975)	One adult alcohol treatment program; Northwest Indians
Weibel-Orlando (1989)	Descriptions of 26 adult alcohol treatment programs; Far West
Ferguson (1968, 1970, 1976) Savard (1968)	Etiology and description of treatment and intervention (including use of disulfiram [Antabuse]) with adults who abuse alcohol; Navajo
Westermeyer and Peake (1983)	Etiology and evaluative follow-up of adults who abuse alcohol; Chippewa
Albaugh and Anderson (1974) Pascarosa and Futterman (1976) Blum, Futterman, and Pascarosa (1977)	The use of Native American church rituals and the sacramental use of peyote to treat alcoholism among adults; Plains tribes
Masis and May (1991)	Fetal alcohol syndrome (FAS) prevention through focus on chronic alcohol-abusing women at high risk for causing FAS; Navajo

The articles by Ferguson (1968, 1970, 1976) and Savard (1968) describe the use of Antabuse (disulfiram), arrest diversion, milieus change, and other tertiary methods of prevention and intervention for people who chronically abuse alcohol. Ferguson (1970) reports on a Navajo treatment program involving detoxification, court-ordered use of disulfiram, staff monitoring and assistance in taking the disulfiram, counseling with the assistance of interpreters, and employment and welfare aid. A key outcome used for this study was cessation of destructive drinking as measured by a decrease in drinking-related arrests. During the 18-month treatment period, arrests fell by 78 percent, with about one-third of the 115 people in treatment having no arrests.

The subjects of this study were extreme examples of alcohol abuse. However, given that this type of subject accounts for much of the official American Indian alcohol arrest data, the positive results from the use of disulfiram along with social supports are important. It was also found that those who had stronger ties to more traditional culture fared better than those with weaker traditional ties.

Ferguson (1976) elaborates on this latter point in a second article, in which she applies "stake theory" to the Navajo subjects in the chronic alcoholic study. Stake theory holds that those who have a stake in society will conform to society's norms and demonstrate less deviance such as alcohol abuse. Applying this lens to the subjects who chronically abuse alcohol produced the following results: those with a stake in the Navajo society or a stake in Western society responded better than those with a stake in neither. However, those with a stake in both Navajo society and Western society had the most success in terms of the 24-month outcome. This is an important finding and one that corresponds with the findings of Oetting and Beauvais (1990–1991) and Moran and colleagues (in press) regarding bicultural competence. These authors found increased levels of psychological well-being, such as higher self-esteem and more internal locus of control, and fewer problem behaviors among American Indian adolescents who identified strongly with both their American Indian culture and Western culture versus those who identified with only one or with neither. The implication here is that programs at all prevention levels can probably benefit by consciously addressing issues of culture in a manner that fosters stronger identification and thus enhances participants' stake in both their American Indian society and Western society.

Westermeyer and Peake's (1983) study is unique in that it consists of a 10-year treatment follow-up interview with 45 American Indians who abuse alcohol. At the time of the 10-year interview, seven had improved, seven remained unchanged in their alcohol use, 19 were doing worse, nine had died, and three could not be located. Factors associated with doing better were stable employment, good economic and living conditions, strong interpersonal relationships, and little depression. These factors were not present for those doing worse. Although not a causal argument, these data point to the importance of some components of primary prevention efforts described later in this chapter.

Also included in the tertiary level literature are three articles describing the therapeutic efficacy of using the values, beliefs, structure, and rituals of the Native American church to treat and prevent further problems from alcoholism. Albaugh and Anderson (1974), Blum and colleagues (1977), and Pascarosa and Futterman (1976) describe Native American church practices and peyote as therapeutic agents that can treat problems with alcoholism. The latter two articles, however, emphasize the pharmacology more than Albaugh and Anderson, who emphasize the social and behavioral aspects.

The final article in Table 1-1, Masis and May (1991), describes a fetal alcohol syndrome (FAS) prevention program in Arizona that is focused on women who chronically abuse alcohol. The tertiary goals are to prevent alcohol damage (FAS or lesser alcohol-related birth defects) among children yet to be born to mothers who have already had one damaged child or are drinking heavily while pregnant. The program provides extensive case management using counseling, social support, birth control, and treatment for alcoholism.

Secondary Prevention Programs

Secondary prevention uses measures available to individuals and populations for early detection within high-risk groups and prompt and effective intervention to correct or minimize alcohol abuse in the earliest years of onset (Last, 1983). The secondary prevention resources presented here focus on groups and individuals within those groups, rather than on the entire community, environment, or structural conditions.

Alcohol and Mental Health Programs

The articles in Table 1-2 concern secondary AOD abuse prevention conducted within the context of mental health programs. Many, if not most, of the people in mental health programs have problems that involve comorbidity with AOD consumption (May, 1982). Therefore, AOD abuse prevention has often been developed in mental health programs. Of the eight articles of this nature, six are in a mental health or suicide prevention context, one is in an alcoholism treatment context (Silk-Walker, Walker, & Kivlahan, 1988), and two are in the context of a community mental health initiative (Parker, Jamons, Marek, & Camacho, 1991; Shore & Kofoed, 1984). These articles underscore the many possibilities for initiating prevention in all mental health and alcoholism programs. For example, Silk-Walker and colleagues (1988) describe the necessity for prevention of alcohol problems to be undertaken within families. Stabilization of at-risk families through skills training of spouses and broader community ties should reduce drinking in American Indian communities. Furthermore, centers for social detoxification and halfway houses are described as prevention possibilities for American Indian communities (Silk-Walker et al., 1988). Shore and Kofoed (1984) advocate programs for identifying and diverting alcohol-impaired drivers as well as programs for the public inebriate and a greater emphasis on outpatient and social detoxification. The article by Parker and colleagues (1991) takes the problem of youth AOD abuse as it is affected by a poor self-concept and lack of understanding of traditional culture and traditions. They describe a program of alcohol education and alcohol abuse resistance through the use of an alcohol abuse education curriculum and active participation in traditional tribal activities such as artwork, crafts, songs, and lore.

Table 1-2. Secondary Level Prevention—Mental Health Programs

Author	Topic and Target Groups
Silk-Walker et al. (1988)	issues in an alcohol treatment program; adults who abuse alcohol
Levy and Kunitz (1987)	High-risk factors for suicide and alcohol problems for secondary prevention; Hopi
Shore and Kofoed (1984)	Five secondary prevention programs for communities; adults
Kahn and Stephan (1981) Kahn and Fua (1985) Ward (1984) Fox, Manitowabi, and Ward (1984)	Alcohol abuse prevention as an effective community-based mental health or suicide prevention program; Tono O'Odam and Canadian Indian adults
Parker et al. (1991)	An American Indian culture–based prevention program to build self-esteem and reduce substance abuse; Northeastern Indians

School-Based Programs

The articles in Table 1-3 are school-based programs. Most prevention programs aimed at American Indians in recent years have been school-based initiatives that emphasize information about the effects and consequences of AOD abuse. Programs such as "Here's Looking at You," "Project Charley," and "Babes" have been used in many American Indian communities, both on and off reservations. However, the effectiveness of such programs has been infrequently studied and published. The 15 articles listed in Table 1-3 represent the published evaluations of programs in American Indian community schools. IHS documents describe the most frequently used school-based prevention efforts (IHS, 1986, 1987).

The consistent themes in school-based AOD abuse prevention programs are building bicultural competence (LaFromboise & Rowe, 1983), increasing self-esteem and self-efficacy (IHS, 1987), improving resistance to peer pressure and overall discriminatory and judgment skills (Duryea & Matzek, 1990; Gilchrist, Schinke, Trimble, & Cvetkovich, 1987; Schinke et al., 1988; Schinke, Mancher, Holden, Botvin, & Orlandi, 1989), and increasing the perception of the riskiness of AOD abuse (Bernstein & Woodall, 1987). The current etiological literature supports these thematic efforts if undertaken in the proper context. That is, building self-esteem alone will not solve the AOD use and abuse problems, yet building new perceptions, values, skills, and support systems along with self-esteem may be essential. Therefore, these programs must also affect the social and cultural aspects of life and mitigate the effects of abusive peer clusters in the lives of these youths (Newcomb & Bentler, 1989). Whether this is accomplished by direct or indirect influence, the sociocultural aspects must be addressed along with the mental health and psychological issues (Oetting & Beauvais, 1989).

The articles that document school-based prevention can be used as guides and models for health promotion. Long-term follow-up of the adolescents who participated in these programs should be pursued aggressively, particularly after they leave school and enter adulthood. Studies of health promotion among American Indian youths will have to use long-term outcome evaluation that pinpoints factors associated with low AOD abuse and overall health and success in life (Neumann, Mason, Chase, & Albaugh, 1991).

Primary Prevention

Primary prevention is the promotion of health and elimination of alcohol abuse and its consequences through communitywide efforts, such as

Table 1-3. Secondary Level Prevention—School-Based Programs

Author	Topic and Target Groups
Indian Health Service (1986, 1987)	A description and summary of the several hundred school-based alcohol abuse prevention programs of the Indian Health Service; American Indian youths and parents
Manson, Beals, Dick, and Duclos (1989)	School-based suicide prevention programs with alcohol prevention components; youths
Duryea and Matzek (1990)	Prevention among elementary school children through resistance to peer pressure; Pueblo
Okwumabua, Okwumabua, and Duryea (1989)	Health decision making among seventh graders, as influenced by knowledge of the consequences of their behavior; Pueblo
Bernstein and Woodall (1987)	Perceptions of riskiness in a program combining health education and life experience; New Mexican Indians in grades 6–8
Murphy and DeBlassie (1984)	Counselor intervention strategies; Mescalero Apache elementary school children
Scott and Meyers (1988)	Fitness training to stabilize alcohol and other drug use; Canadian Indian youths ages 12–18
Schinke et al. (1989) Schinke, Shilling, Gilchrist, Asby, and Kitajima (1989) Schinke et al. (1988) Gilchrist et al. (1987) Schinke et al. (1985)	Skills training and health education to provide American Indian youths with greater knowledge of drug effects, better peer pressure management, and lower rates of substance use; Northwest Indian youths
LaFromboise and Rowe (1983)	Culturally appropriate skills training for bicultural competence and assertiveness; American Indian youths
Carpenter, Lyons, and Miller (1985)	A peer-managed self-control program for teaching responsible drinking to teenagers; American Indian teenagers
Davis, Hunt, and Kitzes (1989)	Integrated health services, including alcohol education and counseling, at a school-based teen center; Pueblo teens

improving knowledge; altering the environment; and changing the social structure, norms, and values (Last, 1983). General approaches and overview articles are presented in Table 1-4. The rationale and philosophy of primary prevention among American Indian people are described in these articles. Rhoades, Mason, Eddy, Smith, and Burns (1988) and the IHS (1986) call for broad programs of health promotion, particularly those that emphasize community change. May (1986) stresses primary prevention through social policy, environmental change, and broad-based action for normative change. The Office of Substance Abuse Prevention (1990) focuses on both mental health and AOD abuse programs for prevention and concludes with an emphasis on comprehensive prevention. Mail (1985) lays out a rationale and some specific considerations for primary prevention initiatives in American Indian communities, and Mail and Wright (1989) indicate that successful prevention programs will have to come from the communities themselves.

Marum (1988) describes the community-generated prevention process with one program in Alaska. Public education on AOD abuse was undertaken to increase the pool of knowledgeable and skilled people who would be working on preventing AOD abuse. Specifically, the Alaskan efforts emphasized community mobilization and empowerment through volunteer networks to increase knowledge of AOD abuse and interventions, communitywide awareness of AOD abuse, AOD education for youths, problem solving at the local level, and increased involvement and empowerment of the elders.

Table 1-4. Primary Level Prevention—General Literature

Author	Topic and Target Groups
Rhoades et al. (1988) Indian Health Service (1986)	IHS programs and philosophy in the treatment and prevention of alcoholism for more than 300 reservations; American Indians
May (1986)	An overview of the existing alcohol abuse problems, especially mortality, and detailed suggestions for comprehensive prevention programs; American Indians
Office of Substance Abuse Prevention (1990)	A comprehensive review of the literature, prevention programs instituted past and present, and recommendations; American Indians
Mail (1985) Mail and Wright (1989)	Two works on the concepts for, and necessity of, designing comprehensive prevention from the indigenous cultural point of view; American Indians
Beauvais and LaBoueff (1985)	Advocates that prevention must come from the ground up; all American Indians
Marum (1988)	Community mobilization through workshops and training; Alaska native communities
Beauvais (1992a)	A model based on key, individual substance abuse etiology variables (peer, psychological, social structure, and socialization factors); American Indian youths
Maynard and Twiss (1970)	A comprehensive study and plan for primary prevention of mental health and substance abuse problems; Oglala Sioux

Beauvais (1992a) pinpoints socioeconomic conditions as the major factors that have contributed greatly to AOD abuse among the youths of most American Indian communities. He therefore proposes a four-level integrated model of prevention. True prevention of many AOD problems will come from improvement in social structure (economic, family structure, and cultural integrity), socialization (family caring, sanctions, and religiosity), psychological factors (self-esteem and reduced alienation), and peer clusters (peer encouragement and sanctions against promoting AOD). Ultimately, this improvement will lead to lower levels of AOD use. This approach is similar to the one advocated by Beauvais and LaBoueff (1985) in an earlier article, an approach that should be implemented in a collaborative manner from within the community rather than from the top down.

Maynard and Twiss (1970) describe a pilot model community mental health program at Pine Ridge, South Dakota, in the 1970s. Research was generated on social and environmental conditions that were related to mental health, AOD abuse, and other health and behavioral health conditions. Their monograph summarizes those studies. It details the historical, demographic, economic, social, and cultural conditions among the Oglala Lakota (Sioux) at Pine Ridge and analyzes their significance for behavioral health. A large part of the concern is related to AOD abuse. Each section of the monograph concludes with suggestions for prevention, most of them geared to primary prevention. Most solutions involve communitywide, structural issues. Maynard and Twiss (1970) advocate a major social and economic development program that eliminates dependent poverty through providing culturally approved employment opportunities on the reservation, upgrading the educational system, and fostering leadership through strengthening the authority and dignity of the tribal leadership and tribal council.

Alcohol-Related Injury Programs

The four articles listed in Table 1-5 relate to the prevention or control of alcohol-related injury. The May (1989b) article is a literature review that documents the close tie between alcohol and deaths and injuries, that result from motor vehicle accidents, and outlines a variety of suggestions for prevention. May advocates the following primary prevention efforts: social and economic improvement; traffic safety education and highway improvement; public education; and new tribal alcohol policies, laws, norms, and values. Improving alcohol education in schools, working to break abusive drinking subgroups and peer clusters, and increasing use of safety belts and infant car seats for injury reduction were advocated as secondary prevention level efforts. Tertiary prevention efforts included improving emergency medical systems, medical care, and alcohol abuse treatment programs.

Similarly, the Smith (1991) and IHS (1990) documents outline specific strategies for the prevention of injury and present detailed data to guide and support these efforts. The IHS initiatives emphasize surveillance to pinpoint problem topics and environments in need of prevention, as well as increased community awareness of injuries and their alcohol-related nature. Recommended prevention activities include multiple-media "None for the Road" campaigns, training of local community experts and advocates, and infant car seat and adult safety belt usage programs to prevent serious injury and death despite alcohol-related crashes.

Finally, the Macedo (1988) article provides a primary prevention perspective on whole communities that are "injured" and traumatized by modern forces, particularly alcohol abuse, and offers a paradigm for recovery. Macedo emphasizes the concept that these communities must first work through their collective trauma and then begin to develop their own internal interventions.

Fetal Alcohol Syndrome Programs

FAS has been upheld by many as a perfect motivation for primary prevention among American Indians (May, 1986). Indeed, some would say that American Indian communities and some American Indian organizations

Table 1-5. Primary Level Prevention—Alcohol-Related Injury Control

Author	Topic and Target Groups
May (1989b)	A literature review and overview of alcohol and motor vehicle crashes among American Indians with primary, secondary, and tertiary prevention suggestions; all American Indians and Alaska natives
Smith (1991) Indian Health Service (1990)	An article and a data monograph that lay out the details of the American Indian injury problem and the IHS initiative to implement primary prevention and tools for prevention; all American Indians and Alaska natives
Macedo (1988)	A description of communitywide change and prevention of alcohol-related social trauma and injury in two communities and a framework for analysis; Canadian Indians

are leading the way in the area of FAS prevention. The three articles on FAS prevention in Table 1-6 are all examples of using public education, awareness, research, and some diagnostic clinic work to change perceptions and behaviors around this issue. These American Indian FAS prevention efforts have been unique in that they have been initiated in conjunction with clinical screening efforts that were designed to elicit the nature, prevalence, and epidemiological characteristics of the problem before initiating full-scale prevention programs (May & Hymbaugh, 1983). They represent targeted approaches based on the clinical and epidemiological findings on the mothers and infants. Furthermore, the baseline prevalence of the problem as established by the screening will allow for eventual determination of prevention program success (May & Hymbaugh, 1983, 1989). In the coming years, it will be vital to evaluate the long-term effects of health promotion programs in some of the communities that participated in the first FAS prevention efforts described in these articles.

Policies and Laws

The final primary prevention area is that of alcohol control policy and laws. Table 1-7 lists the major articles in this area. The principal policy regarding American Indians and alcohol has been prohibition (Mail & McDonald, 1980). In 1832 the U.S. Congress prohibited the sale of liquor to any American Indian. This law remained in effect until 1953, when each reservation was given the power to regulate alcohol within its own borders (May, 1976). Because only about 30 percent of all reservations have passed laws making alcohol legal, more than two-thirds continue to operate under a policy of prohibition (May, 1992). However, it is clear from the

Table 1-6. Primary Level Prevention—Fetal Alcohol Syndrome

Author	Topic and Target Groups
May and Hymbaugh (1989)	Nationwide primary prevention program directed at FAS that uses public education through the training of trainers; all American Indians and Alaska natives
May and Hymbaugh (1983)	A comprehensive FAS research/clinical assessment and primary prevention program for a number of tribal communities; Southwestern Indians
Plaisier (1989)	A primary and secondary FAS prevention program using health education as a vehicle; American Indians in Michigan

information presented in this chapter that this policy has not been effective. Bootleggers and the off-reservation purchase of alcohol have largely circumvented this policy. In fact, some see the policy as encouraging such alcohol-abusive behavior as passing a bottle among group members and drinking quickly until the alcohol is gone (Bach & Bornstein, 1981; Dozier, 1966; Mail & McDonald, 1980). Some scholars have suggested new laws to allow legalization and control of alcohol sales on reservations (Dozier, 1966; Stewart, 1964).

Other policy options discussed in the literature include the following:

◆ Increase the price of alcohol through taxation (Moore & Gerstein, 1981). Many western states have relatively low tax rates on alcohol. It is estimated that a 33.6 percent increase in price would result in an 11 percent to 32 percent decline in alcohol consumption (U.S. Surgeon General, 1989). However, reducing availability of alcohol through price can also have the unintended result of increasing the use of alternative and more toxic substances such as hair sprays, solvents, and inhalants (Beauvais et al., 1985b; Oetting & Beauvais, 1989).

◆ Reduce the number of establishments licensed to sell alcohol and regulate the type and location of licenses issued. For example, alcohol sold

Table 1-7. Primary Level Prevention—Policy and Laws

Author	Topic and Target Groups
May (1975, 1976, 1977)	Two articles and a doctoral dissertation on alcohol legalization and prohibition policies on eight reservations and the effects of these laws on alcohol-related mortality; Northern Plains tribes
Back (1981)	Effectiveness of prohibition on the Navajo reservation and a new policy as a preventive measure; Navajo
Bellamy (1984)	Comparison of the behavorial and attitudinal characteristics of youths growing up on three reservations: one with prohibition, one with long-term alcohol legalization, and one with alcohol recently legalized; Plains Indians
May and Smith (1988)	A survey of opinions about alcohol and alcohol policy with subsequent recommendations for alcohol policy and prevention; Navajo
May (1992)	A comprehensive survey of alcohol control policy and primary prevention measures applied to American Indians and border town communities; all American Indians and Alaska natives

in bars has generally been found to produce more cases of alcohol-impaired driving, yet alcohol sold in grocery stores results in the lowest level of drinking and driving (O'Donnell, 1985).

◆ Ban or limit alcohol advertising. For many years, beer companies advertised heavily at events such as powwows. Many American Indian communities are now refusing advertising from beer companies, and powwows have generally become alcohol-free events.

There is a rich literature regarding approaches to policy, that may provide useful examples for American Indian communities (Blose & Holder, 1987; Colon, Cutter, & Jones, 1981; Gliksman & Rush, 1986; MacDonald & Whitehead, 1983; Mosher & Jernigan, 1989). For example, authors writing about non-Indian populations call for policies to be instituted in a comprehensive, community-generated way that affects norms and values (Institute of Medicine, 1989). Beauchamp (1980, 1990) advocates for improved understanding of the epidemiological nature of alcohol use patterns and problems to initiate new norms that are encouraging and less tolerant of alcohol abuse. Holder and Stoil (1988), Moore and Gerstein (1981), and Pittman and White (1991) have compiled and written extensive literature on policy approaches to alcohol abuse, some of which have been evaluated and found effective. Non-Indian literature on policy-oriented primary prevention is extensive and may inform health promotion among American Indians as well. New approaches to community definitions and policy need to be further integrated into both research and application in American Indian communities.

Although the potential for communitywide policy and normative change is immense, implementing such change is treacherous and slow. As Gordis (1991) has pointed out, going from science to social policy is an "uncertain road," highly affected by the type of scientific evidence, cultural and social influences, timing, and many other factors. Similar, or even greater, pitfalls have been recorded in many American Indian and Alaskan native communities (Foulks, 1989; Levy & Kunitz, 1981; Manson, 1989; Moran, 1995). For example, one edition of the journal *American Indian and Alaska Native Mental Health Research* was devoted to the pitfalls of an alcohol research and prevention initiative in an Alaskan community. In this community, research on alcohol use patterns and plans for prevention created tremendous misunderstanding and turmoil perceived as frustrating, painful, and destructive. The purpose of this volume of the journal was to solicit and print commentaries by established researchers and prevention professionals who describe how such problems could be avoided in the future (Manson 1989). The conclusion reached by the contributors was that it is vital for professionals working in alcohol problem prevention in American Indian communities to be patient, culturally sensitive, and responsive to local leaders and citizens alike (Beauchamp, 1980; Beauvais & Trimble, 1992).

Summary and Conclusion

As a group, American Indians experience many health problems that are related to alcohol abuse. Alcohol-involved mortality data are worse for American Indians than overall U.S. averages. The age of first involvement with alcohol is younger, the frequency and amount of drinking is greater, and negative consequences are more common for American Indian than non-Indian youths. The literature summarized in this chapter shows that programs do attempt to promote health in the face of the problem of alcohol abuse among American Indians. A theme emerging from this literature is that programs that address these issues must consider American Indian heterogeneity as it is reflected in tribal affiliation, cultural groups, language, and blood quantum. Prevention programs must also consider the young age composition of the American Indian population and the observation that most American Indian people live off, rather than on, reservations.

Programs implemented in American Indian communities must be designed to allow the content to be shaped and molded to fit the local culture. Furthermore, programs must assist people in their efforts at empowerment (Beauvais & LaBoueff, 1985). Prevention programs can be initiated by outside "experts" working with tribal leaders, but the continuation and entrenchment of the activities must be carried on by individuals in the local community (Moran, 1995; Office of Substance Abuse and Prevention, 1990). This requirement does not imply that programs designed for one tribe cannot be transferred to others. Programs should be made relevant to local norms, values, and conditions through particular, culturally sensitive adaptations (May & Hymbaugh, 1989).

A comprehensive, community approach to health promotion and alcohol abuse prevention must always keep the issue of adapting to the specific culture in mind. Such an approach should focus on a public health perspective. In a public health approach, the goal is to apply comprehensive strategies and programs to reduce the rates of affliction and early death among total groups and aggregates of individuals (Beauchamp, 1980). The focus should be on communities and particular geographic areas and *not* on individuals. No single type of alcohol abuse prevention should be championed, but rather various programs and approaches should be fit or bound together in a mutually supportive and beneficial manner (May, 1992). Different levels of prevention dealing with alcohol-involved behaviors should be used and coordinated (Bloom, 1981; Manson, Tatum, & Dinges, 1982). For example, prevention efforts must have plans to involve and strengthen the community and family. American Indian families that are strong and well integrated produce children with better indicators of adjustment and, in most cases, fewer indicators of deviance (Jensen, Stauss, & Harris, 1977). Conversely, disorganized, multiproblem families have higher alcohol use and more health and deviance problems (Lujan, DeBruyn, May, & Bird, 1989; Spivey, 1977). The various programs described in this chapter, then, are not mutually exclusive but can be mutually supportive if orchestrated by a comprehensive communitywide plan and approach. Any community will have to have prevention programs and standard health and AOD treatment programs. Once the problems and priorities of a community are identified from research, data analysis, and local wisdom, proper programs and approaches can be established that draw heavily on the literature presented in this chapter.

References

Albaugh, B. J., & Anderson, P. O. (1974). Peyote in the treatment of alcoholism among American Indians. *American Journal of Psychiatry, 131,* 1247–1250.

Bach, P. J., & Bornstein, P. H. (1981). A social learning rationale and suggestions for behavioral treatment with American Indian alcohol abusers. *Addictive Behaviors, 6,* 75–81.

Bachman, J. G., Wallace, J. M., O'Malley, P. M., Johnston, L. D., Kurth, C. L., & Neighbors, H. W. (1991). Racial/ethnic differences in smoking, drinking, and illicit drug use among American Indian high school seniors, 1976–1989. *American Journal of Public Health, 81,* 372–377.

Back, W. D. (1981). The ineffectiveness of alcohol prohibition on the Navajo Indian reservation. *Arizona State Law Journal, 4,* 925–943.

Beauchamp, D. E. (1980). *Beyond alcoholism: Alcohol and public health policy.* Philadelphia: Temple University Press.

Beauchamp, D. E. (1990). Alcohol and tobacco as public health challenges in a democracy. *British Journal on Addiction, 85,* 251–254.

Beauvais, F. (1992a). An integrated model for prevention and treatment of drug abuse among American Indian youth. *Journal of Addictive Diseases, 11*(3), 68–80.

Beauvais, F. (1992b). Trends in Indian adolescent drug and alcohol use. *American Indian and Alaska Native Mental Health Research, 5*(1), 1–12.

Beauvais, F., & LaBoueff, S. (1985). Drug and alcohol abuse intervention in American Indian communities. *International Journal of the Addictions, 20*(1), 139–171.

Beauvais, F., Oetting, E. R., & Edwards, R. W. (1985a). Trends in drug use of Indian adolescents living on reservations: 1975–1983. *American Journal on Drug and Alcohol Dependence, 11*(3–4), 209–229.

Beauvais, F., Oetting, E. R., & Edwards, R. W. (1985b). Trends in the use of inhalants among American Indian adolescents. *White Cloud Journal of American Indian Mental Health, 3*(4), 3–11.

Beauvais, F., & Trimble, J. E. (1992). The role of the researcher in evaluating American Indian drug abuse prevention programs. In M. Orlandi (Ed.), *Cultural competence for evaluations: A guide for alcohol and other drug prevention practitioners working with ethnic/racial communities* (pp. 173–201). Rockville, MD: Office of Substance Abuse Prevention.

Bellamy, G. R. (1984). *Policy implications for adolescent deviance: The case of Indian alcohol prohibition.* Unpublished doctoral dissertation, The Johns Hopkins University.

Bernstein, E., & Woodall, W. G. (1987). Changing perceptions of riskiness in drinking, drugs, and driving: An emergency department-based alcohol and substance abuse prevention program. *Annals of Emergency Medicine, 16*, 1350–1354.

Bloom, M. (1981). *Primary prevention: The possible science.* Englewood Cliffs, NJ: Prentice Hall.

Blose, J., & Holder, H. (1987). Liquor by the drink and alcohol-related traffic crashes: A natural experiment using time series analysis. *Journal of Studies on Alcohol, 48*, 52–60.

Blum, K., Futterman, S. L., & Pascarosa, P. (1977). Peyote, a potential ethnopharmacologic agent for alcoholism and other drug dependencies: Possible biochemical rationale. *Clinical Toxicology, 11*, 459–472.

Carpenter, R. A., Lyons, C. A., & Miller, W. R. (1985). Peer-managed self-control program for prevention of alcohol abuse in American Indian high school students: A pilot evaluation. *International Journal of the Addictions, 20*(2), 299–310.

Colon, I., Cutter, H., & Jones, W. (1981). Alcohol control policies, alcohol consumption, and alcoholism. *American Journal on Alcohol and Drug Abuse, 8*, 347–362.

Davis, S. M., Hunt, K., & Kitzes, J. M. (1989). Improving the health of Indian teenagers—A demonstration program in rural New Mexico. *Public Health Reports, 104*, 271–278.

Dozier, E. P. (1966). Problem drinking among American Indians: The role of sociocultural deprivation. *Quarterly Journal of Studies on Alcohol, 27*, 72–84.

Duryea, E. J., & Matzek, S. (1990). Results of a first-year pilot study in peer pressure management among American Indian youth. *Wellness Perspectives: Research, Theory, and Practice, 7*(2), 17–30.

Ferguson, F. N. (1968). Navajo drinking: Some tentative hypotheses. *Human Organization, 27*, 159–167.

Ferguson, F. N. (1970). A treatment program for Navajo alcoholics: Quantity. *Journal of Studies on Alcohol, 31*, 898–919.

Ferguson, F. N. (1976). Stake theory as an explanatory device in Navajo alcohol treatment response. *Human Organization, 35*(1), 65–77.

Fleming, C. (1992). American Indians and Alaska natives: Changing societies past and present. In M. Orlandi (Ed.), *Cultural competence for evaluations: A guide for alcohol and other drug prevention practitioners working with ethnic/racial communities* (pp. 147–171). Rockville, MD: Office of Substance Abuse Prevention.

Forslund, M. A., & Cranston, V. A. (1975). A self-report comparison of Indian and Anglo delinquency in Wyoming. *Criminology, 12*(2), 193–197.

Forslund, M. A., & Meyers, R. E. (1974). Delinquency among Wind River Indian reservation youth. *Criminology, 12*(1), 97–106.

Foulks, E. F. (1989). Misalliances in the Barrow alcohol study and commentaries. *American Indian and Alaska Native Mental Health Research, 2*(3), 7–17 (entire volume).

Fox, J., Manitowabi, D., & Ward, J. A. (1984). An Indian community with a high suicide rate—five years after. *Canadian Journal of Psychiatry, 29*, 425–427.

Gilchrist, L., Schinke, S. P., Trimble, J. E., & Cvetkovich, G. (1987). Skills enhancement to prevent substance abuse among American Indian adolescents. *International Journal of the Addictions, 22*, 869–879.

Gliksman, L., & Rush, B. (1986). Alcohol availability, alcohol consumption, and alcohol-related damage. *Journal of Studies on Alcohol, 47*, 11–18.

Gordis, E. (1991). From science to social policy: An uncertain road. *Journal of Studies on Alcohol, 52*, 101–109.

Guyette, S. (1982). Selected characteristics of American Indian substance abusers. *International Journal of the Addictions, 17*, 1001–1014.

Hirschfelder, A., & Montano, M. (1993). *The Native American almanac.* Englewood Cliffs, NJ: Prentice Hall.

Hisnanick, J., & Erickson, P. (1993). Hospital resource utilization by American Indians and Alaska natives for alcoholism and alcohol abuse. *American Journal of Drug and Alcohol Abuse, 19*, 387–396.

Hodgkinson, H. L., Outtz, J. H., & Obarakpor, A. M. (1990). *The demographics of American Indians: One percent of the people; fifty percent of the diversity.* Washington, DC: Institute for Educational Leadership.

Holder, H. D., & Stoil, M. J. (1988). Beyond prohibition: The public health approach to prevention. *Alcohol Health and Research World, 12*(4), 292–297.

Hughes, S. P., & Dodder, R. A. (1984). Alcohol consumption patterns among American Indians and white college students. *Journal of Studies on Alcohol, 45*, 433–440.

Indian Health Service. (1986). *Alcoholism, substance abuse prevention initiative.* Rockville, MD: U.S. Department of Health and Human Services.

Indian Health Service. (1987). *School- and community-based alcoholism/substance abuse prevention survey.* Rockville, MD: U.S. Department of Health and Human Services.

Indian Health Service. (1990). *Injuries among American Indians and Alaska natives, 1990.* Rockville, MD: U.S. Department of Health and Human Services.

Indian Health Service. (1991). *Regional differences in Indian health*. Rockville, MD: U.S. Department of Health and Human Services.

Indian Health Service. (1992). *Trends in Indian health*. Rockville, MD: U.S. Department of Health and Human Services.

Indian Health Service. (1993). *Trends in Indian health*. Rockville, MD: U.S. Department of Health and Human Services.

Institute of Medicine. (1989). *Prevention and treatment of alcohol problems: Research opportunities*. Washington, DC: National Academy Press.

Jensen, G., Stauss, J., & Harris, V. (1977). Crime, delinquency, and the American Indian. *Human Organization, 36*(3), 252–257.

Jessor, R., Graves, T., Hanson, R., & Jessor, S. (1968). *Society, personality, and deviant behavior: A study of tri-ethnic community*. New York: Holt, Rinehart, & Winston.

Kahn, M. V., & Fua, C. (1985). Counselor training as a therapy for alcohol abuse among aboriginal people. *American Journal of Community Psychology, 13*, 613–616.

Kahn, M. V., & Stephan, L. S. (1981). Counselor training as a treatment method for alcohol and other drug abuse. *International Journal of the Addictions, 16*, 1415–1424.

LaFromboise, T. D., & Rowe, W. (1983). Skills training for bicultural competence: Rationale and application. *Journal of Counseling Psychology, 30*, 589–595.

Last, J. M. (1983). *A dictionary of epidemiology*. New York: Oxford University Press.

Leland, J. (1976). *Firewater myths: North American Indian drinking and alcohol addiction*. New Brunswick, NJ: Rutgers Center on Alcohol Studies.

Levy, J. E., & Kunitz, S. J. (1974). *Indian drinking*. New York: Wiley Interscience.

Levy, J. E., & Kunitz, S. J. (1981). Economic and political factors inhibiting the use of basic research findings in Indian alcoholism programs. *Journal of Studies on Alcohol, 9*, 60–72.

Levy, J. E., & Kunitz, S. J. (1987). A suicide prevention program for Hopi youth. *Social Science and Medicine, 25*, 931–940.

Liban, C. B., & Smart, R. G. (1982). Drinking and other drug use among Ontario Indian students. *Drug Alcohol Dependence, 9*, 161–171.

Longclaws, L., Barnes, G., Grieve, L., & Dumoff, R. (1980). Alcohol and other drug use among the Brokenhead Ojibwa. *Journal of Studies on Alcohol, 41*(1), 21–36.

Lujan, C. C., DeBruyn, L., May, P. A., & Bird, M. E. (1989). Profile of abused and neglected Indian children in the Southwest. *Child Abuse and Neglect, 13*(4), 449–461.

Lurie, N. O. (1971). The world's oldest ongoing protest demonstration. *Pacific History Review, 40*(3), 311–332.

MacDonald, S., & Whitehead, P. (1983). Availability of outlets and consumption of alcoholic beverages. *Journal of Drug Issues, 13*, 477–486.

Macedo, H. (1988). Community trauma and community interventions. *Arctic Medical Research, 47*(Suppl. 1), 94–96.

Mail, P. D. (1985). Closing the circle: A prevention model for Indian communities with alcohol problems. *IHS Primary Care Provider, 10*(1), 2–5.

Mail, P. D., & Johnson, S. (1993). Boozing, sniffing, and toking: An overview of the past, present, and future of substance use by American Indians. *American Indian and Alaska Native Mental Health Research, 5*(2), 1–33.

Mail, P. D., & McDonald, D. R. (1980). *Tulapai to Tokay.* New Haven, CT: Human Resource Area Files Press.

Mail, P. D., & Wright, L. J. (1989). Point of view: Indian sobriety must come from Indian solutions. *Health Education Research, 20*(5), 15–19.

Manson, S. M. (Ed.). (1989). *American Indian and Alaska Native Mental Health Research, 2*(3), 7–90.

Manson, S. M., Shore, J., Barron, A., Ackerson, L., & Neligh, G. (1992). Alcohol abuse and dependence among American Indians. In J. Helzer & G. Canino (Eds.), *Alcoholism in North America, Europe, and Asia* (pp. 119–130). New York: Oxford University Press.

Manson, S. M., Tatum, E., & Dinges, N. G. (1982). Prevention research among American Indian and Alaska native communities: Charting future courses for theory and practice in mental health. In S. M. Manson (Ed.), *New directions in prevention among American Indian and Alaska native communities* (pp. 1–64). Portland, OR: Oregon Health Sciences University.

Marum, L. (1988). Rural community organizing and development strategies in Alaska native villages. *Arctic Medical Research, 47*(Suppl. 1), 354–356.

Masis, K. B., & May, P. A. (1991). A comprehensive local program for the prevention of fetal alcohol syndrome. *Public Health Reports, 106*(5), 484–489.

May, P. A. (1975). Arrests, alcohol, and alcohol legalization among an American Indian tribe. *Plains Anthropologist, 20*(68), 129–134.

May, P. A. (1976). *Alcohol legalization and Native Americans: A sociological inquiry.* Unpublished doctoral dissertation, University of Montana.

May, P. A. (1977). Alcohol beverage control: A survey of tribal alcohol statutes. *American Indian Law Review, 5*, 217–228.

May, P. A. (1982). Substance abuse and American Indians: Prevalence and susceptibility. *International Journal of the Addictions, 17*, 1185–1209.

May, P. A. (1986). Alcohol and other drug misuse prevention programs for American Indians: Needs and opportunities. *Journal of Studies on Alcohol, 47*(3), 187–195.

May, P. A. (1989a). Alcohol abuse and alcoholism among American Indians: An overview. In T. D. Watts & R. Wright (Eds.), *Alcoholism in minority populations* (pp. 95–119). Springfield, IL: Charles C. Thomas.

May, P. A. (1989b). Motor vehicle crashes and alcohol among American Indians and Alaska natives. In U.S. Surgeon General (Ed.), *The Surgeon General's workshop on drunk driving: Background papers* (pp. 207–223). Washington, DC: U.S. Department of Health and Human Services.

May, P. A. (1992). Alcohol policy considerations for Indian reservations and border town communities. *American Indian and Alaska Native Mental Health Research, 4*(3), 5–59.

May, P. A. (1995). The prevention of alcohol and other drug abuse among American Indians: A review and analysis of the literature. In P. Langton (Ed.), *The challenge of participatory research preventing alcohol-related problems in ethnic communities* (pp. 183–243). Washington, DC: National Institute on Alcohol Abuse and Alcoholism and Center for Substance Abuse Treatment.

May, P. A. (1996). Overview of alcohol abuse epidemiology for American Indian populations. In G. D. Sandefur, R. R. Rundfass, & B. Cohen (Eds.), Changing numbers, changing needs: American Indian demography and public health. Washington, DC: National Academy Press.

May, P. A., & Hymbaugh, K. J. (1983). A pilot project on fetal alcohol syndrome among American Indians. *Alcohol Health Research World, 7*(2), 3–9.

May, P. A., & Hymbaugh, K. J. (1989). A macro-level fetal alcohol syndrome prevention program for Native Americans and Alaska natives: Description and evaluation. *Journal of Studies on Alcohol, 50*(6), 508–518.

May, P. A., Miller, J. H., & Wallerstein, N. (1993). Motivation and community prevention of substance abuse. *Experimental and Clinical Psychopharmacology, 1*(1), 68–79.

May, P. A., & Smith, M. B. (1988). Some Navajo Indian opinions about alcohol abuse and prohibition: A survey and recommendations for policy. *Journal of Studies on Alcohol, 49*, 324–334.

Maynard, E., & Twiss, G. (1970). *That these people may live.* Washington, DC: U.S. Government Printing Office.

Moore, M. H., & Gerstein, D. R. (Eds.). (1981). *Alcohol and public policy: Beyond the shadow of prohibition.* Washington, DC: National Academy Press.

Moran, J. (1995). Culturally sensitive alcohol prevention research in ethnic communities. In P. Langton (Ed.), *The challenge of participatory research: Preventing alcohol-related problems in ethnic communities* (pp. 43–56). Washington, DC: National Institute on Alcohol Abuse and Alcoholism and Center for Substance Abuse Treatment.

Moran, J., Fleming, C., Somervell, P., & Manson, S. (in press). Measuring ethnic identity among American Indian adolescents. *Journal of Adolescent Research.*

Mosher, J., & Jernigan, D. (1989). New directions in alcohol policy. *Annual Review of Public Health, 10*, 245–279.

Murphy, S., & DeBlassie, R. D. (1984). Substance abuse and the Native American student. *Journal of Drug Education, 14*(4), 315–321.

National Institute on Alcohol Abuse and Alcoholism. (1981). *Alcohol and health* (4th ed.). Washington, DC: U.S. Government Printing Office.

Neumann, A. K., Mason, V., Chase, E., & Albaugh, B. (1991). Factors associated with success among Southern Cheyenne and Arapaho Indians. *Journal of Community Health, 16*(2), 103–115.

Newcomb, M. D., & Bentler, P. M. (1989). Substance abuse among children and teenagers. *American Psychologist, 44*(2), 242–248.

O'Donnell, M. (1985). Research on drinking locations of alcohol-impaired drivers: Implications for prevention policies. *Journal on Public Health Policy, 6*, 510–525.

Oetting, E. R., & Beauvais, F. (1989). Epidemiology and correlates of alcohol use among Indian adolescents living on reservations. In *Alcohol use among U.S. ethnic minorities*

(NIAAA Research Monograph No. 18, pp. 239–267). Rockville, MD: U.S. Public Health Service.

Oetting, E. R., & Beauvais, F. (1990–1991). Orthagonal cultural identification theory: The cultural identification of minority adolescents. *International Journal of the Addictions, 25*(5a and 6a), 655–685.

Oetting, E. R., Beauvais, F., & Edwards, R. W. (1988). Alcohol and Indian youth: Social and psychological correlates and prevention. *Journal of Drug Issues, 18*, 87–101.

Oetting, E. R., Swaim, R. C., Edwards, R. W., & Beauvais, F. (1989). Indian and Anglo adolescent alcohol use and emotional distress: Path models. *American Journal of Drug and Alcohol Abuse, 15*(2), 153–172.

Office of Substance Abuse Prevention. (1990). *Breaking new ground for American Indian and Alaska native youth at risk: Program summaries* (Technical Report, No. 3). Rockville, MD: U.S. Department of Health and Human Services.

Okwumabua, J. O., & Duryea, E. J. (1987). Age of onset, periods of risk, and patterns of progression in drug use among American Indian high school students. *International Journal of the Addictions, 22*, 1269–1276.

Okwumabua, J. O., Okwumabua, T. M., & Duryea, E. J. (1989). An investigation of health decisionmaking skills among American Indian adolescents. *American Indian and Alaska Native Mental Health Research, 3*(1), 42–52.

Parker, L., Jamons, M., Marek, R., & Camacho, C. (1991). Traditions and innovations: A community-based approach to substance abuse prevention. *Rhode Island Medical Journal, 74*, 281–285.

Pascarosa, P., & Futterman, S. (1976). Ethnopsychedelic therapy for alcoholics: Observations in the peyote ritual of the Native American church. *Journal of Psychedelic Drugs, 8*(3), 215–221.

Pittman, D. J., & White, H. R. (Eds.). (1991). *Society, culture, and drinking patterns reexamined.* New Brunswick, NJ: Rutgers Center on Alcohol Studies.

Plaisier, K. J. (1989). Fetal alcohol syndrome prevention in American Indian communities of Michigan's upper peninsula. *American Indian and Alaska Native Mental Health Research, 3*(1), 16–33.

Reed, T. E. (1985). Ethnic differences in alcohol use, abuse and sensitivity: A review with genetic interpretation. *Social Biology, 32*(3–4), 195–209.

Rhoades, E. R., Mason, R. D., Eddy, P., Smith, E. M., & Burns, T. R. (1988). The Indian Health Service approach to alcoholism among American Indians and Alaska natives. *Public Health Reports, 103*(6), 621–627.

Sage, G. P., & Burns, G. L. (1993). Attributional antecedents of alcohol use in American Indian and Euroamerican adolescents. *American Indian and Alaska Native Mental Health Research, 5*(2), 46–56.

Savard, R. J. (1968). Effects of disulfiram therapy on relationships within the Navajo drinking group. *Quarterly Journal of Studies on Alcohol, 29*, 909–916.

Schaefer, J. M. (1981). Firewater myths revisited. *Journal of Studies on Alcohol, 9*, 99–117.

Schinke, S. P., Mancher, M. S., Holden, G. W., Botvin, G. J., & Orlandi, M. A. (1989). American Indian youth and substance abuse: Tobacco use problems, risk factors and prevention interventions. *Health Education Research, 4*(1), 137–144.

Schinke, S. P., Orlandi, M. A., Botvin, G. J., Gilchrist, L., Trimble, J. E., & Locklear, V. S. (1988). Preventing substance abuse among American Indian adolescents: A bicultural competence skills approach. *Journal of Counseling Psychology, 35*(1), 87–90.

Schinke, S. P., Shilling, R. F., Gilchrist, L., Asby, M. R., & Kitajima, E. (1989). Native youth and smokeless tobacco: Prevalence rates, gender difference, and descriptive characteristics. *National Cancer Institute Monographs, 8,* 39–42.

Schinke, S. P., Shilling, R. F., Gilchrist, L., Barth, R. P., Bobo, J. K., Trimble, J. E., & Cvetkovich, G. T. (1985). Preventing substance abuse with American Indian youth. *Social Casework, 66,* 213–217.

Scott, K. A., & Meyers, A. M. (1988). Impact of fitness training on native adolescents' self-evaluation and substance use. *Canadian Journal of Public Health, 79,* 424–428.

Shore, J. H., & Kofoed, L. (1984). Community intervention in the treatment of alcoholism. *Alcoholism: Clinical and Experimental Research, 8*(2), 151–159.

Shore, J. H., & Von Fumetti, B. (1972). Three alcohol programs for American Indians. *American Journal of Psychiatry, 128,* 1454–1459.

Silk-Walker, P., Walker, D., & Kivlahan, D. (1988). Alcoholism, alcohol abuse, and health in American Indians and Alaska natives. In S. Manson & N. Dinges (Eds.), *Behavioral health issues among American Indians* (American Indian and Alaska Native Mental Health Research, Monograph, No. 1, pp. 65–92). Denver: University of Colorado Press.

Smith, R. J. (1991). Injuries and injury control. In N. Poland & L. Berger (Eds.), *Frontiers of community health.* Albuquerque, NM: Lovelace Medical Foundation Proceedings.

Snipp, C. M. (1989). *American Indians: The first of this land.* New York: The Russell Sage Foundation.

Spivey, G. H. (1977). The health of American Indian children in multiproblem families. *Social Science and Medicine, 11,* 357–359.

Stewart, O. C. (1964). Questions regarding American Indian criminality. *Human Organization, 23*(1), 64–76.

Swaim, R. C., Oetting, E. R., Edwards, R. W., & Beauvais, F. (1989). Links from emotional distress to adolescent drug use: A path model. *Journal of Consulting and Clinical Psychology, 57*(2), 227–231.

Swaim, R. C., Oetting, E. R., Thurman, P. J., Beauvais, F., & Edwards, R. W. (1993). American Indian adolescent drug use and socialization characteristics: A cross-cultural comparison. *Journal of Cross-Cultural Psychology, 24*(1), 53–71.

U.S. Bureau of the Census. (1991). *American Indian and Alaska native areas: 1990.* Washington, DC: U.S. Government Printing Office.

U.S. Surgeon General. (1989). *Surgeon General's workshop on drunk driving: Recommendations.* Rockville, MD: U.S. Department of Health and Human Services.

Walker, D., Howard, M., Anderson, B., & Lambert, M. (1994). Substance-dependent American Indian veterans: A national evaluation. *Public Health Reports, 109*(2), 235–242.

Ward, J. A. (1984). Preventive implications of a Native American mental health program. *Journal of Preventive Psychiatry, 2*(3–4), 371–385.

Weibel-Orlando, J. (1989). Treatment and prevention of Native American alcoholism. In T. D. Watts & R. Wright (Eds.), *Alcoholism in minority populations* (pp. 121–139). Springfield, IL: Charles C. Thomas.

Weisner, T. S., Weibel-Orlando, J. C., & Long, J. (1984). Serious drinking, white man's drinking, and teetotaling: Drinking levels and styles in an urban American Indian population. *Journal of Studies on Alcohol, 45*(3), 237–250.

Westermeyer, J. (1974). The drunken Indian stereotype: Myths and realities. *Psychiatry Annual, 41*(11), 29–36.

Westermeyer, J., & Peake, E. (1983). A ten-year follow-up of alcoholic Native Americans in Minnesota. *American Journal of Psychiatry, 140*(4), 189–194.

Whittacker, J. O. (1962). Alcohol and the Standing Rock Sioux Tribe. *Quarterly Journal of Studies on Alcohol, 23*, 468–479.

Whittacker, J. O. (1982). Alcohol and the Standing Rock Sioux Tribe: A 20-year follow-up study. *Journal of Studies on Alcohol, 43*, 191–200.

Wilson, L. G., & Shore, J. H. (1975). Evaluation of a regional Indian alcohol program. *American Journal of Psychiatry, 132*, 255–258.

Wilson, T. (1992). Blood quantum: Native American mixed bloods. In M. Root (Ed.), *Racially mixed people in America* (pp. 108–125). Newbury Park, CA: Sage Publications.

Winfree, L. T., & Griffiths, C. T. (1983a). Social learning and adolescent marijuana use: A trend study of deviant behavior in a rural middle school. *Rural Sociology, 48*(2), 219–239.

Winfree, L. T., & Griffiths, C. T. (1983b). Youth at risk: Marijuana use among Native American and white youth. *International Journal of the Addictions, 18*, 53–70.

Wingert, J. L. (1982). *Inhalant use among Native American adolescents: A comparison of users and nonusers at Intermountain Intertribal School.* Unpublished dissertation, Utah State University.

Hispanics/ Latinos   2

Melvin Delgado

Historical Context of AOD Use

The problem of alcohol and other drug (AOD) abuse cannot be viewed simply within the present-day context in which we are studying it. As noted by Gerbner (1990), "Alcohol, tobacco, and other drugs of various kinds have a long history of remedial and ceremonial functions." Gerbner continues:

> Improvements in production and marketing, and the cultural changes we associate with the industrial and media revolutions, swept away most of the traditional controls of scarcity, custom, and ritual. Except where coherent ideological and other cultural (usually religious) rules inhibit or forbid their uses, many palliative and addictive substances have become commodities marketed to serve individual desires and institutional and geopolitical interests. (p. 55)

This problem must be viewed within a historical context to better understand the issues associated with this topic for various Latino subgroups. This chapter, therefore, does not attempt to provide an in-depth understanding for each major Latino subgroup. Instead, it synthesizes the major threads common to Latinos with respect to three key drugs: alcohol, cocaine, and marijuana.

Alcohol

It is impossible to examine the role of alcohol in isolation from the political economy associated with sugar cane (Mintz, 1985). Alcohol was not only another product to market, but also served as an important tool for social control, particularly among low-skilled workers with minimal recreational and advancement opportunities. This point was particularly evident in Cuba, the Dominican Republic, and Puerto Rico, where rum has been and continues to be relatively inexpensive.

Cocaine

The importance of the coca leaf in South America has been established (Benjamin & Miller, 1991; Wisotsky, 1990). This plant has exerted prodigious influence in several South American countries. The coca plant has been grown in the Andes Mountains for thousands of years and been used by indigenous people to minimize the pains associated with hunger and to increase worker endurance (Benjamin & Miller, 1991).

The leaves of the coca bush had been chewed by Andean peasants for at least 4,000 years before the early Spanish explorers arrived in South America. Coca leaves have nutritional value as food, and the cocaine alkaloid in them acts as a powerful appetite suppressant, an effective antidote for altitude sickness, a potent local anesthetic, and a central nervous system stimulant. It is little wonder that the Incas revered coca leaves as a gift of the gods.

In addition to the qualities of the coca leaves, coca cultivation represents an important product for the economy of several nations; these nations have a strong tradition of agriculture with workers who cannot make the transition to a postindustrialized market (Wisotsky, 1990). Consequently, the eradication of cocaine cannot be separated from the social–political–economic context of coca in the lives of countless numbers of Latin American workers and farmers.

Marijuana

The history of marijuana in Latin America is different from that of alcohol and cocaine. Marijuana was introduced to this part of the world by Spain in the 16th century (Benjamin & Miller, 1991). Attempts to review the literature on the history of marijuana in Latin America, and more specifically Mexico, were disappointing. Unfortunately, the literature on this topic does not provide details on the plant's role in the economy of the region and how the Spaniards used it to make their conquest and occupation profitable and easier to accomplish. The literature, however, does note that Mexican Americans played an influential role in introducing the drug into the United States (Benjamin & Miller, 1991; Doweiko, 1993; Ray & Ksir, 1990).

Latino Demographics

The 1990 U.S. census indicates approximately 22 million Latinos resided in the United States (U.S. Bureau of the Census, 1991); this figure represents approximately a 50 percent increase over the 1980 figures (U.S. Bureau of the Census, 1983). The 1980 figure, in turn, represented an increase of 61 percent over 1970 (U.S. Bureau of the Census, 1971). Population growth estimates indicate that Latinos will continue to increase in numbers over the next 60 years—29 million by the year 2000, accounting for approximately 10 percent of the total population, and 128 million by the year 2050, making Latinos the largest ethnic group in the United States (U.S. Bureau of the Census, 1986). The Latino population is represented in all 50 states and is heavily concentrated in six states (California, Florida, Illinois, New Jersey, New York, and Texas), accounting for 78 percent of all Latinos in the United States (U.S. Bureau of the Census, 1991).

Mexican Americans are the largest Latino subgroup, accounting for approximately 63 percent of all Latinos in the United States (13,421,000), followed by Central and South Americans with 2,951,000 (21 percent), Puerto Ricans with 2,382,000 (11 percent), and Cubans with 1,055,000 (5 percent) (U.S. Bureau of the Census, 1991). Latinos are the most urbanized ethnic group in the United States, with approximately 92 percent residing in urban areas, compared with the national average of 74 percent; Puerto Ricans and Cubans, in turn, are the most urbanized subgroups, with 95 percent residing in cities, followed by Mexican Americans with approximately 91 percent (U.S. Bureau of the Census, 1991).

The Latino population is young, with a median age of 26, compared with 34 for the non-Latino population. Mexican Americans are the youngest of the subgroups with a median age of 24, followed by Puerto Ricans (27); Cubans are by far the oldest subgroup, with a median age of 39 (U.S. Bureau of the Census, 1991).

Poverty rates for Latinos are high compared with non-Latino whites. Twenty-five percent of Latino families fall below the poverty level versus approximately 9 percent for non-Latino white families. However, it is necessary to examine Latino subgroups, where wide disparity exists, with Puerto Rican families having the highest poverty rate (approximately 38 percent), followed by Mexican Americans (28 percent), and Cubans (17 percent) (U.S. Bureau of the Census, 1991). Household income patterns are similar to poverty rates, with Latinos having a median household income of $22,300 versus $30,500 for non-Latino households. Puerto Ricans have the lowest income ($16,200), followed by Mexican Americans ($22,439); Cubans have the highest income ($25,900) (U.S. Bureau of the Census, 1991).

Only 51 percent of Latinos have completed four years or more of high school versus 80 percent of non-Latinos. Puerto Ricans had a graduation rate of 58 percent; Cubans had a rate of 61 percent; and Mexican Americans had the lowest rate with only 44 percent completing high school (U.S. Bureau of the Census, 1991). Finally, the family composition of Latinos indicates that most consist of married couples (69 percent, compared with 79 percent of non-Latino families), with 24 percent headed by women, compared to 16 percent for non-Latino households (U.S. Bureau of the Census, 1991). Again, significant differences existed among Latino subgroups, with Puerto Rican families having the lowest percentage of married couples (41 percent) and the highest percentage of female heads (34 percent) (U.S. Bureau of the Census, 1991).

Extent of the Problem

Culture covers many key factors, making generalizations about racial and ethnic groups difficult, if not impossible. Latinos are no exception. The social construct of the term "Latino/Hispanic" brings together many subgroups on the basis of nationality (Castex, 1994). According to Alcocer (1993), "the term is meant to include the diverse nationalities from North, Central, and South America, as well as the Caribbean area, that supposedly share a common heritage. But it is a very unsatisfactory term since these people are, in fact, quite diverse and not easily comparable" (p. 37). Latino/Hispanic may be based on criteria such as country of origin, location of birth, primary language, surname, parent's country of origin, and self-disclosure (Hayes-Bautista & Chapa, 1987; Humm-Delgado & Delgado, 1983a). Mayers and Kail (1993) note that wide disparities exist among Latino subgroups on "indices such as educational attainment, socioeconomic status, and labor force participation. There are also disparities in patterns of drug use because there is a clustering of the various Hispanic subgroups in different parts of the country, just as types of drug use vary around the country" (p. 5).

Assessing the nature and extent of the problem of AOD is also complicated by definitional and methodological limitations (Booth, Castro,

& Anglin, 1990; Delgado & Rodriguez-Andrew, 1990; Mayers & Kail, 1993). These limitations, in turn, make generalizations impossible, as noted by Booth and colleagues (1990):

> Until recently, little scientific information on [AOD abuse] and Hispanics was available. What scattered data that did exist generally failed to note the differences among various Hispanic cultural groups. Thus, what was known was based largely on poorly defined populations or related only to selective subgroups within a particular Hispanic group . . . stereotypes were fostered by generalizations from some of these early studies. (p. 21)

According to the Hispanic Health and Nutrition Examination Survey (HHANES, 1987), AOD use among Latinos increases with age, as in the general population. Nevertheless, contrary to popular opinion, Latinos generally have lower rates of lifetime use of alcohol, phencyclidine (PCP), hallucinogens, and stimulants than do non-Latino whites (Booth et al., 1990). Use of cocaine is an exception (Mayers & Kail, 1993). African Americans, in turn, have a higher rate of lifetime use of heroin than do Latinos and non-Latino whites (National Institute on Drug Abuse, 1985).

The problem of AOD abuse, however, must be examined for each respective Latino subgroup, considering many key factors to avoid false generalizations. The variable of age plays a strong role among Latinos. Latino youths ages 12 to 17 have a higher rate of cocaine use than their African American and non-Latino white counterparts (National Clearinghouse for Alcohol and Drug Information, 1993). More specifically, Puerto Rican youths have a higher use rate than Mexican Americans or Cubans (Booth et al., 1990). However, in turning to marijuana, the HHANES noted that Mexican Americans ages 12 to 17 have the highest percentage of lifetime use among Latinos—31 percent, versus 26 percent among Puerto Ricans and 21 percent among Cubans (the latter represents the combination of two age categories, 12 to 24 and 25 to 44, because of a small sample size). The non-Latino white and African American populations have use rates of 25 percent and 24 percent, respectively.

Differences can also be found based on gender when examining use for cocaine and marijuana. Puerto Rican men have the highest rate of lifetime use of cocaine (28 percent) of all groups surveyed; Puerto Rican women have the highest rate of cocaine use (close to 17 percent), a rate still lower than their male counterparts. As already noted, however, Mexican American men have the highest rate of lifetime use of marijuana among Latinos, almost double the use rate of Mexican American women (approximately 54 percent versus 28 percent).

The study of alcohol use among Latinos has received increased attention in the past 10 years (Alcocer, 1993; Caetano, 1987, 1988, 1989; Gilbert,

1993). In a fashion similar to lifetime use rates of PCP, hallucinogens, and stimulants, Latino men (87 percent) and women (72 percent) report a lower rate of alcohol use than do non-Latino white men (91 percent) and women (83 percent) (National Institute on Drug Abuse, 1989). Caetano (1985) indicates that drinking decreases with age. Puerto Rican women have a lower rate of abstention and a higher proportion of less frequent, heavy drinkers than other Latino populations (Alcocer, 1993). Alcocer, in his summary of the literature on youths and alcohol, indicates that Latino youths (both male and female) start drinking at a later age than other ethnic or racial groups, with boys having a tendency to drink more often than girls.

Cultural Considerations

AOD abuse does not happen in a social vacuum; it transpires in a social context with definitions of what constitutes an AOD problem and with explicit expectations of what constitutes intervention. Culture is part of that context and must be considered in the development of prevention and intervention strategies. The literature on culture-specific services has identified six important principles that must form the basis of any successful program: (1) commitment to providing culture-specific services, (2) awareness and acceptance of the concept of diversity, (3) staff self-awareness and self-appreciation, (4) understanding of the dynamics of cultural differences and how they influence the development of relationships and interventions, (5) knowledge of client and community cultural background and values, and (6) flexibility in the adaptation of methods and skills to match client and community needs and background (Cross, 1988).

The professional literature on Latinos traces the etiology of AOD abuse to one or more of the following sources: stress, familial discord or disruption, and peer pressure (Mayers & Kail, 1993). These sources, in turn, have been affected by uprooting, acculturation, and limited resources for prevention, early identification, and treatment.

Stress

Some Latino scholars have identified the increased amount of stress Latinos face in this society (Barrera, Zautra, & Baca, 1984; Cervantes & Castro, 1985; Mayers & Kail, 1993; Vega & Miranda, 1985). Stressors associated with poor economic conditions, as already noted, combined with low educational achievement, limited English-language skills, high crime rates, high drug availability, and the impact of racism on self-esteem make Latinos particularly vulnerable to AOD use and abuse.

Familial Discord and Disruption

The literature is in general agreement that the Latino family forms the cornerstone of any effort at understanding and treating AOD abuse (Booth et al., 1990; Delgado & Rodriguez-Andrew, 1990; Mayers & Kail, 1993; Padilla, Snyder, & de Salgado, 1992; Santisteban & Szapocznik, 1982; Szapocznik & Kurtines, 1989). Familial difficulties might arise as a result of children acculturating to life in the United States. They are increasingly exposed to new values through education, media, and contact with members of other ethnic and racial groups. These values may be diametrically different from those of their parents (independence versus interdependence or cooperation versus competition, for example). These differences in values manifest themselves when children stop embracing their parents' values and begin behaving in ways that seriously undermine family structure and role expectations. Latino youths, in turn, must reconcile living in two different worlds (parents and society), making them more vulnerable to AOD use.

Peer Pressure

The literature has shown that peer influence is strong in initial and subsequent drug use (Booth et al., 1990; Mayers & Kail, 1993; Padilla & Snyder, 1992; Robles, Martinez, & Moscoso, 1979). Peer influence is particularly strong during the adolescent and early childhood developmental phases; consequently, a youth's chances of using AOD go up dramatically if any peer group members are also involved in drug taking. This situation is compounded when youths feel isolated from the greater society because of ethnicity, language preferences, or geographical isolation that limit the nature and extent of the social network.

As a result of these etiological themes, the literature of Latino AOD use has stressed using the following cultural factors as a foundation for any assessment and intervention: (1) natural support systems, particularly family; (2) urban–rural context; and (3) perceptions of etiology.

Natural Support Systems

The influence of natural support systems in Latino families and communities is formidable (Barrera & Reese, 1993; Delgado, 1994, 1995; Humm-Delgado

& Delgado, 1993; Gfoerer & De La Rosa, 1993; Valle & Vega, 1980). Natural support system frameworks and definitions are in the literature. However, the definition developed by Delgado (1995) is the basis for this analysis:

> Hispanic natural support systems are composed of a constellation of individuals who relate to you, although not necessarily to each other, on a familiar or even intimate basis. These individuals are an important basis for self-definition and identity formation, and can be accessed freely on a casual basis or for the purposes of meeting specific expressive, and/or instrumental needs. The concept of natural support systems extends far beyond the existence of mechanisms that can be utilized as support systems and includes the individuals that comprise the support system (that is, while a church has the potential to be utilized as a natural support system, its utility lies in the personality of its religious leader); consequently, support systems are only as good as the individuals (natural support providers) providing the assistance. Hispanic natural support systems involve extended family (both related and non-related), neighbors, friends, healers, institutions (including religious and other indigenous types), local self-help groups, and community leaders. (p. 23)

This encompassing definition addresses the importance of the personality and ability of the individual in a position to be a natural support, and it identifies the key natural support system types.

The family, which can consist of blood relatives, relatives by marriage, and "adopted" relatives (key friends and important neighbors who are considered family), is the center of any natural support system in this community (Vega, 1990). The other natural supports will fall into the following types: religious, folk healing, merchants or social clubs (that is, grocery stores, botanical shops, sporting teams, and so on), and community leaders. These supports may exert a wide range of influence, depending on circumstance and needs.

Urban–Rural Context

The geographical context in which AOD abuse takes place has enormous implications for how the problem is viewed, both by the community and the social service system. Most research on Latinos and AOD abuse has been urban based; three cities have been extensively covered in the literature—Los Angeles, Miami, and New York (Humm-Delgado & Delgado, 1983b). As a result of this focus on large cities, it is easy to draw implications and generalizations for Latinos without seriously considering their fate in small cities, towns, and rural areas. For example, although there are higher rates of AOD abuse among urban-based Latino youths, indications show that rates are also increasing in rural areas among some Latino sub-groups (Mata & Rodriguez-Andrew, 1988; Rodriguez-Andrew, 1988). Geographical context will probably exert influence over the types of drugs available, cost, and use patterns (Booth et al., 1990).

Perceptions of Etiology

As indicated by McNeece and DiNitto (1994), culture-bound definitions of AOD abuse among Latinos must be considered in defining whether AOD abuse is a perceived problem. As a result, AOD abuse may be viewed as being caused by external, metaphysical forces such as God or spirits (Comas-Diaz, 1986; Singer, 1984). The power of this belief system can be formidable, influencing how an individual or family responds to an AOD abuse problem. In this case, the individual or family may believe that intervention can be effective only if it involves metaphysical forces and cannot be addressed through earthly means such as counseling.

Culture-Specific Intervention

As noted by Delgado (1989), it is essential for culture-specific interventions to occur throughout the entire continuum of AOD-related services. These services must be grounded in the value system, traditions, and language of the client, family, and community. Marin (1993), in his article on designing culture-specific interventions with Latinos, notes that

> differences predicate the notion that in order to be effective, community interventions need to take into consideration the specific characteristics of the group being targeted. Culturally appropriate interventions are defined, therefore, as meeting each of the following characteristics: (1) The intervention is based on the cultural values of the group, (2) the strategies that make up the intervention reflect the subjective culture (attitudes, expectations, norms) of the group, and (3) the components that make up the strategies reflect the behavior preferences and expectations of the group's members. (p. 149)

Failure to provide culture-specific services throughout the entire continuum will in all likelihood result in poor use of services. Furthermore, these human services *must* use Latino natural support systems whenever and wherever possible. The professional literature on intervention in Latino communities is in general agreement on the following key strategies for reaching and assisting this population group: (1) assessment (both assets and needs); (2) collaboration between formal and informal systems whenever possible; (3) community education; (4) multimodality intervention; (5) bilingual and bicultural staffing of all services; and (6) community capacity development.

Assessment

It is essential that organizations hoping to serve the needs of Latinos have an in-depth understanding of whom they are trying to reach. As already noted, it is too simplistic just to say "Latino" population; it is necessary to develop an accurate profile of the target population. This profile has a profound impact on assessment throughout all intervention strategies. Assessment is not restricted to needs (that is, what is needed or missing in the community), but must start with an assessment of assets (that is, what is available to the individual, family, organization, and community). Given that only a relatively small percentage of Latinos have displayed risk-taking behaviors, the concept of resiliency must be considered because it plays an influential part in the development of any intervention strategy. Rutter (1987) sums up the basis for resiliency quite nicely:

> Protection does not reside in the psychological chemistry of the moment but in the ways in which people deal with life changes and in what they do about their stressful or disadvantageous circumstances. Particular attention needs to be paid to the mechanisms operating at key points in people's lives when a risk trajectory may be redirected onto a more adaptive path. (p. 329)

According to Newcomb (1992), resiliency factors are, in essence, the flip side of risk factors. However, starting with an assessment of assets and resiliency establishes the context for viewing the need or problem and invariably casts a prodigious influence on how an intervention strategy is conceptualized and implemented.

Delgado's case study (Delgado, 1995a) of an asset assessment in a New England city (Holyoke, Massachusetts) involving a Puerto Rican community is an excellent example of this type of approach. In essence, a community that can mobilize its collective resources to address a communitywide problem increases its chances of solving it; these communities have an advantage at the outset when residents have personal resources and high self-esteem. The Holyoke study focused on a 40-block area with a high concentration of Puerto Ricans and addressed the following goals:

◆ Providing a detailed description and location of Puerto Rican natural support systems with a specific focus on houses of worship and merchants and social clubs. (The study did not attempt to identify folk healers and significant community leaders. The former would be difficult to access without relationship building; key community leaders had already been identified.)

◆ Providing youths with a resilient perspective on this community.

◆ Raising the consciousness of human services organizations and providers concerning positive aspects of the Puerto Rican community.

◆ Creating a resource directory specifically focused on community assets.

Data on available resources were collected on five dimensions: (1) geographical location and category of resource (that is, commercial, religious, recreational, and other); (2) identity of key contact person and years in operation; (3) hours and days of operation; (4) type of support services provided (for example, referral, financial assistance, information, and so on); and (5) general reactions of the interviewer to the receptivity of the institution for collaboration on community activities and projects.

Collaboration between Formal and Informal Services

Interagency collaboration increases in importance when the needs of Latinos are examined with respect to AOD abuse. Collaboration serves to coordinate existing resources and tie AOD services with the general social services community, minimizing isolation of these programs (Delgado, 1989). However, as already noted, collaboration must also bring in natural support systems (Delgado & Humm-Delgado, 1980). Delgado's asset study revealed a wealth of resources that could be mobilized to assist the Latino community and be a part of an agency's collaborative network (Delgado, 1995a):

> Eighteen institutions stated that people were welcome to come in and converse and not have to purchase goods or services in order to do so. Six institutions provided information on social services and made appropriate referrals to social service agencies. Several establishments ($N = 4$) indicated that they provided crisis counseling as needed, food for the hungry ($N = 4$), loans ($N = 3$), and credit ($N = 6$) as needed. One botanical institution indicated a willingness to take care of children in case of a crisis. Thus, the survey revealed an extensive array of social services being provided by these natural support systems. Twenty establishments noted a willingness to become involved in community events such as festivals, parades, contests, health fairs, and collaborating with human service agencies. Collaboration would take the form of making referrals for services,

distributing information, donating food, services and/or money. In short, these institutions were willing to become more involved with social agencies. (p. 70)

Community Education

The need for AOD abuse education is recognized by providers and consumers. The Latino community must develop a greater awareness of the impact of AOD abuse on individuals, families, and the community. For a campaign to have impact, it must stress prevention, early identification, and rehabilitation options.

Unfortunately, little research has been undertaken on Latino media use: "One of the most glaring gaps in the literature is the absence of reliable, in-depth data on Hispanic/Latino media use. Although various studies have asked questions about respondents' sources of information, the availability of viewer, listener, and reader data from commercial courses has been ignored" (Office of Substance Abuse Prevention, 1990, p. 187).

The availability of AOD abuse services to Latinos in the United States is seriously limited by lack of culture-specific services. In addition, the community has not had a well-conceptualized educational campaign, particularly for alcohol and marijuana. Much attention in the media has focused on cocaine and heroin, two drugs that have had the most visible impact on families and communities.

Several important principles must guide the development of community education campaigns focused on Latinos: use of multimedia outlets, in-depth knowledge of target audiences, use of local resources, and use of cultural themes.

Use of Multimedia Outlets

The use of all sources of information should be stressed; reliance on any one method may systematically exclude significant sectors of the Latino community. For example, illiteracy in both Spanish and English may severely limit who can read flyers, newspapers, and billboards. The research undertaken by Greenberg and colleagues (1983) with Mexican Americans has highlighted this point.

In-depth Knowledge of Target Audience

Knowledge of who constitutes the target group not only enhances the likelihood of a message being received, but it also influences how the message is delivered and who should deliver it. Programming that targets youths, for example, may not appeal to adults; the inverse may also be true. Educational campaigns should target four specific Latino groups: (1) Latino adults, both men and women; (2) Latino families; (3) Latino women of childbearing age; and (4) Latino men who drink heavily, ages 19 to 39 (OSAP, 1990).

Use of Local Resources

To make an anti-AOD campaign more relevant to a Latino community, local resources should be used to develop and implement AOD abuse messages:

> Communications programs or strategies should neither begin nor end with information campaigns. Within communities, they should seek to build the desire, resources, and mechanisms to promote prevention-associated behaviors. There are appropriate national roles in developing leadership, research and data, and prototypes of programs, but without the community base, the national component will not fulfill its potential. (OSAP 1990, p. 205)

Use of Cultural Themes

AOD community education campaigns should be conceived in a cultural context—not in a social vacuum. Thus, key cultural themes should be used in educational campaigns. Casas (1992) provides an excellent example of this point:

> In providing educational programs, all relevant personnel must be aware that, for more traditional Hispanics, the concept of simpática (a central cultural value and social script that mandates politeness and respect) may require Hispanic listeners to appear to agree with a message even though they do not understand it or have no intention of following the advice. . . . This makes it crucial that . . . personnel ask questions to ensure that AOD-related information has been correctly understood. (p. 105)

The use of cultural symbols and themes increases the likelihood that a message will not offend a community and will achieve its goal of properly informing.

Multimodality Intervention

Individual-based treatment is not without merit. However, the literature on Latinos and AOD abuse highlights the need for the use of multimodality interventions (Comas-Diaz, 1986; Delgado, 1988; Gilbert & Cervantes, 1986; Singer 1984; Santisteban, Szapocznik, & Rio, 1993). Delgado (1989) summarizes the literature on intervention: "Literature on this topic stresses use of a wide range of treatment modalities . . . the treatment of choice should be family focused, complemented by individual therapy, whenever possible. . . . However, the use of groups represents an added dimension to treatment that is often overlooked or dismissed by providers" (p. 90).

The research undertaken by Szapocznik and Kurtines (1989) best highlights the importance of involving Latino families in treatment. Familial disruption or conflict, as already indicated, can often be a direct consequence of youth, particularly men, being better educated and more highly acculturated than their parents (Booth et al., 1990; Szapocznik et al., 1989). Consequently, every effort must be made to involve Latino families in treatment.

The literature on group intervention with Latinos, for example, has shown that this method is effective and may be the best method (Delgado & Humm-Delgado, 1984). This approach is conducive to mutual help (expressive and instrumental), casting group members in both helper and helpee roles. In addition, it places the problem of AOD intervention into a broader context—namely, other individuals sharing similar needs and hopes. Comas-Diaz (1986) has reported on the importance of using group modality with low-income Puerto Rican women with alcoholism: "The success of interventions for alcoholism may be in the positive restructuring of the lives of the significant members. The group program made contact with significant others and included them in treatment" (pp. 56–57). Multimodality interventions provide the options of making treatment available to all Latinos, regardless of predisposition to any one type of intervention.

Bilingual and Bicultural Staffing of All Services

The effectiveness of multimodality interventions is predicated on the qualifications of the staff entrusted to conduct treatment. Qualifications, in this instance, are not limited to professional or educational credentials; they also entail cultural competence. Cultural competence is dramatically increased when staff share the same cultural background as their clients. This background, it should be emphasized, is not restricted to Latino subgroups but also covers such key factors as language abilities, socioeconomic status, and sexual orientation.

Programs must make every effort to have Latino representation at *all* levels of an organization, including the board of directors, and should have more than one Latino representative. Delgado (1979) states:

> Human service agencies very often employ just one Hispanic staff member who, in turn, is faced with prodigious obstacles within the setting and in the

Hispanic community. Hispanic staff, when hired, are usually paraprofessional and are often entrusted with virtually every Hispanic case the agency sees, regardless of the complexity of the presenting problem. Hispanic staff in predominantly non-Hispanic settings often experience frustration in carrying out their job responsibilities, which often results in low staff morale and high staff turnover. (pp. 465–466)

In discussing the field of AOD abuse, Booth and colleagues (1990) raise an important point when examining the mixed success rate of Latinos in treatment programs:

Treatment efforts with Hispanic clients have not met with much success. Whether due to economic or other factors, many Hispanics in treatment are disproportionately enrolled in the programs that emphasize pharmacological treatment. And much of the failure of treatment programs can be attributed to the lack of bilingual or bicultural personnel qualified to address . . . Hispanic communities in the United States. (p. 40)

Thus, availability of Latino staff increases the likelihood that available resources are used to the maximum extent and increases the likelihood of therapeutic success.

Fitzpatrick (1990), commenting on the importance of bilingual personnel, states: "Language continues to be a problem on every level of Puerto Rican or Hispanic experience . . . things have improved . . . but the problem of language and the need for bilingual personnel in the addiction prevention or correction efforts is very clear. . . . It is surprising how widely this elementary point is neglected" (p. 200). As researchers have indicated, success at recruiting and retaining Latinos in treatment cannot be separated from the necessity of having Latino staff.

Community Capacity Development

National campaigns declaring war on drugs appear and disappear depending on political climate. This, however, does not mean that the problems associated with AOD abuse disappear. Consequently, it is important that any effort to address AOD abuse in Latino communities focus on community capacity development. Community capacity development is the philosophical foundation for developing intervention strategies that build on and use individual, family, and community strengths.

These strategies must stress infrastructure development, both social and physical. No community exists without indigenous resources, and these resources, in turn, represent avenues for validating and engaging significant sectors of a community. According to McKnight and Kretzman (1991), two significant reasons exist for developing capacity:

1. Significant community development can transpire only when local community members are committed to investing themselves and their resources to change efforts. Communities, as a result, can be developed only from the bottom up.
2. Development, as a result, must commence from within because the government may not make needed resources available.

Government resources are never committed without restrictions attached to the funds, which can seriously compromise a community.

McKnight and Kretzman's work in the area of community capacity development clearly applies to the Latino community. Their framework for assessing community capacity stresses organizations and businesses and consists of three stages:

1. Primary building blocks—assets and capacities located inside the neighborhood, largely under neighborhood control (individual, associational, and organizational).
2. Secondary building blocks—assets located within the community but largely controlled by outsiders, such as private and nonprofit organizations, public institutions and services, and physical resources such as vacant lands, houses, and so forth.
3. Potential building blocks—resources originating outside the neighborhood and controlled by outsiders (welfare expenditures, public capital improvement expenditures, public information).

Workers in the field of AOD prevention and treatment can use this framework for increasing the capacity of the Latino community to meet its own needs. The use of primary building blocks as the foundation of all services will identify and develop a comprehensive system of culture-specific services that use Latinos as providers and leaders in the field. Furthermore, it will increase community participation in development, both organizational and community.

Evaluation of Outcome Measures

Outcome measures, although hoping to reflect an AOD-free existence, will also reflect the nature of the setting offering services, either inpatient or outpatient. The development of outcome measures for Latinos is influenced by the theories of etiology an agency subscribes to in establishing services. These outcome measures cannot be developed without significant input from both providers and the community. Consequently, measures must be based on a solid understanding of the goals of a program and an in-depth understanding of whom it is designed to assist (Casas, 1992; Padilla & Snyder, 1992).

Unfortunately, the literature on treatment outcomes for Latinos is seriously lacking: "While we have recently learned much about the epidemiology of Hispanic substance abuse, we still know little about what is effective treatment for this problem. . . . Treatment centers need to build in more efficient monitoring and evaluating systems to measure the results of their efforts. More effort needs to take place in the long-term follow-up of treatment effects among Hispanic abusers" (Mayers & Kail, 1993, p. 15).

Mayers and Kail (1993, p. 15) have developed key questions that should be a part of any effort to evaluate treatment outcomes for Latinos:

◆ What factors enter into decisions to seek treatment, to stay in treatment, and to maintain new lifestyles after treatment?
◆ What are the differences between those Latinos who seek treatment and those who do not?
◆ What are the critical factors or predictors of successful adjustment after treatment?
◆ What role does gender play in treatment decisions?
◆ How are the responses to these questions unique to Latinos compared with whites, and what intercultural differences exist?

Barrera and Reese (1993) raise an important treatment question related to natural support systems: How can natural support systems be positive factors that protect Latinos from AOD abuse as well as influences that can increase their risk for abusing drugs? Santisteban and colleagues (1993) have focused their measures on family functioning. No "standard" outcome measures are universal for use with Latinos, but numerous measures reflect specific settings, subgroups, drugs, and contexts.

Conclusion

Fortunately, the professional literature and the social work profession have started to notice Latinos and the field of AOD problem prevention and treatment. Culture-specific interventions necessitate a clear understanding of this population and its subgroups. This chapter provided the reader with a foundation on the topic, issues related to service delivery, and a framework for assessing and developing interventions. The dynamic changes occurring in the Latino population make generalizations difficult, if not dangerous. Practitioners must endeavor not to stereotype this diverse ethnic group. The development of culture-specific interventions must be systematically planned and implemented, with input from providers and community whenever possible.

References

Alcocer, A. M. (1993). Patterns of alcohol use among Hispanics. In R. S. Mayers, B. L. Kail, & T. D. Watts (Eds.), *Hispanic substance abuse* (pp. 37–49). Springfield, IL: Charles C. Thomas.

Barrera, Jr., M., & Reese, F. (1993). Natural support systems and Hispanic substance abuse. In R. S. Mayers, B. L. Kail, & T. D. Watts (Eds.), *Hispanic substance abuse* (pp. 115–130). Springfield, IL: Charles C. Thomas.

Barrera, Jr., M., Zautra, A., & Baca., L. M. (1984). Some research considerations in studying stress and distress of Mexican-Americans. In J. L. Martinez & R. H. Mendoza (Eds.), *Chicano psychology* (pp. 223–247). Orlando, FL: Academic Press.

Benjamin, D. K., & Miller, R. L. (1991). *Undoing drugs: Beyond legalization.* New York: Basic Books.

Booth, M. W., Castro, F. G., & Anglin, M. D. (1990). What do we know about Hispanic substance abuse? A review of the literature. In R. Glick & J. Moore (Eds.), *Drugs in Hispanic communities.* New Brunswick, NJ: Rutgers University Press.

Caetano, R. (1985). *Drinking patterns and alcohol problems in a national sample of U.S. Hispanics.* Paper presented at National Institute of Alcohol Abuse and Alcoholism Conference, Epidemiology of Alcohol Use and Abuse Among U.S. Minorities, Bethesda, MD.

Caetano, R. (1987). Acculturation, drinking, and social setting among U.S. Hispanics. *Drug and Alcohol Dependence, 19,* 215–226.

Caetano, R. (1988). Alcohol use among Hispanic groups in the United States. *American Journal of Drug and Alcohol Abuse, 14,* 293–308.

Caetano, R. (1989). Differences in alcohol use between Mexican-Americans in Texas and California. *Hispanic Journal of Behavioral Sciences, 11,* 58–69.

Casas, J. M. (1992). A culturally sensitive model for evaluating alcohol and other drug abuse prevention programs: A Hispanic perspective. In M. A. Orlandi, R. Weston, & L. G. Epstein (Eds.), *Cultural competence for evaluators* (pp. 75–116). Rockville, MD: U.S. Department of Health and Human Services.

Castex, G. M. (1994). Providing services to Hispanic/Latino populations. *Social Work*, *39*, 288–296.

Cervantes, R. C., & Castro, F. G. (1985). Stress, coping, and Mexican-American health: A systemic review. *Hispanic Journal of Behavioral Sciences*, *7*, 1–73.

Comas-Diaz, L. (1986). Puerto Rican alcoholic women: Treatment considerations. *Alcoholism Treatment Quarterly*, *3*, 47–57.

Cross, T. L. (1988). Services to minority populations. *Focal Point*, *3*, 1–4.

Delgado, M. (1979). Hispanic staff in non-Hispanic settings: Issues and recommendations. *Administration in Social Work*, *3*, 465–475.

Delgado, M. (1988). Alcoholism treatment and Hispanic youth. *Journal of Drug Issues*, *18*, 33–48.

Delgado, M. (1989). Treatment and prevention of Hispanic alcoholism. In T. D. Watts, & R. Wright (Eds.), *Alcoholism in minority populations* (pp. 77–92). Springfield, IL: Charles C. Thomas.

Delgado, M. (1994). Hispanic natural support systems and the AOD field: A developmental framework for collaboration. *Journal of Multicultural Social Work*, *3*, 11–37.

Delgado, M. (1995a). Community asset assessment and substance abuse prevention: A case study involving the Puerto Rican community. *Journal of Child and Adolescent Substance Abuse*, *4*, 57–77.

Delgado, M. (1995b). Natural support systems and AOD services: Challenges and rewards for practice. *Alcoholism Treatment Quarterly*, *12*, 17–31.

Delgado, M., & Humm-Delgado, D. (1980). Interagency collaboration to increase community resources in serving Hispanics. *Hispanic Journal of Behavioral Sciences*, *2*, 269–285.

Delgado, M., & Humm-Delgado, D. (1984). Hispanics and group work: A review of the literature. *Social Work with Groups*, *7*, 85–96.

Delgado, M., & Humm-Delgado, D. (1993). Chemical dependence, self-help groups, and the Hispanic community. In R. S. Mayers, B. L. Kail, & T. D. Watts (Eds.), *Hispanic substance abuse* (pp. 145–156). Springfield, IL: Charles C. Thomas.

Delgado, M., & Rodriguez-Andrew, S. (1990). *Alcohol and other drug use among Hispanic youth* (OSAP technical report 4). Rockville, MD: Office of Substance Abuse Prevention.

Doweiko, H. E. (1993). *Concepts of chemical dependency*. Pacific Grove, CA: Brooks/Cole Publishers.

Fitzpatrick, J. P. (1990). Drugs and Puerto Ricans in New York City. In R. Glick & J. Moore (Eds.), *Drugs in Hispanic communities* (pp. 195–201). New Brunswick, NJ: Rutgers University Press.

Gerbner, G. (1990). Stories that hurt: Tobacco, alcohol, and other drugs in the mass media. In H. Resnick (Ed.), *Youth and drugs: Society's mixed messages* (pp. 53–127). OSAP Prevention Monograph 6. Rockville, MD: Office of Substance Abuse Prevention.

Gfoerer, J., & De La Rosa, M. (1993). Protective and risk factors associated with drug use among Hispanic youth. *Journal of Addictive Diseases, 2*, 87–107.

Gilbert, M. J. (1993). Intercultural variation in alcohol-related cognition among Mexican-Americans. In R. S. Mayers, B. L. Kail, & T. D. Watts (Eds.), *Hispanic substance abuse*. Springfield, IL: Charles C. Thomas.

Gilbert, M. J., & Cervantes, R. (1986). Alcohol services for Mexican-Americans: A review of utilization patterns, treatment considerations, and prevention activities. *Hispanic Journal of Behavioral Sciences, 8*, 1–60.

Greenberg, B. S., Burgoon, M., Burgoon, J. K., & Korzenny, F. (1983). *Mexican Americans and the mass media*. Norwood, NJ: Ablex Publishing Corp.

Hayes-Bautista, D. E., & Chapa, J. (1987). Latino terminology: Conceptual bases for standardized terminology. *American Journal of Public Health, 77*, 61–68.

Hispanic Health and Nutrition Examination Survey. (1987). *Use of selected drugs among Hispanics: Mexican Americans, Puerto Ricans, and Cuban Americans*. Rockville, MD: U.S. Department of Health and Human Services.

Humm-Delgado, D., & Delgado, M. (1983a). Assessing Hispanic mental health needs: Issues and recommendations. *Journal of Community Psychology, 11*, 363–375.

Humm-Delgado, D., & Delgado, M. (1983b). Hispanic adolescents and substance abuse: Issues for the 1980's. *Child and Youth Services, 6*, 71–87.

Marin, G. (1993). Defining culturally appropriate community interventions: Hispanics as a case study. *Journal of Community Psychology, 21*, 149–158.

Mata, A., & Rodriguez-Andrew, S. (1988). Inhalant abuse in a small rural South Texas community. In R. A. Crider & R. A. Rouse (Eds.), *Epidemiology of inhalant abuse: An update* (pp. 91–98) (NIDA Research Monograph 85). Rockville, MD: U.S. Government Printing Office.

Mayers, R. S., & Kail, B. L. (1993). Hispanic substance abuse: An overview. In R. S. Mayers, B. L. Kail, & T. D. Watts (Eds.), *Hispanic substance abuse* (pp. 5–16). Springfield, IL: Charles C. Thomas.

McKnight, J. L., & Kretzman, J. (1991). *Mapping community capacity*. Evanston, IL: Northwestern University.

McNeece, C. A., & DiNitto, D. M. (1994). *Chemical dependency: A systems approach*. Englewood Cliffs, NJ: Prentice Hall.

Mintz, S. (1985). *Sweetness and power: The place of sugar in modern history*. New York: Viking Press.

National Clearinghouse for Alcohol and Drug Information. (1993). *Prevention primer: An encyclopedia of alcohol, tobacco, and other drug prevention terms*. Rockville, MD: Author.

National Institute on Drug Abuse. (1985). *Demographic characteristics and patterns of drug use of clients admitted to drug abuse treatment facilities in selected states: Annual data*. Rockville, MD: U.S. Government Printing Office.

National Institute on Drug Abuse. (1989). *National household survey on drug abuse: 1988 population estimates*. Rockville, MD: U.S. Department of Health and Human Services.

Newcomb, M. D. (1992). Understanding the multidimensional nature of drug use and abuse: The role of consumption, risk factors, and protective factors. In M. Glantz & R. Pickens (Eds.), *Vulnerability to drug use* (pp. 235–298). Washington, DC: American Psychological Association.

Office of Substance Abuse Prevention. (1990). *Communicating about alcohol and other drugs: Strategies for reaching populations at risk* (OSAP Prevention Monograph 5.) Rockville, MD: Author.

Padilla, A. M., & Salgado de Snyder, N. (1992). Hispanics: What the culturally informed evaluator needs to know. In M. A. Orlandi, R. Weston, & L. G. Epstein (Eds.), *Cultural competence for evaluators* (pp. 117–146). Rockville, MD: U.S. Department of Health and Human Services.

Ray, O., & Ksir, C. (1990). *Drugs, society, and human behavior.* St. Louis, MO: Times Mirror/Mosby.

Robles, R. R.; Martinez, R.; & Moscoso, M. (1979). Drug use among public and private secondary school students in Puerto Rico. *International Journal of the Addictions, 14,* 243–258.

Rodriguez-Andrew, S. (1988). Research and evaluation of primary prevention efforts with Mexican-American children and adolescents. In R. Urby & J. H. Flores (Eds.), *Hispanic health status symposium* (pp. 98–106). San Antonio, TX: Center for Health Policy Development, Inc.

Rutter, M. (1987). Psychological resilience and protective mechanisms. *American Journal of Orthopsychiatry, 37,* 317–331.

Santisteban, D., & Szapocznik, J. (1982). Substance abuse disorders among Hispanics: A focus on prevention. In R. M. Becerra, M. Karno, & J. I. Escobar (Eds.), *Mental health and Hispanic Americans: Clinical perspectives* (pp. 83–100). New York: Grune & Stratton.

Santisteban, D., Szapocznik, J., & Rio, A. T. (1993). Family therapy for Hispanic substance-abusing youth. In R. S. Mayers, B. L. Kail, & T. D. Watts (Eds.), *Hispanic substance abuse* (pp. 157–186). Springfield, IL: Charles C. Thomas.

Singer, M. (1984). Spiritual healing and family therapy: Common approaches to treatment of alcoholism. *Family Therapy, 11,* 155–162.

Szapocznik, J., & Kurtines, W. M. (Eds.) (1989). *Breakthroughs in family therapy with drug-abusing and problem youth.* New York: Springer Publishing Co.

Szapocznik, J., Santisteban, D., Rio, A., Perez-Vidal, A., Santisteban, D., & Kurtines, W. M. (1989). Family effectiveness training: An intervention to prevent drug abuse and problem behavior in Hispanic adolescents. *Hispanic Journal of Behavioral Sciences, 11,* 3–27.

U.S. Bureau of the Census. (1971). *Persons of Spanish origin in the United States: November 1969* (Population Characteristics, Series P-20, Nos. 2, 3). Washington, DC: U.S. Government Printing Office.

U.S. Bureau of the Census. (1983). *Projections of the Hispanic population: 1983–2080* (Current Population Reports, Series P-25, No. 995). Washington, DC: U.S. Government Printing Office.

U.S. Bureau of the Census. (1986). *Projections of the Hispanic population: 1983–2028* (Current Population Report, Series P-25, No. 995). Washington, DC: U.S. Government Printing Office.

U.S. Bureau of the Census. (1991). *The Hispanic population in the United States: March 1990* (Current Population Reports, Series P-20, No. 449). Washington, DC: U.S. Government Printing Office.

Valle, R., & Vega, W. (Eds.) (1980). *Hispanic natural support systems.* Sacramento, CA: State of California.

Vega, W. A. (1990). *Hispanic families in the 1980's: A decade of mental health: Relating research to service delivery.* Rockville, MD: National Institute of Mental Health.

Vega, W. A., & Miranda, M. R. (Eds.). (1985). *Stress and Hispanic mental health: Relating research to service delivery.* Rockville, MD: National Institute of Mental Health.

Wisotsky, S. (1990). *Beyond the war on drugs.* Buffalo, NY: Prometheus Books.

African Americans 3

Muriel Gray

Solutions to alcohol and other drug (AOD) abuse as a societal problem and as an individual problem must include an understanding of their historical role and of the influence these substances have on contemporary society. This chapter explores AOD use among African Americans in a historical and cultural context. It also includes an overview of epidemiological data, examples of culturally sensitive and appropriate programs, and an analysis of outcome measures. Because a historic analysis is included, the terms *Negro*, *Black*, and *African American* are used as they reflect the sociopolitical context of the various eras.

Most of the literature related to African Americans and AOD use defines African Americans as a homogeneous population with a single culture; therefore, historic and contemporary differences within the group have been largely ignored. Consequently, there is a paucity of data that focus on the diversity within the African American population in general or the diversity of attitudes and behaviors regarding AOD use among African Americans in particular. This lack of information highlights the problems inherent in research methodologies that study "race" rather than "culture" or "ethnicity" (Gaines, 1985).

Historical Context of AOD Use

Contemporary patterns of AOD use are believed to be influenced by historical events (Herd, 1985; Wright, Kail, & Creecy, 1990). The history of Africans in the United States is marked by specific social, economic, and political movements. This section of the chapter examines the role that AOD use played during the following social movement eras: precolonial Africa, slavery, abolition, after emancipation, and after the civil rights movement.

Precolonial Africa

Differences among African Americans as a group existed before slavery in that slaves came from various tribes, spoke different languages, practiced different religions, and held different values (Stevenson, 1993).

It is believed that most—though not all—African Americans in the United States share a West African ancestry. This non-Islamic tribal culture had a long tradition of using fermented grains and palm sap to make beer and wine (Herd, 1985). Kola nuts and vegetables were also used as intoxicants or stimulants (McNeese & DiNitto, 1994). However, the use of these substances was not seen as a problem. To the contrary, the consumption of alcohol—especially beer—was an integral part of collective social activities and associated with cultural practices of medicine, religion, and rites of passage celebrations. This tradition valued moderate drinking and disapproved of intoxication and any related disruptive behaviors (Herd, 1985; Umunna, 1967). Hence, although AOD use was an integral part of West African (non-Islamic) culture, its use was not a social problem.

Slavery: Rural South

One of the most profound historical events for African Americans is slavery. Although slaves were held by Northern slaveholders, most slaves were held in the South. There were many class differences within the slave culture based on social status, gender, physical health and physique, the nature of assigned jobs, and skin color. The slaves also differed in their religious beliefs (Joyner, 1991). Although some slaveholders instructed slaves in Christianity, others actively opposed efforts to Christianize the slaves. In spite of Christianity, many slave funerals drew on African tradition and were seen as a celebration of the person's life. Such celebrations included singing, dancing, and drinking (Goldfield, 1991). However, there was a strong Islamic presence that did not include the consumption of alcohol.

Slaves believed in the supernatural, which incorporated African spirit beliefs and Christianity. Nothing in the literature suggests that alcohol was used by the conjurers who practiced voodoo. However, according to Charles Joyner (1991), conjurers used natural herbs, roots, and chemicals (especially sulfur) in their rituals, a practice that now exists among some African American cultures.

For the most part, the continuation of drinking in moderation and the disapproval of socially disruptive behavior that was a part of the West African way of life were reinforced in slavery. However, conflicting accounts are found in the literature regarding alcohol use during slavery. On the one hand, Wright and colleagues (1990) describe alcohol as an integral part of the slaves' life, with weekend drinking as a reward for hard work described as one identifiable pattern. On the other hand, Joyner (1991) suggests that drinking was not an integral part of slave life when he quotes slaves saying, "The men would save money out of crops to buy their Christmas whiskey. It was all right for the slaves to get drunk on Christmas and New Year's day; no one was whipped for getting drunk on those days" (p. 82). During this era, many believed that slaveholders used alcohol to manipulate slaves and minimize unrest. According to Joyner, Frederick Douglass believed that such holidays were "among the most effective means in the hands of slaveholders in keeping down the spirit of insurrection" (p. 82), and in 1892 he argued that sobriety was necessary for freedom because one had to be alert to plan and execute an escape to freedom. This is also a sentiment shared by contemporary author Amuleru-Marshall (1993), who refers to "chemical slavery" as the result of the impact of AOD use on the contemporary African American community. Although debate exists regarding the role that alcohol played during slavery, all accounts seem to agree on the absence of alcohol-related problems. The literature attributes the absence of such problems to the slaves' precolonial culture and the slave culture, both of which negatively reinforced disruptive drinking behavior (Herd, 1985). This phenomenon was so pervasive that African Americans were thought to be physiologically immune to alcoholism.

Slavery: Urban South

Not all blacks were slaves. Some were born as Free Blacks. However, most slaves lived on plantations in the rural South, while most Free Blacks lived in urban areas. Many urban Free Blacks held relatives as slaves with the intent of freeing them. Hence, class differences have existed among African Americans since slavery. As these socioeconomic class differences emerged among African Americans, differences in attitudes and behavior regarding AOD use became more apparent. African Americans in urban areas (whether free or enslaved) frequented taverns, even though it was illegal to serve liquor to slaves throughout the urban South. According to Goldfield (1991) in *Before Freedom Came*, "the problem was less the sale of alcohol to slaves than the alleged plots that might be hatched in such a convivial and heady atmosphere" (p. 141).

Not only did a distinction exist between Free Blacks and slaves, but also distinctions existed based on skin color and on class and ethnicity. Hence, "Latin Negroes" of Creole descent were distinguished from "American Negroes," and "elite Free Blacks" were distinguished from "poor Blacks." Differences also were based on religion. Creole Blacks were usually Catholic. Slaves or poor Free Blacks usually attended the African-Methodist or African-Baptist churches. These class and religious differences were also reflected in drinking norms. For instance, African Americans who were active in fundamentalist churches were likely to hold an anti-alcohol ideology, which included a ban on drinking alcohol, whereas "elite Free Blacks" used alcohol as a way of displaying wealth. Even in 1993 frequent church attendance was found to serve as a protective factor against heavy drinking among African American women (National Institute on Alcohol Abuse and Alcoholism, 1993).

The Abolition Movement

The temperance movement and the abolition movement were intrinsically connected. Churches (black and white) played a major role in both the anti-slavery and the temperance movements (Herd, 1985). On the one hand, the black church reinforced temperance and abstinence among African Americans throughout the 19th century; on the other hand, the white reformist Protestant churches denounced slavery and the consumption of alcohol (Herd, 1985). The popularity of the temperance movement among African Americans resulted in the formation of several "colored" temperance societies throughout the United States between 1829 and 1838 (Herd, 1985).

After Emancipation

Johnson and Nishi (1976) suggest that society's definition of the problem of addiction among racial minorities resembles equivalent definitions from other American social reform movements, in that reform movements often symbolically associate the vulnerability of people of color with the social problem under attack. This association has been a common thread in the history of African Americans and society's approach to alcohol, cocaine, and heroin abuse as a social problem (Gaines, 1985; Herd, 1990; Ray & Ksir, 1993).

Just as the consumption of alcohol by African Americans was used as a social tool of control during slavery (Herd, 1985), it became a political tool of control following slavery. It was used as an argument for segregation and denying African Americans the right to vote. According to Herd (1985), during Prohibition, whites described the black vote as being corrupted by liquor and Blacks themselves as liquor crazed. This turn of events was seen as symbolic of larger social problems, with blacks being scapegoats for the existing political factions and economic strife.

The "Negro problem" became a central issue in liquor reform, wherein alcohol use—especially "Nigger gin"—was used to exacerbate racial tensions by associating consumption of alcohol by blacks with the rape of white women. The African Americans who once embraced the prohibition movement began opposing prohibition as the movement embraced racist propaganda and white supremacy ideologies.

After the Civil Rights Movement

The civil rights movement spans almost a half a century. According to *The State of Black America* (Jacobs, 1993), this social movement can be conceptualized as two movements: one ended segregated schools, the other ended the remaining traditional segregation practices. The historical literature does not directly address AOD use among African Americans during the civil rights era. However, recent studies show that as people of color and women become acculturated into the majority culture, their AOD use approximates that of whites (Gilbert, 1991; Vega, Gil, & Zimmerman, 1993a).

Alcohol

Whether or not AOD were used, they played and continue to play a major economic and social role in African American life. Bootlegging became a major activity that offered economic and social stability. Many families used this new industry to finance their children's education. Individual entrepreneurship in the form of liquor stores and nightclubs influenced the development of an African American entertainment culture (Daniels, 1980). Alcohol emerged as a symbol of sociability, sophistication, and wealth.

The fact that alcohol continues to be a part of the social life of some African Americans is evidenced by the liquor industry's current practice of targeting African Americans as a major market in its advertising. Although the sales of AOD result in a thriving economy, they also result in myriad related problems. As in slavery, some contemporary authors also believe that AOD and arrests for behaviors associated with them are a means of social control (Amuleru-Marshall, 1993; Staples, 1988). Therefore, ambivalent attitudes have emerged as African Americans benefited from the alcohol economy yet experience the emergence of alcohol-related medical, social, and legal problems (Herd, 1985).

Cocaine

After emancipation, cocaine and opiate addiction also emerged as a problem. It was a problem among soldiers of the Civil War and became a part of the entertainment culture.

As in the case of alcohol, post-Reconstruction fear-provoking ideas about African Americans were also associated with cocaine use. Whites referred to African Americans as "cocaine crazed" and blamed them for the crime problem, although cocaine was used by both African Americans and whites. Around the turn of the century it was an ingredient in Coca-Cola (Johnson & Nishi, 1976).

Heroin

Heroin use in the African American community was also accompanied by a belief by whites that African Americans were peculiarly susceptible to heroin addiction. Hence, the "drug problem" was seen primarily as a "black problem." Consequently, the identification of African Americans with heroin use in a hostile political environment resulted in punitive drug control legislation in the 1950s (Ray & Ksir, 1993). The 1956 Narcotics Drug Control Act, which permitted the death penalty for the sales of narcotics to minors, is an example. Drug use as a problem outside the African American community was not identified as such until after 1965 and the emergence of the counterculture exemplified by Dr. Timothy Leary.

Demographic Overview of Contemporary African Americans

It is difficult to get an accurate picture of the African Americans whose descendants were brought to the United States as slaves because the most recent census data (1990) do not distinguish among African Americans, African Caribbeans, Africans from the other Americas, and Africans from Africa who emigrated to the United States. Hence, "black" is used as the official designation (U.S. Bureau of the Census, 1993).

The 1990 census provides the following data:

◆ There were 30 million blacks in the United States, a 13 percent increase over the 1980 census. This population growth includes immigrants from the Caribbean and Africa.
◆ The median age of the black population is six years younger than that of the white population, with black women living longer than black men.
◆ Most blacks live in large metropolitan areas; however, by 1990 more were buying homes in the suburbs than had done so in 1980.
◆ More black women than black men have completed college.
◆ Blacks are unemployed at more than twice the rate of whites; however, more black women are employed than white women, and the proportion of employed black women was higher than employed black men.
◆ The median income of black families improved over the decade but in 1990 was still only 83 percent of the median income of comparable white families.
◆ Poverty levels for blacks were about the same at the beginning of the decade and at the end of the decade.
◆ The number of black female-headed households increased from 1980 to 1990.
◆ The number of professional blacks increased over the decade.

In summary, the 1990 census report identified differences among blacks according to income and age when compared with whites and gender differences among blacks in relation to education and unemployment. These generalizations give a demographic overview but do not add to an understanding of the differences among the subgroups of African Americans, especially in relation to cultural identification.

Cultural Identification

It is difficult and unfair to characterize a group as diverse as African Americans by race, because race is an inadequate measure of cultural or ethnic identification (Cheung, 1991; Gray & Barrow, 1993). Therefore, it is necessary to consider collective group cultural similarities and intragroup cultural differences. The similarities result from the collective and historical experiences that result from being of African descent in America. These similarities reflect characteristics that identify African Americans as a group with a heritage that is necessarily African (Butler, 1992). However, the characteristics may not be readily identified as African because, unlike other American groups, African Americans do not have a direct, identifiable kinship group and cultural link that can be traced to a particular tribal group, village, or family in Africa. Therefore, African Americans may not understand that some similarities result from a common heritage because that heritage bond was deliberately broken by the slave trade economy. It was replaced with a ban on education, a dissolution of individual family units, and economic dependence—the same issues that are identified with contemporary AOD abuse.

Similarities among African Americans Regarding AOD Use

The historical context and accompanying positive and negative influences that AOD use has had on the African American community have resulted in the ambiguity of drinking norms that is reflected in contemporary literature and current epidemiological studies. Studies (National Institute on Alcohol Abuse and Alcoholism, 1993) show both a high number of abstainers yet a disproportionate number of African Americans in the using population.

A discussion of AOD use must consider the socioeconomic conditions in which the behavior occurs because research has found racial differences in drinking patterns associated with such sociodemographic characteristics. Some theories of etiology hypothesize a relationship between AOD abuse and stress associated with such problems as living with unemployment and poverty. The frustration associated with racism and discrimination and the availability of substances are believed to contribute to the widespread AOD problems (Primm, 1987). According to the National Urban League *State of Black America* (Jacobs, 1993), unemployment, poverty, economic instability, and discrimination beset African Americans disproportionately, and this may, in part, explain why African Americans are disproportionately represented among the AOD-abusing population.

As implied from the history of African Americans in the United States in previous sections of this chapter, the following similarities and themes regarding AOD have resulted, in part, from the collective and historical experiences of African Americans. Many are carried over from African customs.

◆ African Americans have been victimized by societal and institutional practices of racism, and the resultant consequences of racism lead to a distortion of the reality of African American addiction manifested in research methodology (Cook, 1987; Feagin, 1987; Johnson & Nishi, 1976).

◆ African Americans distinguish alcohol from food and view its taste as unsuitable for consumption with meals (Gaines, 1985).

◆ African Americans tie the consumption of alcohol to celebrations and sociability (Gaines, 1985).

◆ African Americans who drink also associate alcohol with the "blues" and use it as a psychological remedy for "bad times" (Gaines, 1985).

◆ The consumption of high-priced, high-proof brands of alcohol is often viewed as a status symbol, which media advertising perpetuates (Center for Substance Abuse Prevention, 1993; Gaines, 1985).

◆ AOD are more accessible in urban communities where liquor stores are the most common type of small business and where drug trafficking is a rewarding economic activity among some subcultures (Center for Substance Abuse Prevention, 1993).

Other Similarities among African Americans

Any generalizations that could be reliably made about African Americans as a group are related to the influence of "race" on quality of life and the quest for identity within this society. Butler (1992) states that "the quest for identity could easily be considered the major theme of African American existence in the Western world" (p. 26). Several other authors (Amuleru-Marshall, 1993; Bell & Evans, 1981; Butler, 1992; Gaines, 1985) also identify racial consciousness as a theme among African Americans. Most of them describe the complex nature of maintaining an identity as an African American while simultaneously responding to the expectations of adjusting to a majority European American culture. The stress associated with this process has also been associated with the use of AOD as a way of medicating "racial pain" (Bell & Evans, 1981; Goddard, 1993; Neff & Hoppe, 1992; Rhodes & Jason, 1990). Although this process of cultural adaptation is a shared experience among African Americans, the nature of the acquired cultural identity results from a dynamic process that varies among African Americans. These variations reflect an example of the heterogeneity among the group.

Differences and Heterogeneity among African Americans

Intragroup differences reflect the heterogeneity among African Americans and also represent the nature of cultural identity. Bell and Evans's (1981) model of heterogeneity among blacks describes the use of a "double consciousness" (awareness of being black in a white society) as a dynamic of protection against racism. They identify four primary, interpersonal styles often adopted by African Americans: acculturated, bicultural, culturally immersed, and traditional. They note that these styles are dynamic and may change over time or as interpretations of personal experiences dictate. This concept stresses the importance of assessing one's interpersonal style to intervene in a culturally appropriate way. It focuses on the importance of matching client and worker according to interpersonal styles rather than race.

Implicit in the Bell and Evans model is the concept of different worldviews associated with the different interpersonal styles because each style has adopted a different way of interpreting and responding to being black in a predominantly white society. According to Butler (1992), "the worldview of African Americans represents their general design for living and patterns for interpreting reality. It is how they make sense of their world and their experiences . . . and provides the process by which those events are made harmonious with their lives" (p. 29).

Using the Bell and Evans model, it may be assumed that differing worldviews can be associated with the differing interpersonal styles. For instance, the acculturated style that rejects African customs could be associated more with a European worldview; however, a culturally immersed style that embraces African customs could be more closely associated with an African-centered worldview. Of course these examples represent extremes with other worldviews representing various mutations of those views. Hence, not all African Americans share the same worldview. This realization raises questions about the extent to which all African Americans should share such a worldview.

Given that most AOD prevention programs are designed from European American values and most approaches have been less effective with African Americans who abuse AOD than with whites, several authors (Amuleru-Marshall, 1993; DeLeon, Melnick, Schoket, & Jainchill 1993; Rowe & Grills, 1993; Smith, Buxton, Bilal-Rafiq, & Richard, 1993) suggest that the prevailing prevention and treatment strategies are insensitive to African American behavioral patterns and are therefore inappropriate for African Americans. Because differing worldviews exist among African

Americans, appropriate interventions must consider worldview and inter-personal style.

The following behavioral patterns have been associated with an African orientation and may aid in assessing interpersonal style. In "Of Kindred Minds: The Ties that Bind," Butler (1992) describes the six trends developed by Na'im Akbar as descriptive of African American behavioral patterns that are different from those of people of European descent. These trends are manifested in language, oral patterns, people orientation, interactive style, African thought, and spontaneity.

African American language is highly affective and rhythmic and uses pantomime-like body movements. Oral patterns rely more on the spoken word than on the written word. The value placed on the spoken word results in a sensitivity to subtleties in other's expressions and intonation. Orientation toward people is a value believed to be an African carryover that places a higher value on the group than on the individual. The African American interactive style of communicating, referred to as "call and respond" and often seen in traditional African American churches, is one in which the listeners immediately respond in support of the speaker. African thought refers to a respect for "hunches" as a means of problem solving. Some people may also associate a spiritual component with these internal cues. Spontaneity is seen as a strength and refers to an ability to rapidly adapt to different situations. These behavioral patterns are rooted in Africa and in part distinguish African Americans from other American groups. An African American worldview is another distinguishing characteristic.

The importance of determining worldview among African Americans when considering culturally appropriate intervention strategies is pointed out in a study of cultural relevance in a therapeutic community, which found that African American AOD abusers who reject the values of mainstream society may be poorly assimilated into therapeutic communities that reinforce mainstream values, whereas recovering AOD abusers who value success in the larger society demonstrate better adjustment to the mainstream-oriented therapeutic community (DeLeon et al., 1993).

A study of attitudes about AOD abuse (Gary & Berry, 1985) found that racial consciousness was highly correlated with attitudes about drug use. An African-centered worldview has been suggested as a more appropriate approach because racial and cultural consciousness is the basis for helping African Americans understand what identifies them as a group distinct from other groups in the United States (Butler, 1992). Such a worldview is suggested as a means of "transformative healing" from AOD abuse (Rowe

& Grills, 1993). As a result, many primary prevention programs designed for African Americans include interventions directed at racial consciousness and self-determination.

According to the African American worldview, AOD abuse results, in part, from the cultural and political imbalance that denies African Americans the opportunity to work toward self-determination (Wilson, 1990). Therefore, it would appear that the appropriateness of the Afrocentric approach may also be related to perceptions of self-determination.

In summary, AOD use occurs in a social–cultural–political context. Racism (individual and institutional) as a part of the African American experience is the thread that runs through the collective experiences of the group. Consequently, attempts to understand individual and group behavior in general and AOD-related behavior in particular must acknowledge the role that racism plays (Amuleru-Marshall, 1993; Bell & Evans, 1981). These cultural experiences not only help understand the existing trends and patterns of AOD use, but also they have implications for the inclusion of culturally appropriate strategies in the formulation of prevention, treatment, and policy development.

Extent of the Problem

Research on AOD problems tends to focus on either the general population or treatment populations. Differences exist among the two populations, and methodological differences exist among the research on these populations. Treatment population research is often conducted on small, nonrepresentative, and convenient samples. General population research has a large representative sample; however, it typically uses a survey instrument and may lack sufficient numbers of problem users and clinically relevant variables to generalize (Lee, Mavis, & Stoffelmayr, 1991). Although each approach has advantages and disadvantages, the research limitations result in a research "gap" (Wilsnack, Wilsnack, & Klassen, 1985).

Most data on AOD and African Americans are derived from large, national samples. This research typically adheres to traditional epidemiological research, biological theories of etiology, and racial and social classification categories. For the most part, researchers do not use a cultural theory of human difference (Gaines, 1985) or an ethnographic approach. Hence, the information is more useful in intergroup social comparisons than in intragroup cultural comparisons. Therefore, the capacity to understand intragroup variation is limited.

Alcohol

In the *Eighth Special Report to the U.S. Congress on Alcohol and Health* (National Institute on Alcohol Abuse and Alcoholism, 1993), Herd (1990) observes that drinking norms continue to be ambiguous among African Americans, as reflected in a pattern of abstinence by most African Americans and heavy drinking by a small subsample of the entire population. African American drinkers also have identifiable drinking patterns: African Americans tend to be group drinkers or weekend drinkers, and street drinking has emerged among some young men as a social custom (Goddard, 1993). These patterns seem to be consistent with the description of the precolonialization pattern described by Herd (1985). Unlike previous historical periods and despite African Americans' higher rates of alcohol abstinence than whites, African Americans currently have higher rates of alcohol-related medical problems and mortality rates than do whites (Goddard, 1993; National Institute on Alcohol Abuse and Alcoholism, 1994). However, a treatment population study comparing problems in living for black and whites entering AOD abuse treatment programs (Lee et al., 1991) found no black–white difference in severity of medical problems. However, they did find that black clients were more likely to be unemployed and were more likely to use other drugs in combination with alcohol.

Illicit Drugs

Most official data regarding illicit drug use are derived from the National Household Survey on Drug Abuse; the Drug Abuse among American High School Seniors, College Students, and Young Adults Survey; the Drug Abuse Warning Network; the Drug Use Forecasting System; and law enforcement and clinical treatment statistics. The data from the surveys are taken from samples in which African Americans are underrepresented; therefore, the findings may not accurately reflect the extent of the problem (Primm, 1987).

Marijuana

Marijuana is seen as the least risky of the illicit drugs, and it is the most commonly used (Substance Abuse and Mental Health Services Administration, 1993). Different patterns and trends of marijuana use exist among African Americans. Research involving young African American men and Vietnam veterans (Robins, 1980) found a natural developmental history of illicit drug use starting with marijuana, alcohol, and cigarettes. Studies of patterns of drug use have found that African American drug users tend to progress from marijuana to heroin, yet whites tend to progress from marijuana to hallucinogens. Similarly, according to the most recent National Household Survey, African Americans, as a group, were more likely to have used marijuana during the past month than whites or Latino Americans. However, a survey of high school seniors, college students, and young adults found that African American students had lower usage rates for most drugs, licit or illicit, than did white or Latino students.

Powdered Cocaine and Crack Cocaine

According to the National Household Survey on Drug Abuse (Substance Abuse and Mental Health Services Administration, 1993), African Americans and Latino Americans have similar rates of cocaine use. Both rates were significantly higher than that of whites. Young African American adult women have been identified as the fastest growing group of crack cocaine users in the United States (Boyd, 1993). However, the National Household Survey on Drug Abuse found that both powdered cocaine and crack cocaine use declined among African American, Latino American, and white American high school seniors.

However, statistics do not capture the nature of the economy associated with illicit drugs in general and crack cocaine in particular. An ethnographic study in a metropolitan area cites several respondents who were drawn to selling crack cocaine by the "lure of making quick, extravagant profits" and "the payoff of being able to emulate the American dream through the purchase and display of high-tech commodities" (Carlson & Siegal, 1991, p. 13).

Heroin and Other Opiates

Historically, African Americans have been overrepresented in the heroin-using population (Kleinman and Lukoff, 1978), which is particularly alarming because heroin is most often injected and needles are often shared. The sharing of needles is one of the major means of transmission of the human immunodeficiency virus (HIV), the virus that causes acquired immune deficiency syndrome (AIDS). However, the prevalence of AIDS is not limited to drug injection. The higher risk of unprotected sexual behaviors as a consequence of AOD abuse also increases the risk of contracting HIV (Center for Substance Abuse Prevention, 1993). Unfortunately, heroin use among adults in the general population older than 35 years of age has significantly increased (Substance Abuse and Mental Health Services Administration, 1993).

Theories of Etiology

Although most African Americans do not have a problem with AOD use, they are overrepresented among the population that has a related problem. For the most part, research—because of methodological limitations—does not explain this phenomenon nor do etiological theories of addiction. The cause of AOD abuse continues to be debated. However, the theories or explanations regarding African American AOD abuse include biochemical and genetic factors, psychological factors, environmental and cultural factors, and a multifactorial perspective (Straussner, 1993). Although these are the same theories used to explore the phenomena among the general population of abusers, this chapter will identify those perspectives that specifically focus on African Americans.

Biochemical Perspective

Research that has explored issues of genetic susceptibility and neurochemical involvement in AOD abuse has not explained why African Americans are overrepresented among the addicted population. In fact, such research has met with skepticism among many African Americans because the research does not consider the sociocultural environment the person experiences. However, Newton (1993) uses a social context that explores the impact of dietary patterns, physiological structure, and neurochemical composition of African Americans in an article discussing African American biological vulnerability to alcohol and other drug abuse.

Although acknowledging that research on the health effects of melanin is relatively unexplored by Western scientists, Newton cites advances in melanin research that suggest that melanin (which everyone has but which people classified as blacks have in higher concentrations) has neurochemical and physiological attributes associated with altered states of consciousness. This research purports to show a relationship between melanin and toxins that causes the release of neurotransmitters into the body that are associated with AOD use. It is also hypothesized that licit food chemical addictions (to such substances as fat and sugar found in fast food and junk food) may be a precursor to addiction to illicit substances. Another possible precursor is the unconscious incentive to use liquor and cigarettes, as shown by the availability of liquor stores in communities heavily populated by African Americans.

Psychological Perspective

Theoretical models that explore a relationship between psychological disturbances and addiction require more rigorous research in general, and research that considers cultural and ethnic differences among African Americans is particularly needed. However, from a conceptual viewpoint, approaches that emphasize deviancy and pathological perspectives lend little to an understanding of how being African American in the United States affects AOD abuse among African Americans.

Theoretical models of cultural identification and the role of acculturation have been explored in relation to patterns of AOD abuse among people of color (Oetting, 1993). This concept focuses on the adjustment of people of color (in the United States) trying to exist in and adapt to a predominant European American culture.

According to Oetting (1993), several models describe different aspects of this process. This theory maintains that an individual's cultural identification can be described along different dimensions that are independent of one another. Therefore, it is possible to identify with aspects of more than one culture. However, Long (1993) believes that a bicultural identity might be damaging for African Americans because in reality African Americans have not been able to maintain their own culture while taking on the values of the mainstream European culture. The orthogonal theory acknowledges no clear relationship between cultural identification and AOD use, but it does acknowledge that "a high level of identification can lead to substance use if the culture approves." Similarly, "it can prevent use if the culture disapproves" (National Institute on Drug Abuse, 1993, p. 51).

The prevailing Eurocentric model may be thought of as a deficit-oriented model because it often identifies individual and group problems at the expense of identifying assets and positive outcomes. Hence, many studies have identified or focused on deficits such as low self-esteem, identity confusion, and self-destructive behavioral patterns. Long (1993) points out that these deficits are often described as such without considering the socialization process. He quotes Perkins, who described the black socialization process as one composed of "three conditions, socially determined and institutionally supported [that] characterize the black experience: social injustice, societal inconsistency, and personal impotence" (p. 88). Few specific interventions to address this type of black experience are sensitive to these social experiences. The extent that these experiences have been individually internalized and result in reactive behavior is the extent to which an approach that specifically focuses on addressing these conditions may be appropriate.

However, the Afrocentric model is purported to be an approach that includes the sociopolitical reality of being black in the United States and according to Long (1993), it attempts to develop a positive personality by developing individuals with "a strong sense of discipline, well-defined roles in family and community, a positive self-concept, and self-appreciation" (p. 89). Afrocentric intervention strategies have only recently been adopted by the prevention and treatment communities; therefore, effectiveness has not been systematically studied. However, given that several studies have found a relationship between low self-esteem and low cultural identification and low self-esteem and AOD use among African American youths, an Afrocentric approach may be appropriate for individuals who are confused about cultural self-identity and who have manifested low self-esteem. Implicit in this model is the assumption that a positive self-concept and self-appreciation may be protective factors in preventing AOD abuse and that positive self-concept and self-appreciation are healing factors in the treatment of AOD abuse.

Multifactorial Perspective

Numerous environmental, biological, economic, political, and cultural factors have been linked to AOD abuse (Amuleru-Marshall, 1993; Straussner, 1993). For instance, much debate remains about the relative influence of such factors as the availability of AOD, biological vulnerability, economic insecurity, unemployment, and psychological stress. It is likely, however, that all are involved in either the etiology or the maintenance of AOD abuse.

Suggested Prevention Strategies

African Americans have shared experiences and circumstances that result in general themes that reflect a collective sociocultural context. Chestang, as cited in Butler (1992), believes that historical experiences shape what may be thought of as an African American character and personality that is needed to adapt and survive in a "hostile environment." Only recently have prevention and treatment strategies incorporated the sociocultural context of most African Americans. However, even when there is sensitivity to the need of considering culture, many programs continue to approach African Americans as a homogeneous group. Therefore, culturally sensitive strategies do not necessarily result in culturally appropriate strategies.

Prevention

The literature on primary prevention mainly focuses on youths and adolescents, whereas the literature on adults primarily focuses on treatment interventions. There is also a focus on risk factors and protective factors that are a part of the adolescent life experience. Risk factors increase the probability of drug use, and protective factors mitigate against risk factors, thereby leading to lower probability of drug use (Brook, 1993).

Vega and colleagues (1993b) studied risk factors for early adolescent drug use and found low self-esteem, depressive mood, low family pride, family AOD abuse, perceptions of peer approval for use, and involvement in delinquent behavior to be risk factors for African American adolescents. Kleinman and Lukoff (1978), in a study of ethnic differences in factors associated with drug use, found that peer drug use was an important risk factor and religious involvement was a barrier. However, the adolescent population comprises many subcultures. Several studies (Clayton & Voss, 1981; Kleinman & Lukoff, 1978) have found drug subcultures and risk factors related to drug availability, involvement in drug selling, and other forms of illegal behavior.

Culturally appropriate interventions must address risk factors for African American adolescents and specific factors associated with various subcultures to be effective in preventing and treating AOD abuse among African American adolescents.

Few studies or articles have focused on the strengths of African Americans. Long (1993) states that interventions must consider the following group strengths:

◆ Ability to adapt to an oppressive environment.
◆ Ability to survive with little family guidance as a result of forced separation.
◆ Desire to be free.

Several authors (Dawkins, 1988; Gross, 1993) have identified external and internal factors that contribute to AOD use among inner-city adolescents. External risk factors include exposure to images and social patterns that are associated with drug abuse, limited access to neighborhood employment, poor neighborhood schools, overcrowded and substandard housing, low rates of home ownership, few vocational education opportunities, the lure of the drug sales economy, and the targeting of the inner-city community for sales by the alcohol industry. However, family support was identified as a critical protective factor in the elevation of adolescent self-esteem, which is identified as another protective factor.

Other researchers (Catalano et al., 1993), studying rates of early initiation to drug use, levels of exposure to risk factors, and the degree to which risk factors predict AOD use, found differences between African American youths and European American youths. African Americans had earlier exposure to such risk factors as aggression and delinquent behavior, but they had lower early initiation rates than European American youths.

An evaluation of primary prevention programs funded by the Center for Substance Abuse Prevention (CSAP) and targeting African American youths found that the effective Afrocentric and non-Afrocentric programs shared the following common themes, which were identified as aspects of African American experiences: values of the traditional African American community, emphasis on extended community involvement, and emphasis on spirituality.

Values of the African American community and involvement of the extended community were part of effective programs in that community leaders were directly involved with the youths in the program and were visible in the entire community. These programs organized communities to become actively involved in day-to-day programming.

A focus on spirituality was also a part of the most effective programs. Without focusing on any specific religion, the programs focused on the concept of spirituality and how it works in the lives of Africans and African Americans.

In addition to the aforementioned African American themes, Warfield-Coppock, as cited by Long (1993), suggests that prevention components should also include interventions that build self-esteem by developing an identity that begins with African origins rather than with slave origins. This approach is the foundation of the Afrocentric model and includes specific interventions that do the following:

- ◆ Deprogram, reeducate, and train youths in the skills needed to be responsible adults.
- ◆ Include older generations to serve as respected elders and role models.
- ◆ Assist in crises by having a team identified to fulfill this function.

Treatment

Most treatment data on AOD abuse focus on adult populations. Treatment data, by their nature, focus on a treatment population, a selected population that does not allow generalizing about AOD abusers who are not in treatment. This distinction is critical for African Americans because they are underrepresented in treatment programs (Gordon, 1993). This underrepresentation is, in part, a result of cultural responses in determining a need for treatment, accessing treatment services, and forming expectations of treatment outcomes.

Cultural differences—in defining AOD problems, in explaining the causes of these problems and in forming expectations about appropriate interventions and outcomes—influence the decisions about the need for treatment and accessing treatment services. Expectations about appropriate interventions and treatment outcomes often influence the extent of treatment involvement (Brisbane, 1992).

Biomedical definitions of AOD problems often differ from the definition of such problems by some African American users and nonusers. These differences may exist, in part, because of cultural influences. The treatment community uses diagnostic instruments and behavioral indicators to determine the nature of AOD use but seldom uses the norms of the individual's primary cultural group. However, African Americans examine drinking and drug-using behaviors in the context of subcultural norms. For instance, Gaines (1985) has identified "respectable drinking" and "problem drinking" as classifications used by African Americans to describe various drinking patterns. According to this classification, drinking becomes a "problem" when it results in behaviors not valued by respectable people. The organizing themes of this classification include the quality of the substance consumed or used, the place of use, and the context of use. Most people use personal or informal support systems to help define what is a problem. It is likely that the recognition of an AOD problem will be within the context of a person's subculture. This phenomenon may help explain why African Americans tend to enter treatment programs with more severe problems than European Americans (Gordon, 1993).

Brisbane (1992) has identified the following cultural differences of African Americans that may also influence treatment accessibility and effectiveness: (1) attitudes toward receiving mental health care, (2) language and verbal expressions in talking about problems, (3) the need for culturally specific intervention strategies, (4) styles of interventions preferred, (5) treatment process and outcome, and (6) definitions of appropriate helpers.

AOD prevention and treatment occurs in many different settings. Although it is beyond the scope of this chapter to give an exhaustive overview of treatment settings serving African Americans, some settings stand out because African American treatment involvement appears disproportionately low. For instance, African Americans are typically not represented in therapeutic communities (DeLeon et al., 1993) and are underrepresented in many prison and jail programs.

In a study of the cultural relevance of therapeutic communities, DeLeon and colleagues (1993) found that dropout rates were related to ethnicity and culture. Although the technical component of AOD treatment may be similar for most abusers, effective treatment must be within a culturally specific milieu and include cultural realities (Smith et al., 1993).

The jail and prison populations have grown considerably. This growth is in large part the result of drug-related arrests (Peters & May, 1992). A nationwide survey conducted by the American Jail Association of in-jail treatment programs found that drug treatment programs varied in size and quality. Larger jails had larger treatment populations, but it concluded that most programs (large or small) did not provide adequate services. It was also found that most programs had more people requesting services than available treatment slots.

Brown (1992) identified the following five program models available to AOD abusers in correctional settings: (1) incarceration without specialized services, (2) incarceration with drug education or drug abuse counseling, (3) incarceration with residential units dedicated to drug abuse counseling, (4) incarceration with client-initiated or client-maintained services, and (5) incarceration with specialized services that do not directly target users' drug abuse problems. The most prevalent program model was incarceration without specialized services.

Although this survey found approximately 23 percent of the treatment participants to be African Americans, little information was found about ethnicity except that the 12-step program of Narcotics Anonymous and the adoption of the Muslim faith and practice of its tenets were cited as "programs" positively regarded by correctional staff, in part because they require few prison resources and help to maintain peace in the setting. Evidence of effectiveness is largely anecdotal, but the author suggests that in-prison religious conversions and AOD abuse merit more study (Brown, 1992).

Evaluation of Outcome Measures

Research has not typically been an integral part of primary prevention and treatment programs. Therefore, there is a paucity of research on the effectiveness of traditional and population-specific treatment programs and on culturally sensitive strategies within traditional programs (National

Institute on Alcohol Abuse and Alcoholism, 1993). The research literature on cultural sensitivity and AOD use is seriously flawed by the use of a social classification system using race (and not culture) and ethnic identification as objects of study (Gaines, 1985; Herd, 1985; Pena & Koss-Chioino, 1992).

Outcome measures are influenced by program goals. In many instances, culture and ethnic identification may be one of the desired outcomes. The goals of primary prevention and treatment are often the subject of debate. These debates are greatly influenced by the guiding theories of etiology and the sociopolitical context of the interventions. Therefore, some programs have abstinence as a goal, whereas others have improved social functioning as a goal. However, culturally sensitive prevention and treatment interventions require culturally sensitive research.

By necessity, culturally sensitive research must be guided by integrative models that view AOD abuse as the result of complex interactions between multiple biological and social factors (Pena & Koss-Chioino, 1992). Therefore, researchers conducting such studies must also be knowledgeable of cultural nuances that may influence research findings. As noted in *Cultural Competence for Evaluators* (Grace, 1992), the ethnicity and such personal characteristics as age, race, sex, and credentials of the researcher may significantly affect evaluation research. It would therefore seem that incorporating cultural sensitivity throughout the research process—defining the problem, establishing sampling procedures, selecting the instrument, and interpreting the data—while respecting and capturing cultural and ethnic expectations of program goals is a challenge, but is also essential to culturally sensitive research.

For instance, a generally accepted outcome for an African-centered primary prevention program, as described in *An African-Centered Model of Prevention for African American Youth at High Risk* (Center for Substance Abuse Prevention, 1993), is the development of "a human being who is spiritually rejuvenated, has love of self, family, and community and is willing and able to respect, protect, and defend self, family, and community" (p. 128). Such program goals seem to beg for culturally sensitive measures of outcome that address threats to validity while being sensitive to issues of generalizability. As in the previous example, cultural values are reflected in such goals, and the measurement of outcome expectations may be more challenging than, for instance, a study by Woody (1987) that examined more European-oriented variables such as legal status, employment, psychopathology, and drug use. Although these variables are important social indices, they imply a different worldview than that of the African-centered prevention program.

Conclusion

The emergence of culture and ethnicity as study topics will fill a void in the existing body of knowledge on AOD use among African Americans. This chapter has attempted to provide an overview of the similarities and differences among African Americans and their historic underpinnings as a way of understanding current patterns and trends, while challenging the reader to consider future program, policy, and research implications. The incorporation of culturally and ethnically sensitive and appropriate interventions that are not based on stereotypes of African or European Americans may constitute an important paradigm shift in social work practice and research.

References

Amuleru-Marshall, O. (1993). Political and economic implications of alcohol and other drugs in the African-American community. In L. Goddard (Ed.), *CSAP technical report 6* (pp. 23–34). Rockville, MD: U.S. Department of Health and Human Services.

Bell, P., & Evans, J. (1981). *Counseling the black client: Alcohol use and abuse in black America.* City Center, MN: Hazelden Foundation.

Boyd, C. (1993). The antecedents of women's crack cocaine abuse: Family substance abuse, sexual abuse, depression, and illicit drug use. *Journal of Substance Abuse Treatment, 10,* 433–438.

Brisbane, F. (1992). *Working with African-Americans: The professional handbook.* Chicago: HRDI International.

Brook, J. (1993). Interactional theory: Its utility in explaining drug use behavior among African-American and Puerto Rican youths. In M. La Rosa, & J. Adrados (Eds.), *Drug abuse among minority youth: Methodological issues and recent research advances* (Research Monograph Series 130, pp. 79–101). Rockville, MD: U.S. Department of Health and Human Services.

Brown, B. (1992). Program models. In C. Leukefeld, & F. Tims (Eds.), *Drug abuse treatment in prisons and* jails (NIDA Research Monograph 118, pp. 31–37). Rockville, MD: U.S. Department of Health and Human Services.

Butler, J. (1992). Of kindred minds: The ties that bind. In M. Orlandi, R. Weston, & L. Epstein (Eds.), *Cultural competence for evaluators: A guides for alcohol and other drug abuse prevention* (pp. 23–54). Rockville, MD: U.S. Department of Health and Human Services.

Carlson, R., & Siegal, H. (1991). The crack life: An ethnographic overview of crack use and sexual behavior among African-Americans in a midwest metropolitan city. *Journal of Psychoactive Drugs, 23,* 11–20.

Catalano, R., Hawkins, D., Krenz, C., Gillmore, M., Morrison, D., Wells, E., & Abbott, R. (1993). Using research to guide culturally appropriate drug abuse prevention. *Journal of Consulting and Clinical Psychology, 61,* 804–811.

Center for Substance Abuse Prevention. (1993). *The second national conference on preventing and treating alcohol and other drug abuse, HIV infection, and AIDS in black communities* (CSAP Prevention Monograph 13). Rockville, MD: U.S. Department of Health and Human Services.

Cheung, Y. (1991). Ethnicity and alcohol/drug use revisited: A framework for future research. *International Journal of the Addictions, 25*, 581–605.

Clayton, R. & Voss, H. (1981). *Young men and drugs in Manhattan: A causal analysis* (NIDA Research Monograph 39). Rockville, MD. U.S. Department of Health and Human Services.

Cook, S. (1987). Behavior change implications of low involvement in an issue. *Journal of Social Issues, 43*, 105–112.

Daniels, D. (1980). *Pioneer urbanites*. Philadelphia: Temple University Press.

Dawkins, M. (1988). Alcoholism prevention and black youth. *The Journal of Drug Issues, 18*, 15–20.

DeLeon, G., Melnick, G., Schoket, D., & Jainchill, N. (1993). Is the therapeutic community culturally relevant? Findings on race/ethnic differences in retention in treatment. *Journal of Psychoactive Drugs, 25*, 77–86.

Feagin, J. (1987). Changing Black Americans to fit a racist system. *Journal of Social Issues, 43*, 85–89.

Gaines, A. (1985). Cultural conceptions and social behavior among urban Blacks. In L. Bennett, & G. Ames (Eds.), *The American experience with alcohol: Contrasting cultural perspectives* (pp. 171–200). New York: Plenum Press.

Gary, L., & Berry, G. (1985). Predicting attitudes toward substance use in a Black community: Implications for prevention. *Community Mental Health Journal, 21*, 42–51.

Gilbert, M. (1991). Acculturation and changes in drinking patterns among Mexican-American women. *Alcohol Health and Research World, 15*, 234–238.

Goddard, L. (1993). Background and scope of the alcohol and other drug problems. In L. Goddard (Ed.), *CSAP technical report 6: An African centered model of prevention for African-American youth at high risk* (pp. 11–18). Rockville, MD: U.S. Department of Health and Human Services.

Goldfield, D. (1991). Black life in Old South cities. In E. Campbell, & K. Rice (Eds.), *Before freedom came: African-American life in the antebellum south* (pp. 123–153). Richmond, VA: The Museum of the Confederacy.

Gordon, J. (1993). A culturally specific approach to ethnic minority young adults. In E. Freeman (Ed.), *Substance abuse treatment: A family systems approach* (pp. 71–99). Newbury Park, CA: Sage Publications.

Grace, C. (1992). Practical consideration for program professionals and evaluators working with African-American communities. In M. A. Orlandi (Ed.), *Cultural competence for evaluators* (OSAP Cultural Competence Series 1, pp 55–74). Rockville, MD: U.S. Department of Health and Human Services.

Gray, M., & Barrow, F. (1993). Ethnic, cultural, and racial diversity in the workplace. In P. Kurzman, & S. Akabas (Eds.), *Work and well-being: The occupational social work advantage* (pp. 138–152). Washington, DC: NASW Press.

Gross, S. (1993). Treatment issues associated with adolescents who abuse alcohol and other drugs. In *The second national conference on preventing and treating alcohol and other drug abuse, HIV infection, and AIDS in black communities* (CSAP Prevention Monograph 13, pp. 147–160). Rockville, MD: U.S. Department of Health and Human Services.

Herd, D. (1985). Ambiguity in Black drinking norms: An ethnohistorical interpretation. In L. Bennett, & G. Ames (Eds.), *The American experience with alcohol: Contrasting cultural perspectives* (pp. 149–170). New York: Plenum Press.

Herd, D. (1990). Subgroup differences in drinking patterns among Black and White men: Results from a national survey. *Journal of Studies on Alcohol, 51*, 221–232.

Jacobs, J. (1993). Black America, 1992: An overview. In B. Tidwell (Ed.), *The state of black America* (pp. 1–10). New York: National Urban League.

Johnson, B., & Nishi, S. (1976). Myths and realities of drug use by minorities. In P. Liyama, S. Nishi, & B. Johnson (Eds.), *Drug use and abuse among U.S. minorities: An annotated bibliography* (pp. 3–68). New York: Praeger Publishers.

Joyner, C. (1991). The world of the plantation slaves. In E. Campbell, & K. Rice (Eds.), *Before freedom came: African-American life in the antebellum south* (pp. 51–99). Richmond, VA: The Museum of the Confederacy.

Kleinman, P., & Lukoff, I. (1978). Ethnic differences in factors related to drug use. *Journal of Health and Social Behavior, 19*, 190–199.

Lee, J., Mavis, B., & Stoffelmayr, B. (1991). A comparison of problems-of-life for Blacks and Whites entering substance abuse treatment programs. *Journal of Psychoactive Drugs, 23*, 233–239.

Long, L. (1993). An Afrocentric intervention strategy. In L. Goddard (Ed.), *CSAP technical report 6* (pp. 87–92). Rockville, MD: U.S. Department of Health and Human Services.

McNeese, C., & DiNitto, D. (1994). *Chemical dependency: A systems approach.* Englewood Cliffs, NJ: Prentice Hall.

National Institute on Alcohol Abuse and Alcoholism. (1993). *Eighth special report to the U.S. Congress on alcohol and health.* Rockville, MD: U.S. Department of Health and Human Services.

National Institute on Alcohol Abuse and Alcoholism. (1994). *Alcohol Alert, 23*, 1–3.

National Institute on Drug Abuse. (1993). *National survey results on drug Use from the monitoring the future study, 1975–1992.* Vol. II. Rockville, MD: U.S. Department of Health and Human Services.

Neff, J., & Hoppe, S. (1992). Acculturation and drinking patterns among U.S. Anglos, Blacks, and Mexican Americans. *Alcohol and Alcoholism, 27*, 293–308.

Newton, P. (1993). Issues of biological vulnerability in alcohol and other drug abuse for the African-American community. In L. Goddard (Ed.), *CSAP technical report 6: An African centered model of prevention for African-American youth at high risk* (pp. 35–46). Rockville, MD: U.S. Department of Health and Human Services.

Oetting, E. (1993). Orthogonal cultural identification: Theoretical links between cultural identification and substance use. In M. La Rosa, & J. Adrados (Eds.), *Drug abuse among minority youth: Methodological issues and recent research advances* (Research Monograph Series 130, pp. 32–56). Rockville, MD: U.S. Department of Health and Human Services.

Pena, J., & Koss-Chioino, J. (1992). Cultural sensitivity in drug treatment research with African-American males. In J. Pena & J. Koss-Chioino (Eds.), *Ethnic and multicultural drug abuse* (pp. 157–179). Binghamton, NY: The Haworth Press.

Peters, R., & May, R. (1992). Drug treatment services in jails. In C. Leukefeld, & F. Tims (Eds.), *Drug abuse treatment in prisons and jails* (NIDA Research Monograph 118, pp. 31–37). Rockville, MD: U.S. Department of Health and Human Services.

Primm, B. (1987). Drug use: Special implications for black America. In J. Dewart (Ed.), *The state of black America 1987* (pp. 145–158). New York: National Urban League.

Ray, O., & Ksir, C. (1993). *Drugs, society, & human behavior.* St. Louis, MO: Times Mirror/Mosby.

Rhodes, J., & Jason, L. (1990). A social stress model of substance abuse. *Journal of Consulting and Clinical Psychology, 58,* 395–40.

Robins, L. (1980). Epidemiological findings in drug abuse. In E. Purcell (Ed.), *Psychopathology of childhood and youth: A cross-cultural perspective* (pp. 223–242). New York: Josiah Macy Foundation.

Rowe, D., & Grills, C. (1993). African-centered drug treatment: An alternative conceptual paradigm for drug counseling with African-American clients. *Journal of Psychoactive Drugs, 25,* 21–33.

Smith, D., Buxton, M., Bilal-Rafiq, S., & Richard, B. (1993). Cultural points of resistance to the 12-step recovery process. *Journal of Psychoactive Drugs, 25,* 97–108.

Staples, R. (1988). The Black American family. In C. Mindel (Ed.), *Ethnic families in America* (pp. 303–324). New York: Elsevier Science Publishing Co., Inc.

Stevenson, J. (1993). Strengths of Black families. In *The second national conference on preventing and treating alcohol and other drug abuse, HIV infection, and AIDS in black communities* (CSAP Prevention Monograph 13, pp. 175–180). Rockville, MD: U.S. Department of Health and Human Services.

Straussner, S. (1993). Assessment and treatment of clients with alcohol and other drug abuse problems: An overview. In S. Straussner (Ed.), *Clinical work with substance-abusing clients* (pp. 3–29). New York: The Guilford Press.

Substance Abuse and Mental Health Services Administration. (1993). *National household survey on drug abuse: Highlights 1991.* Rockville, MD: U.S. Department of Health and Human Services.

Umunna, I. (1967). The drinking culture of a Nigerian community. *Quarterly Journal of Studies on Alcohol, 28,* 529–537.

U.S. Bureau of the Census. (1993). *We the American Blacks.* Washington, DC: U.S. Government Printing Office.

Vega, W., Gil, A., & Zimmerman, R. (1993a). Patterns of drug use among Cuban-American, African-American, and White Non-Hispanic boys. *American Journal of Public Health, 83,* 257–259.

Vega, W., Zimmerman, R., Warheit, G., Apospori, E., & Gil, A. (1993b). Risk factors for early adolescent drug use in four ethnic and racial groups. *American Journal of Public Health, 83,* 185–189.

Wilsnack, S., Wilsnack, R., & Klassen, A. (1985). Drinking and drinking problems among women in a U.S. national survey. *Alcohol Health and Research World, 9,* 3–13.

Wilson, A. (1990). *Black-on-black violence: The psychodynamics of black self-annihilation in service of white domination.* New York: Afrikan World Infosystems.

Woody, G. (1987). Twelve-month follow up of psychotherapy for opiate dependence. *American Journal of Psychiatry, 144,* 590–596.

Wright, R., Kail, B., & Creecy, R. (1990). Culturally sensitive social work practice with Black alcoholics and their families. In S. Logan, E. Freeman, & R. McRay (Eds.), *Social work practice with black families* (pp. 203–222). White Plains, NY: Longman.

Asian Americans
4

Ford H. Kuramoto

History

Asians and Pacific Islanders are frequently combined in discussions of cultural competency. They are, however, diverse populations, and the focus of this chapter is limited to Asian Americans. Asian Americans represent about 95 percent of the 7.2 million U.S. Asians and Pacific Islanders. According to the U.S. Census Bureau (1991), Asian Americans include people from more than 20 countries along the Pacific Rim and in Central, South, and Southeast Asia (O'Hare & Felt, 1991). About 23 percent of the total are Chinese Americans. About 63 percent of the Chinese American population is foreign born (Zane, Takeuchi, & Young, 1994). This chapter focuses on only the largest of the Asian American populations. A brief historical perspective on these populations is presented in this section.

Reports indicate that some Asians lived in parts of the United States as early as 498 A.D. However, most Asians began arriving in America at the time of the California Gold Rush, around 1850. There is a historical connection between the immigration of Asians and the history of drugs in America, specifically opium.

The first group of Asian immigrants to arrive in the United States in large numbers was the Chinese, beginning about 1850 (Zane et al., 1994). According to Zane and colleagues, between 1849 and 1882 more than 275,000 Chinese entered the United States to work in California during the Gold Rush, as well as on the transcontinental railroads. The Chinese laborers, about 90 percent of whom were single men, brought opium with them to smoke. It is estimated that by 1875 opium smoking had become widespread in the United States among all segments of society (Inciardi, 1992).

After the Chinese Exclusion Act of 1882, Japanese laborers were brought to America in increasing numbers from 1885 to about 1910. The National Origins Act barred Japanese and other Asians from entering the United States after 1924. According to the 1990 census, Japanese Americans represented 12 percent of Asians and Pacific Islanders, the third largest subgroup (U.S. Bureau of the Census, 1991).

Although Filipinos are generally considered Asians, some Filipino Americans identify themselves as Pacific Islanders. In contrast to the Chinese and Japanese nationals who immigrated to America, the Filipinos were considered American nationals because of the colonial control the United States held over the Philippines. Filipinos are the second largest Asian and Pacific Islander population in the United States, with 1.4 million or 19 percent of all Asians and Pacific Islanders. More than 64 percent of Filipino Americans are foreign born (Zane & Kim, 1994).

Koreans began immigrating to the United States around the turn of the century as a result of war (for example, the Tonghak Rebellion, the Sino-Japanese War, the Russo-Japanese War), disease, and famine. According to the 1990 census, Korean Americans represented 11 percent of Asians and Pacific Islanders. More than 80 percent of Korean Americans are foreign born (Zane & Kim, 1994).

Relatively few Southeast Asians lived in the United States before 1975. After the fall of Saigon in 1975, Cambodians, Laotians, and Vietnamese tried to escape war, political purges, and famine by relocating to refugee camps, the United States, and other countries. In the 1990 census, the Vietnamese population represented 8 percent of all Asians and Pacific Islanders, Cambodians 2 percent, Laotians 2 percent, Hmong 1 percent, and Thai 1 percent (Zane & Kim, 1994).

South Asians, primarily Asian Indians, began coming to the United States around 1900. The early immigrants were laborers in the lumber industry in Washington State and the farms of California (Takaki, 1989). According to the 1990 census, Asian Indians represented 11 percent of the Asian and Pacific Islander population (U.S. Bureau of the Census, 1991).

Extent of the Problem

The sheer lack of research data on tobacco and alcohol and other drug (AOD) use in these populations is a basic and serious problem for Asian Americans and Pacific Islanders. A review of the available literature will show how much research should be done.

The National Institute on Drug Abuse (NIDA) monograph on people of color by Trimble, Padilla, and Bell (1987) is one of only a few publications with a section on Asians and Pacific Islanders. The NIDA monograph discusses a few studies that give a mixed picture of the incidence and prevalence of AOD abuse among the diverse Asian and Pacific Islander populations. Most studies cited in the monograph are anecdotal or limited to relatively small samples in specific local communities. Although the incidence and prevalence of AOD abuse among Asians and Pacific Islanders is generally considered to be lower than in other groups, the monograph indicates that conclusions should be cautiously drawn because many studies had methodological weaknesses.

One early study on Asian and Pacific Islander populations was conducted by Nakagawa and Watanabe (1973) in Seattle, Washington. An Asian student population was surveyed in junior high and high schools on the personal use of drugs other than marijuana and alcohol. There were 393 male students and 367 female students in the sample. Twelve percent of the men and 7 percent of the women were classified as drug users. By ethnic groups, 45 percent of the drug users were Filipino, 29 percent Japanese, 22 percent Chinese, and 49 percent other Asians. The drugs used by these youths included amphetamines, barbiturates, psychedelics, cocaine, and heroin.

Porter, Vieira, Kaplan, Heesh, and Colyar (1973) surveyed all students in grades 6 through 12 in Anchorage, Alaska. Of the 15,634 students surveyed, 0.6 percent were Asians and Pacific Islanders. Compared with the drug use rates of Native Alaskans (44 percent), whites (36 percent), and African Americans (32 percent), the Asian and Pacific Islander students reported the lowest rate of use of "at least one drug," at 26 percent.

Stimbu, Schoenfelt, and Sims (1973) surveyed college students in a large southeastern state regarding drug use. Asian and Pacific Islander students represented 1 percent of the 20,547 respondents. Asians and Pacific

Islanders in the sample reported the lowest use of alcohol and tobacco, the second lowest use of marijuana and strong stimulants, and the third lowest use of all other substances compared with American Indian, African American, and white respondents. No study specifically identified the Asian and Pacific Islander subgroups with respect to patterns and characteristics of drug use.

Data derived from the treatment of Asian American patients for drug abuse are another source of information. Some of the early focus on Chinese opium users is considered to be influenced by anti-Chinese, xenophobic sentiments around 1900, and the victimization of Chinese immigrants by drug enforcement authorities was motivated by racial and political attitudes of the day (Johnson & Nishi, 1976; Musto, 1973). According to Trimble and colleagues (1987), some studies indicated that Chinese immigrants were overrepresented among drug addict populations receiving treatment between 1920 and 1962. The profile of the typical Chinese addict is telling: "an immigrant from China, English-limited facilities, mean age of 53, a social isolate with a lack of social, recreational, and spiritual outlets."

Chinese narcotic addicts constituted less than 3 percent of the 32,309 male addicts treated at the U.S. Public Health hospital in Lexington, Kentucky, between 1920 and 1962. This figure overrepresented Chinese Americans in proportion to the total population. However, in San Francisco, during the period 1981–1982, Asians and Pacific Islanders represented 3.3 percent of all admissions to drug treatment programs. This proportion is considered low because about 22 percent of the city's population at that time were Asians and Pacific Islanders. Another drug abuse prevalence study based on a key informant needs assessment found that Chinese American drug use and Filipino American drug use were lower than that of the general population, whereas Japanese American drug use was estimated to be about the same (Trimble, Padilla, & Bell, 1987).

The National Institute on Alcohol Abuse and Alcoholism (NIAAA) publication on ethnic minorities (1989) reported studies of alcohol use among Asian and Pacific Islander populations, including surveys in Hawaii and the continental United States. According to Ahern (1989), the prevalence of alcohol use on Oahu in 1960 indicated that whites had the highest prevalence rate (74 percent), followed by Native Hawaiians (62 percent), Chinese (58 percent), Japanese (50 percent), Filipinos (46 percent), and others (62 percent). Subsequent surveys in 1974 and 1979 indicated similar patterns.

Yu, Liu, Xia, and Zhang (1985) studied alcohol use among Chinese in Shanghai and the United States. This study found that the average annual death rates attributed to chronic liver disease and cirrhosis specified as alcoholic (1979–1981) indicated that African Americans had the highest rates (10.5 per 100,000), followed by whites (4.7 per 100,000) and Chinese (1.2 per 100,000).

Murakami (1985) studied alcohol and drug problems in Hawaii among four ethnic groups. The prevalence rates of alcohol consumption in the category of "heavy" drinkers were highest for whites (13.6 percent), followed by Native Hawaiians (11.0 percent), Filipinos (6.7 percent), and Japanese (5.2 percent). Similar alcohol consumption patterns in Hawaii were found by Marchand, Kolonel, and Yoshizawa (1989).

Kitano and Chi (1985) studied Chinese, Japanese, Korean, and Filipino alcohol consumption in Los Angeles. This study found that Japanese had the highest percentage of heavy drinkers (25 percent), followed by Filipinos (20 percent), Koreans (15 percent), and Chinese (10 percent).

Kandel, Single, & Kessler (1976) studied youths in New York state, a small number of whom were Asian American. The Asian American students in the sample reported the lowest use of hard liquor, wine, beer, and cigarettes. For example, only 18 percent reported that they had ever tried hard liquor versus 68 percent of white students. In contrast, a national sample of seventh to 12th graders, studied by Wilsnack and Wilsnack (1978), found that 90 percent of Asian American male youths reported that they drank, compared with 80 percent of white male youths in the sample. Asian American female youths reported less drinking than white female youths reported. In the Barnes and Welte (1985) study of the same grade levels in New York, 45 percent of the Asian American youth reported that they drank, whereas 76 percent of the white students so reported. Yet, Asian American male drinkers consumed more alcohol per day than all other groups except Native American male drinkers. Furthermore, Asian American male students reported the greatest number of drunken episodes per month. Finally, Asian American youths also reported relatively high mean numbers of illicit drug use (a mean of 42 times versus 29 times for white male students).

In a study of drug abuse among African American, white, Hispanic, Native American, and Asian American high school seniors between 1976 and 1989, Bachman, Wallace, Kurth, Johnston, and O'Malley (1991) studied prevalence, trends, and correlates. From 1976 to 1979, 439 Asian Americans represented 0.7 percent of the sample. In the 1980 to 1984 sample, Asian Americans represented 1.5 percent of the sample (1,139 high school seniors) and from 1985 to 1989, 2.6 percent (1,899) of the national sample.

In Bachman et al. (1991), the Asian American sample reported the lowest rates of drug use. Asian Americans also reported the lowest rate of lifetime marijuana use at 29 percent. In all other groups, approximately half of the male students reported some lifetime use of marijuana. Annual, monthly, and daily prevalence rates for marijuana use were also relatively low for Asian American students. Reported cocaine use also indicated the lowest rates for Asian American students on an annual basis. Monthly prevalence rates for cocaine use were consistently lower for Asian American students than for other groups.

Other illicit drug use—including inhalants, hallucinogens, heroin, other opiates, stimulants, sedatives, and tranquilizers—indicated the lowest rates of reported use among African Americans and Asian Americans. With regard to the prevalence of alcohol consumption, the reported use by Asian American seniors was among the lowest, with about half of the male students and one-third of the female students reporting alcohol use during the past month. Heavy drinking (defined as five or more drinks at a single sitting) was also lowest among African American male students and Asian American male students. Asian American female seniors reported heavy drinking at a rate about half that of male seniors.

Cigarette smoking (that is, reported use of a half pack daily) prevalence was highest among Native American seniors and significantly lower for all other groups, including Asians and Pacific Islanders.

The study by Hansen, Johnson, Flay, Graham, and Sobel (1988) of seventh and eighth graders in Los Angeles included a significant sample of 275 Asian American students, who reported a relatively low lifetime marijuana use rate (2.6 percent). However, their lifetime cigarette use (12 percent) and alcohol use (11 percent) were comparable with or greater than the rates for other ethnic groups. Sasao (1987) reported that Asian and Pacific Islanders (n = 596) in Los Angeles had higher rates of lifetime drug use for cigarettes (11 percent), alcohol (14 percent), and marijuana (3 percent) than African Americans, Hispanics, and whites. Similar results were found in a statewide biannual survey of drug and alcohol use among students in grades 7, 9, and 11 (Skager, Fisher, & Maddahian, 1986; Skager, Frith, & Maddahian, 1989). Asian and Pacific Islander students had relatively low rates of alcohol use compared with other groups at all grade levels. However, none of these studies differentiated among the various specific Asian and Pacific Islander subgroups.

Studies of college-age samples have also found similar patterns of AOD use among Asian and Pacific Islander students. Adlaf, Smart, and Tan (1989) studied drug use among eight ethnic groups in Ontario, Canada. The Asian and Pacific Islander sample consisting of Chinese and Japanese respondents reported the lowest rates of tobacco, alcohol, and marijuana use. Sue, Zane, and Ito (1979) studied the drinking patterns of Asian and Pacific Islander and white students in Washington state. The Asian and Pacific Islander students reported lower rates of drinking, had more negative attitudes toward drinking, and needed fewer cues to regulate their own drinking than did the white students. More Asian and Pacific Islander students (15 percent) than whites (9 percent) reported abstinence or light drinking. Akutsu, Sue, Zane, and Nakamura (1989) also found that Asian and Pacific Islander students reported lower levels of alcohol consumption than white students. Self-reported physiological reactions to alcohol and drinking attitudes accounted more for the ethnic differences in use than did generalized cultural values.

Klatsky, Siegelaub, Landy, and Friedman (1983) studied interethnic differences in alcohol consumption of Kaiser Permanente medical patients examined from 1978 through 1980. Klatsky and others found that Asians and Pacific Islanders reported significantly less drinking than individuals from other groups. Significant differences, however, were found in patterns among the Asian and Pacific Islander subgroups. Japanese Americans reported the most alcohol use, and Chinese Americans reported the least drinking. Among women, Filipino women reported the least alcohol use, and Japanese women reported more drinking than the others. Foreign-born respondents more often abstained or drank less than did those who were American born.

McLaughlin, Raymond, Murakami, and Gilbert (1987) studied specific Asian and Pacific Islander groups in Hawaii. The sample included a large number of households, with in-person interviews to assess lifetime prevalence of AOD use. The prevalence rate for Chinese Americans was 4 percent; for Japanese Americans, 22 percent; for Filipino Americans, 11 percent; for Native Hawaiians, 19 percent; and for white Americans, 29 percent. Whites reported higher lifetime prevalence for most drugs than Asians and Pacific Islanders. However, Hawaiians tended to have higher lifetime prevalence rates than other Asians and Pacific Islanders for alcohol, cocaine, amphetamines, and marijuana. Japanese and Chinese Americans had a higher prevalence of tranquilizer use than other Asians and Pacific Islanders. However, it is difficult to generalize these findings to Asians and Pacific Islanders outside Hawaii. Asians and Pacific Islanders in Hawaii differ from their counterparts in the continental United States because of their nonminority status, acculturation levels, English-language proficiency, community cohesiveness, sociopolitical identification, and generational status (Zane & Kim, 1994).

Sasao (1991) also sampled specific Asian and Pacific Islander groups in California. This drug use assessment found that Japanese Americans had the highest percentage of reported lifetime use of cigarettes and tobacco products (45 percent), followed by Filipinos (38 percent), Vietnamese (36 percent), Koreans (36 percent), Chinese (25 percent), and Chinese Vietnamese (24 percent). These rates are lower than the general population rate, which is approximately 80 percent. When asked about lifetime alcohol consumption (at least 10 alcoholic drinks in their lifetime), the Japanese Americans had the highest level of lifetime use at 69 percent, followed by Koreans at 49 percent, Chinese at 42 percent, Vietnamese at 43 percent, Filipinos at 39 percent, and Chinese Vietnamese at 36 percent. These rates are significantly lower than the national prevalence rate of 85 percent. It was reported that most of the Asian and Pacific Islander drinking was related to social occasions. Sasao (1989) also conducted a bilingual telephone survey among Japanese respondents in southern California. Both U.S.-born and Japan-born respondents reported lifetime alcohol use of 73 percent and cigarette use of 55 percent. These rates are slightly lower than those of the general U.S. population. Significant differences were found between the U.S.-born and foreign-born Japanese respondents. For example, the two subgroups defined substance abuse differently. The Japan-born respondents tended to limit the definition of substance abuse to drugs such as marijuana, LSD, and heroin and excluded alcohol and tobacco.

Kitano and colleagues (Kitano & Chi, 1985, 1989; Kitano, Lubben, & Chi, 1988) studied alcohol drinking patterns among several Asian and Pacific Islander subgroups. Their studies found that alcohol drinking patterns of young Asian and Pacific Islander men were comparable with national norms, which was inconsistent with the myth that Asians and Pacific Islanders are basically nondrinkers. The studies also found that many Asian and Pacific Islanders were heavy drinkers. The Japanese respondents (most of whom were American born) had the highest percentage of heavy drinkers at 25 percent, followed by Filipinos at 20 percent, Koreans at 15 percent, and Chinese at 10 percent. The results were attributed to more permissive attitudes associated with greater acculturation. This study reported relatively few problems as a result of the heavy drinking. Few respondents reported being arrested for drinking or other serious results of heavy drinking. Apparently, the emphasis on drinking only at special occasions and the apparent social controls on drinking behavior tended to mitigate against social and legal problems as a result of alcohol consumption. Also, Maddahian, Newcomb, and Bentler (1985) found that Asians and Pacific Islanders were the largest group that tried only alcohol and no other substances.

Some studies have implied that the low rates of alcohol use among Asian and Pacific Islander groups are related to the physiological flushing reaction among some Asians and Pacific Islanders. This flushing response is an alcohol-related physiological sensitivity. Although some researchers attribute the relatively lower drinking rates to this physiological response (Agarwal, Eckey, Harada, & Goedde, 1984), others question this basis for the difference in drinking patterns (Chan, 1986; Johnson & Nagoshi, 1990).

A binational study of alcohol patterns was conducted, sampling Japanese in Japan, Japanese Americans in Hawaii, and Japanese Americans and whites in California (NIAAA & National Institute on Alcoholism in Japan, 1991). The study found that the proportion of current drinkers (those who drank alcohol within the past year) in all those study sites was somewhat higher than rates for the adult population in the United States as a whole. Japanese men in Japan had the highest percentage of current drinkers at 91 percent, followed by white men at 85 percent, Japanese American men in California at 84 percent, and Japanese American men in Hawaii at 80 percent. As is usually the case, women drank less than men. White women had the highest proportion of current female drinkers at 81 percent, followed by Japanese American women in California at 75 percent, Japanese American women in Hawaii at 68 percent, and Japanese women in Japan at 61 percent. Sixty-two percent of Japanese men in Japan reported drinking at least three times per week, followed by 44 percent of white male drinkers. The other respondents drank much less frequently. White women in California had the highest proportion of women who drank three or more times per week at 32 percent, followed by Japanese women in Japan at 21 percent and Japanese American women in Hawaii and California at 9 percent.

Two studies were identified that focused on Southeast Asian respondents. Yee and Thu (1987) used household interviews to sample adult Southeast Asian refugees, mainly Vietnamese, in Texas. A majority of the sample (52 percent) reported problems with alcohol or tobacco use. About half the respondents reported that they used alcohol or smoked tobacco to cope with stressful situations or personal problems. In a study of Job Corps members in San Diego, Indo-Chinese youths had the lowest levels of drinking (use in the past six months) compared with whites, African Americans, and Hispanics (Morgan, Wingard, & Felice, 1984). Sixty-six percent of

Indo-Chinese men and 43 percent of Indo-Chinese women drank, compared with an average of 87 percent for men and 88 percent for women in the other groups. The Indo-Chinese youths who drank reported very low levels of other drug use: None had used cocaine, and only 3 percent reported using marijuana.

A Canadian study of Chinese, Indo-Pakistani, and Latin American subjects (Legge & Sherlock, 1990–1991) found that Chinese subjects reported a low frequency and quantity of alcohol consumption compared with Indo-Pakistanis and Latin Americans (9 percent, 52 percent, and 41 percent, respectively). Chinese and Indo-Pakistani respondents were similar in their self-reports of excessive alcohol use. However, drinking was attributed to coping with failure by more Chinese respondents (52 percent) than Indo-Pakistanis (32 percent). A higher proportion of Indo-Pakistani respondents (30 percent) than Chinese respondents (18 percent) mentioned easy availability of alcohol as a reason for use. Similarly, the low cost of alcohol in Canada was considered a reason for use by more Indo-Pakistani respondents (12 percent) than Chinese respondents (7 percent). Chinese and Latin American respondents indicated that health-related problems were the biggest problems resulting from excessive alcohol use (71 percent for both groups). For the Chinese respondents, family disruption, trouble with the law, child abuse, and wife abuse were the other problems identified as resulting from excessive alcohol use. Among the Indo-Pakistani respondents, the greatest concern was family disruption, followed by wife abuse, child abuse, and family breakup.

A San Francisco study (Wong, 1985) differed from most other studies in that it found relatively high rates of AOD abuse among Chinese youths in San Francisco's Chinatown. Their use of cigarettes, marijuana, cocaine, and diazepam (Valium) was comparable with use by whites, African Americans, and Hispanics. The following percentages of Chinese respondents reported consumption of these substances: beer, 77; cigarettes, 75; marijuana, 59; wine, 54; hard liquor, 49; quaaludes, 42; cocaine, 40; hashish, 22; diazepam, 16; and LSD, 15. Chinese youths had similar levels of use for most drugs; however, although female youths more often reported use of diazepam, codeine, and quaaludes.

Only one study has focused on elderly Asian and Pacific Islander men and alcohol abuse (Yamamoto, Lee, Lin, & Cho, 1987). This study found that Filipinos had the highest rate of alcohol abuse or dependence (11 percent) according to DSM-III diagnostic criteria, followed by Japanese at 6 percent and Chinese at 4 percent.

Austin (1994) pointed out that Asian and Pacific Islander respondents did not always report the lowest incidence and prevalence rates. In a national survey of junior and senior high school students in 1974, African Americans had the highest percentage of lifetime abstainers (41 percent), followed by Asians and Pacific Islanders at 35 percent. A California study conducted in the 1980s found that Asian and Pacific Islander students reported higher drinking rates than African Americans and at times Hispanics (Maddahian, Newcomb, & Bentler, 1986). These alcohol studies found that whites had the highest mean rates, followed by Hispanics, Asians, and African Americans. The differences among Asians, African Americans, and Hispanics were not significant, although the rates were substantially lower for whites. As a result of several estimates regarding the use of illicit drugs or alcohol use, Asians and Pacific Islanders rank higher than African Americans (Barnes & Welte, 1985; Barnes, Welte, & Dintcheff, 1993; Kim, McLead, & Shantzis, 1992; Segal, 1992).

In some categories of the national high school seniors survey, the limited sample of Asians and Pacific Islanders reported rates similar to African Americans in terms of the use of cocaine, stimulants, and LSD. In some cases, Asians and Pacific Islanders reported higher rates than African Americans for inhalants, tranquilizers, sedatives, and other opiates (Austin, 1994). In the Los Angeles longitudinal study (Maddahian et al., 1986), Asians and Pacific Islanders showed only a slightly lower average for drug use (other than alcohol, tobacco, and marijuana) than did whites and Hispanics. There were also indications that the use of nonprescription medication (for example, sleeping pills, stimulants, cough medicines, and cold and allergy medication) was higher for Asians and Pacific Islanders than for other ethnic groups. Asians and Pacific Islanders reported using nonprescription medications and drugs at a higher rate than African Americans. In a 1991 New York survey, Asians and Pacific Islanders reported using marijuana the least (10 percent) compared with whites (27 percent), Hispanics (23 percent), and African Americans (21 percent). Similar rates were found for use of analgesics and cocaine compared with whites and Hispanics only. However, Asians and Pacific Islanders reported the same rates for cocaine use as African Americans. Asian and Pacific Islander inhalant use (at 14 percent) was higher than African American use (11 percent) and similar to the rate for Hispanics (16 percent), although substantially lower than for whites (23 percent). Regional differences were found, so the Asian and Pacific Islander rates for use of marijuana varied significantly depending on the region of the state (Austin, 1994).

In the Mecklenburg County, North Carolina, study the rate of total AOD use among Asians and Pacific Islanders was higher than for African Americans, although lower than for other ethnic groups (Kim et al. 1992). Although marijuana use was relatively low, Asians and Pacific Islanders used inhalants, cocaine, amphetamines, and barbiturates at the same rate as whites and other ethnic groups, or higher.

A West Coast study of secondary schools that participate in a prevention program evaluation indicated that Asians and Pacific Islanders may be at relatively higher risk for use of illicit drugs than for use of alcohol (Ellickson, Hays, & Bell, 1992). The study of drug use patterns among students found that whites used illicit drugs at the highest rate, 72 percent, followed by Asians and Pacific Islanders at 10 percent, Hispanics at 8 percent, and African Americans at 7 percent. Also, the pattern of use among Asians and Pacific Islanders began with pills and other drugs, followed later by regular smoking and drinking. Other groups followed a different pattern, in which weekly alcohol use was followed by use of marijuana and all other illicit drugs.

In the 1991 California Student Substance Abuse Survey, approximately 50 high schools were sampled statewide (Austin, 1994). This study found that Asian and Pacific Islander ninth and 11th graders generally reported lower prevalence rates in 10 categories of legal and illicit drugs. However, in several categories, Asians and Pacific Islanders equaled or exceeded the rates reported by African Americans, including weekly drinking; current and daily cigarette smoking; and the use of cocaine, amphetamines, and LSD. The California study concluded that the results further supported the hypothesis that Asian and Pacific Islander youths may be at relatively high risk for use of stimulants (cocaine and amphetamines), inhalants, LSD or hallucinogens, depressants, and psychotherapeutics in general (Austin, 1994). This study and others have found that Asians and Pacific Islanders have similar or higher use rates than African Americans for cocaine, amphetamines, and stimulants. In addition, Asians and Pacific Islanders also used depressant drugs—such as sedatives, barbiturates, and tranquilizers—more than African Americans, sometimes close to the rates of whites. According to Austin (1994), the alcohol, tobacco, and other drug use rates among Asian and Pacific Islander women may be a concern because although rates are generally low, they may rise as Asian and Pacific Islander women become more acculturated. Some research indicates that the more acculturated Asian and Pacific Islander women become, the more traditional values and the stigma of alcohol, tobacco, and other drug use among them may attenuate (Chi, Lubben, & Kitano, 1989).

The gender patterns indicate that men almost always use alcohol and cigarettes more frequently than women (Austin, 1994). However, the annual prevalence rates among Asian and Pacific Islander men and women are similar with regard to the use of LSD, cocaine, sedatives, barbiturates, stimulants, and marijuana. Asian and Pacific Islander women exceeded the men in use of cocaine and stimulants. Drug use among Asian and Pacific Islander women was relatively higher in relation to women of other groups, compared with their male counterparts. Compared with the current and annual prevalence rates for African American women, Asian and Pacific Islander women had higher use rates for sedatives, marijuana, cocaine, stimulants, and inhalants. Asian and Pacific Islander women are at relatively high risk for marijuana, cocaine, and stimulant use. Asian and Pacific Islander women reported much higher rates of daily smoking than African American women and slightly higher rates of daily smoking than Hispanic women.

Although Asian and Pacific Islander men use marijuana significantly more than women, both men and women had similar rates of use for cocaine, amphetamines, inhalants, and depressants. In all cases except inhalant use by men, Asians and Pacific Islanders exceeded African Americans of the same gender. In terms of sedatives and barbiturates, the Asian and Pacific Islander use rates were similar to those of Hispanics and higher than African American rates.

In the 1991 California student survey, alcohol consumption across Asian and Pacific Islander groups was lower than other ethnic groups. Among the Asian and Pacific Islander groups, Pacific Islanders consistently reported the highest rate of alcohol consumption, followed by Koreans, Filipinos, Japanese, Southeast Asians, and Chinese. A similar pattern held true for cigarette smoking.

With regard to illicit drug use, a similar pattern was reported. However, Southeast Asians reported using illicit drugs at relatively high rates, comparable with those of Filipinos. Southeast Asians ranked first in cocaine use and high in amphetamine use. Pacific Islanders, however, reported relatively low rates of both cocaine and amphetamine use. Pacific Islanders reported the highest rates for use of illicit drugs, marijuana, and inhalants, at rates close to non-Asians and Pacific Islanders. Filipinos and Koreans were relatively high users of marijuana, whereas Filipinos and Japanese were relatively high users of cocaine and amphetamines. Asians and

Pacific Islanders used inhalants at a rate similar to that of non-Asians and Pacific Islanders (Austin, 1994).

Incidence and prevalence estimates based on treated cases may initially appear to indicate a lower need for services. However, the relatively low use rates of existing AOD services by Asians and Pacific Islanders could also mean that the services should be at a higher rate, and various circumstances may make the use and access of services difficult (Murase, 1977; Sue & Morishima, 1982). Through a sample of individuals in treatment for AOD abuse in San Francisco (Asian, Inc., 1978), it was estimated that the AOD abuse rate among Japanese Americans is similar to that of the general population in San Francisco. However, the AOD abuse rates for Chinese and Filipino Americans were lower. A national study of drug abuse programs (Phin & Phillips, 1978) found that 55 percent of Asians and Pacific Islanders in treatment and about 65 percent of whites were admitted primarily for heroin use. Asian and Pacific Islander clients reported higher levels of barbiturate use (45 percent) than whites (11 percent). It was also found (Namkung, 1976) that 95 percent of Asian and Pacific Islander inmates in California prisons were incarcerated for drug-related crimes.

Finally, Zane and Sasao (1992) identified trends based on recent studies. First, the use of drugs such as alcohol, nicotine, cocaine, and marijuana appeared to be lower for Asian and Pacific Islanders than for whites and other groups of color. However, it is important to identify the variations in AOD use among the different Asian and Pacific Islander subpopulations. For example, whereas most Asian and Pacific Islander subgroups reported less alcohol use than whites, Hawaiians reported AOD use at a level comparable with whites. Second, it appeared that alcohol use has been underestimated for some Asian and Pacific Islander groups, such as Japanese American men and Filipino American men. Third, evidence suggests that Chinese and Japanese Americans use barbiturates and tranquilizers more than was expected, and this use may be an increasing problem. Fourth, cultural factors play an important role in limiting and sometimes enhancing AOD use among Asian and Pacific Islander groups.

Cultural Characteristics of the Group

To discuss the cultural characteristics of Asian Americans, it is necessary to understand the diversity and some demographic characteristics of this heterogeneous population.

The O'Hare and Felt (1991) report is used extensively in this section because it captures the contrasts and diversity in the Asian and Pacific Islander populations. In this report, based on the March 1990 U.S. Census Bureau Current Population Survey, references made to Asians and Pacific Islanders include people from China, Mongolia, Pakistan, Sri Lanka, Maldives, India, Nepal, Bhutan, Bangladesh, Burma, Laos, Thailand, Vietnam, Cambodia, North Korea, South Korea, Japan, Hong Kong, Macao, Taiwan, Philippines, Malaysia, Singapore, Indonesia, and the island groups that form Melanesia, Micronesia, and Polynesia.

In 1990 the states with the largest numbers of Asian and Pacific Islander populations were California, with 2,845,659 or 9.6 percent of the state's population; New York, with 693,760 or 3.9 percent; Hawaii, with 685,236 or 61.8 percent; Texas, with 319,459 or 1.9 percent; and Illinois, with 285,311 or 2.5 percent.

The rapid increase in the Asian and Pacific Islander population is a result of immigration and an influx of refugees. During the 1980s, 75 percent of the increase in the Asian and Pacific Islander population was a result of immigration.

In the 1980s the average household income of the Asian and Pacific Islander population was slightly higher than that of non-Hispanic whites. During this same period, however, the poverty rate among Asians and Pacific Islanders increased and is nearly twice that of non-Hispanic whites. This rise is a result of a bimodal income pattern, wherein some immigrants are skilled, educated, and able to develop careers in business, whereas others tend not to have the education and skills necessary to develop similar careers and businesses in the United States as easily.

Asian and Pacific Islander families averaged slightly higher incomes than non-Hispanic white families, and more Asians and Pacific Islanders attended college. However, the personal income of Asians and Pacific Islanders was less than non-Hispanic whites. In all age groups, non-Hispanic white men earned more money than Asian and Pacific Islander men of the same age and educational background. Although Asians and Pacific Islanders had more education than non-Hispanic whites, their return on earnings was 21 percent lower, which indicates that the glass ceiling effect of employment discrimination may be keeping Asians and Pacific Islanders from benefiting appropriately from their education and work performance.

The following discussion addresses the various cultural characteristics of the major Asian and Pacific Islander groups with respect to AOD abuse

issues. The discussion regarding cultural characteristics in relation to alcohol use is based extensively on an Asian and Pacific Islander alcohol peer
consultation and training project needs assessment conducted in California (Hatanaka, Morales, & Kaseyama, 1991). The study hypothesized that
whereas cultural backgrounds and drinking styles among Asian and Pacific
Islander groups differed, these groups were similar in their encouragement of moderate drinking. Thus, culture as a variable is considered by
many to be an important aspect of drinking patterns. Acculturation has
also been identified as having a major influence on drinking patterns, that
is, the greater the acculturation levels, in general the greater the amount of
drinking (Austin, 1989; Austin & Gilbert, 1989). According to this theory,
Asians and Pacific Islanders who are recent immigrants should have a drinking pattern similar to their country of origin, whereas Asians and Pacific
Islanders who are more assimilated should demonstrate drinking patterns
more similar to American culture (Chi et al., 1989). Also, it has been hypothesized that alcohol consumption among Asians and Pacific Islanders
increases as a way of coping with stress that is the result of changes in
social norms, family relationships, and upward mobility (Yu & Liu, 1987).
Note, however, that the extent to which acculturation affects Asian and
Pacific Islander drinking patterns is unclear.

The acculturation hypothesis is supported by a study of younger Japanese men and women who reported heavier drinking and a lower percentage of abstinence than an older Japanese sample (Kitano et al., 1988). Also,
Sue and colleagues (1979) found that highly assimilated Asian and Pacific
Islander college students drank more than less assimilated students. Yuen
and Johnson (1986) found that daughters of Chinese and Japanese ancestry drank significantly more than their mothers. However, the acculturation hypothesis is contradicted by other studies such as Akutsu et al. (1989),
in which Filipino women in Los Angeles retained the drinking patterns of
their culture of origin, whereas Filipino men's drinking resembled that of
the dominant society. Thus, sociocultural factors, including acculturation
and physiological factors (such as the flushing response), do not adequately
explain all aspects of Asian and Pacific Islander drinking patterns. Sue and
Nakamura (1984) have therefore proposed the reciprocity model, a concept that includes the interaction of all pertinent variables. This hypothesis suggests that alcohol consumption is an interactive phenomenon in
which the physiological, social, and psychological factors interact with each
other. The reciprocity model assumes that drinking behavior is influenced

by the native culture, the mainstream American culture, and the generational status of individuals.

The figures from the Hatanaka and colleagues (1991) needs assessment study provide a helpful outline of issues that relate to cultural characteristics. Table 4-1 identifies some risk groups in six Asian and Pacific Islander populations. These risk groups include American-born as well as foreign-born individuals, both genders, college-age students and elderly people, and individuals who may have experienced traumatic wartime refugee trauma. Table 4-2 outlines several culturally based behaviors across Asian and Pacific Islander groups that are barriers to treatment and recovery. The most common and most difficult barrier is denial. Table 4-3 shows data for clients in a program targeting driving under the influence (DUI) of alcohol. This survey asked questions regarding individual drinking behavior. The table illustrates how both the self-perceptions and the drinking patterns of these Asian and Pacific Islander groups varied significantly. Table 4-4 also shows data for clients in a DUI program. This survey asked individuals for their reasons or motivation for drinking. Again, significant differences were found among the six Asian and Pacific Islander groups. Peer influence was a relatively low factor, whereas wanting to feel good or at ease around people, escaping from boredom, reducing anxiety and tension, and drinking to enjoy what the person is doing more ("self-actualizing") were higher.

The following section addresses AOD abuse and the relationship to cultural characteristics by individual Asian and Pacific Islander subgroups. This section relies heavily on a statewide Asian and Pacific Islander drug services needs assessment conducted in California (Sasao, 1991). The statewide drug abuse needs assessment obtained data through many mechanisms. One mechanism was a series of community forums for specific groups. These forums were held in three locations: San Francisco, Los Angeles, and San Diego.

The first forum to be summarized focused on the Chinese American population. The community forums indicated that tobacco and alcohol were the most prevalent substances used by Chinese populations. Chinese populations were reported to use other drugs but not at the prevalence rates reported for tobacco and alcohol.

According to the community forums, Chinese immigrants underestimate the health hazards of alcohol, tobacco, and prescription medication because these drugs are legal and culturally accepted in both China and the United States. High-risk populations among Chinese were older

Table 4-1. Risk Groups as Identified through Key Informant Surveys

Chinese	Japanese	Korean	Pacific Islander	Filipino	Southeast Asian
Businessmen (men)—alcohol an intrinsic part of business transactions. Youths—teens and college-age youths, both male and female. Specific subgroups: new immigrants (Taiwan) and second generation and later. Women—generally agreed there is a greater problem than with men. Hidden cases are a problem among women.	American-born men—pack drinking, keeping up with peers. Youths and young adults—socially expected. Often, the only drug of choice, although polydrug use is also significant. Men are at greater risk than women. Japan-born businessmen ("shosha")—Japanese nationals temporarily living in the United States. Business obligations. Isolated elderly people—widowers, monolingual individuals without a strong social support network.	Men (both American born and foreign born)—high alcohol consumption rates. Pack drinking. College-age men and women—increasing trend among young men and women. Social expectations high. Women in general—increasing trend, but significantly less than men. High-risk subgroup: waitresses and hostesses in Korean bars, encouraged to drink with clients.	Youths—main target group. Excessive drinking noted. Significant problems with drugs and gangs. Mostly men, but increasing problems with women because of erosion of clear-cut familial and sexual roles. High incidence of low-income and poverty-level people. Alcohol and related problems exacerbated.	First-generation seniors, often men. Immigrant youths—exacerbated by other drugs and gang activity. American-born youths and young adults—social pressures, acculturation. Men in general pack drinking, peer pressures. Women in general drink alcohol less than men, although an increasing trend of substance abuse is seen.	Recent immigrants—exacerbated by problems of acculturation and posttraumatic stress syndrome. Men in general—peer and social pressures. Women in general—significantly less than men, although it is a custom to drink alcohol after giving birth to restore the mother's health.

Source: Adapted from Hatanaka, H., Morales, R., & Kaseyama, N. (1991). Asian Pacific alcohol peer consultation and training project. Los Angeles: Special Services for Groups.

adult men, adolescents, young adults, immigrants, and members of low-income households. The specific emphasis on older adult men was interpreted as a cultural factor that places heavy responsibility on men within Chinese households. In addition, the immigration experience and the cultural adjustment from the country of origin to the United States are strongly associated with AOD abuse. In addition, peer pressure, family and marital issues, and juvenile delinquency and gang activity are associated with AOD abuse. Conflicts between the older and younger generations often isolate youths from other family members and can lead to depression. This isolation can lead to juvenile delinquency and AOD abuse as a coping mechanism. In the Chinese community, heavy emphasis is placed on the continuity of generations, harmony, and filial respect. Furthermore, consequences of socially unacceptable behavior focus on the welfare of the family and future generations, as opposed to the individual.

The Japanese American community forums reported that alcohol and marijuana were the most prevalent substance used, although tobacco, crack cocaine, and amphetamines were also commonly abused. The Japanese forums also identified adolescents, young adults, and single adults (especially those who are divorced) as high-risk groups. AOD-related problems included parents who used legal and illegal substances and became negative role models for their children. This negative role modeling was later reinforced by peer pressure. New immigrants often felt isolated from mainstream society and coped with their resulting depressed feelings by using AOD. They sometimes joined a drug-using subculture as a way of finding a peer group and social acceptance.

The Korean American community forums identified whiskey, rice wine, and crack cocaine as the most commonly abused substances. The high-risk groups were reported to be adolescents, young adults, and, to a lesser extent, elderly individuals who abuse prescription or over-the-counter medication bought in Korea. Men are considered at especially high risk because they are encouraged to drink and smoke as a sign of masculinity in Korean culture. AOD-related problems in the community include DUIs, traffic citations, domestic violence, juvenile delinquency and gang activity, school truancy, and runaways (Sasao, 1991).

The Filipino American community forums identified alcohol, marijuana, and cocaine as the most frequently abused substances. The high-risk groups were identified as adolescents, young adults, men, and recent immigrants. The AOD-related problems in the community included family and marital problems, problems associated with immigration and adjustment to the

Table 4-2. Barriers to Alcohol Recovery Services as Identified through Key Informant Surveys

Chinese	Japanese	Korean	Pacific Islander	Filipino	Southeast Asian
Denial—the single most important factor contributing to barriers. Lack of Chinese American counselors and bilingual outreach programs.	Denial—embarrassment is probably the key factor motivating the denial response. Only a few Japanese American counselors and bilingual outreach programs.	Denial—especially because drinking is culturally accepted, and in such a close-knit community, a sense of shame is heightened. Korean media (probably watched by 90 percent of the community) tends to glamorize drinking. Only a few Korean American counselors and bilingual outreach programs.	Denial—especially because a lack of culturally relevant substance abuse education exists. Lack of Pacific Islander (for example, Tongan, Samoan) professionals in all fields.	Denial—unwillingness to admit to any problem of this type. Lack of Filipino counselors and bilingual outreach programs.	Denial—and lack of knowledge about substance abuse, especially among recent immigrants. Also shame for the individual as well as for the family. Lack of Southeast Asian counselors and bilingual outreach programs.

Source: Adapted from Hatanaka, H., Morales, R., & Kaseyama, N. (1991). *Asian Pacific alcohol peer consultation and training project.* Los Angeles: Special Services for Groups.

mainstream culture, juvenile delinquency and gang activity, underemployment, crime, high school dropout rates, broken families, suicides, and alcohol-impaired driving arrests and accidents. Traditional acceptance of drinking and smoking for men in Filipino culture was reported to perpetuate the problem. Filipino women are also vulnerable to AOD abuse when they get involved in gang activity.

The Vietnamese American forums identified cigarettes and marijuana as the most prevalent abused substances. Alcohol is also a problem among the older generation, especially Vietnamese veterans of the Vietnam War. High-risk groups include adolescents, men, and members of low-income households. Adolescents were said to be at risk because they tend to have little parental supervision; most parents are at work for long hours. Immigrant adult men are vulnerable because of the frustration and depression they experience adjusting to mainstream American culture. Men are particularly at risk because they often feel they lose control over their families amid the changing roles that the families experience in the United States. The changing of roles in families and the loss of traditional status create vulnerabilities to AOD abuse. This is particularly true when Vietnamese immigrant fathers who speak little English have to rely on their children to interpret and on their wives to provide much of the financial support. AOD-related problems in the community include peer pressure, juvenile delinquency, gang activity, immigration and cultural adjustment, refugee status, economic hardship, stress on the family related to changing roles, and economic difficulties (Sasao, 1991).

The Cambodian American community forums identified alcohol and tobacco as the two most prevalent substances abused by Cambodians. However, crack cocaine and "ice" (methamphetamine) were also major problems. The high-risk groups included low-income Cambodians of all ages and genders. The AOD-related problems in the community included family or marital conflict, juvenile delinquency, gang activity, and peer pressure (Sasao, 1991).

The Laotian American community forum identified alcohol, tobacco, and marijuana as the most prevalent abused substances. All segments of the community were considered at high risk, particularly men. The AOD-related problems in the community included family and marital conflicts, juvenile delinquency, gang activity, unemployment, and the trauma caused by the refugee experience (Sasao, 1991).

The Hmong American community forum identified alcohol, tobacco, and opiates as the most prevalent substances of use or abuse. The forum

Table 4-3. Self-Perception of Drinking Behavior, by Ethnicity

	Total (n = 204)	Chinese (n = 11)	Japanese (n = 24)	Korean (n = 90)	Pacific Islander (n = 28)	Filipino (n = 27)	Southeast Asian (n = 24)
A. How would you characterize your drinking pattern?							
Always have been a nondrinker	2.0	0.0	0.0	1.1	0.0	7.4	4.2
Nondrinker now, drank in past	19.6	18.2	16.7	22.2	32.1	11.1	8.3
Nondrinker now, was an alcoholic or heavy drinker	4.9	0.0	4.2	1.1	14.3	11.1	4.2
Presently a light drinker	42.6	45.5	37.5	44.4	28.6	37.0	62.5
Presently a moderate drinker	26.5	27.3	29.2	27.8	25.0	29.6	16.7
Presently a heavy drinker	2.9	9.1	4.2	3.3	0.0	0.0	4.2
Presently abusing alcohol	1.5	0.0	8.3	0.0	0.0	3.7	0.0
B. Do you think you have a drinking problem?							
No	63.7	54.5	54.2	68.9	53.6	70.4	62.5
Not sure	23.5	27.3	16.7	18.9	46.4	18.5	25.0
Yes	12.7	18.2	29.2	12.2	0.0	11.1	12.5
C. How serious is your drinking problem?							
Does not apply	22.5	45.5	25.0	14.4	7.1	48.1	29.2
Not at all serious	31.4	18.2	33.3	37.8	25.0	29.6	20.8
Not too serious	27.5	27.3	37.5	27.8	32.1	14.8	25.0
Somewhat serious	13.7	9.1	4.2	14.4	28.6	0.0	20.8
Serious	3.9	0.0	0.0	5.6	3.6	3.7	4.2
Very serious	1.1	0.0	0.0	0.0	3.6	3.7	0.0
D. How many times have you sought help for a drinking problem?							
Never	68.1	82.8	54.2	74.4	39.3	70.3	83.3
Once	27.9	18.2	37.5	22.2	57.1	25.9	12.5
Twice	1.5	0.0	0.0	1.1	3.6	0.0	4.2
Three times or more	2.5	0.0	8.3	2.2	0.0	3.7	0.0

Note: Values are given as percentages.

Source: Adapted from Hatanaka, H., Morales, R., & Kaseyama, N. (1991). *Asian Pacific alcohol peer consultation and training project.* Los Angeles: Special Services for Groups.

Table 4-4. Reported Reasons for Drinking, by Ethnicity

	Total (n = 204)	Chinese (n = 11)	Japanese (n = 24)	Korean (n = 90)	Pacific Islander (n = 28)	Filipino (n = 27)	Southeast Asian (n = 24)
A. Social/peer influence							
Because everyone else drinks	26.4	30.0	19.0	16.9	33.3	25.9	60.9
To feel good around people	40.7	45.5	40.9	41.6	44.4	14.8	60.9
To get along better with friends	38.7	27.3	43.5	47.7	25.9	14.8	47.8
Because friends pressure me into drinking	26.1	18.2	40.9	23.9	14.3	26.9	37.5
B. Escapist							
To stop boredom	37.7	36.4	40.9	31.5	29.6	55.6	47.8
To reduce anxiety and tension	33.8	36.4	36.4	36.4	11.1	33.3	47.8
Because I feel bad when I do not drink	8.5	0.0	4.5	7.9	0.0	14.8	21.7
Because I feel sad or depressed	30.7	18.2	40.9	36.0	18.5	22.2	30.4
Because it helps me with problems	27.0	36.4	27.3	19.1	33.3	40.7	30.4
C. Self-actualizing							
To enjoy what I am doing more	43.0	9.1	77.3	38.2	53.6	37.0	39.1
To help me through the day	15.7	9.1	18.2	15.9	7.7	18.5	21.7
To know myself better	15.1	9.1	13.6	16.9	14.8	14.8	13.0
To be more creative and productive	11.6	0.0	27.3	12.4	7.4	7.4	8.7
To understand things differently	16.1	0.0	27.3	20.2	3.7	14.8	13.0
To feel better about myself	27.0	0.0	36.4	27.0	39.3	18.5	26.1

Notes: Values are given as percentages. Percentages refer to mutually exclusive within-group responses to each item. Thus, row totals and column totals do not equal 100 percent.

Source: Adapted from Hatanaka, H., Morales, R., & Kaseyama, N. (1991). Asian Pacific alcohol peer consultation and training project. Los Angeles: Special Services for Groups.

reported that the use of these substances seemed to be declining in the previous five years because of substance users becoming ill and voluntarily discontinuing use of the drugs. The high-risk groups were identified as adolescents and adults, particularly those under stress or peer pressure (Sasao, 1991).

The Thai American community forum identified alcohol, tobacco, marijuana, and amphetamines as the most often abused substances. Those considered to be in the high-risk group were immigrants; those who were monolingual, Thai-speaking, single adults; less educated Thais; and young adults. AOD-related problems in the community included immigration and cultural adjustment, family and marital conflicts, and unemployment. The forum also reported that an increase in fights among community members had occurred as a result of participants being intoxicated. Also there had been an increase in smoking American-made cigarettes.

The tables that follow outline AOD-related factors, including social and cultural aspects. Tables 4-5 and 4-6 list the motivations cited for six Asian and Pacific Islander groups, including Chinese Vietnamese. These tables illustrate the diversity among the groups in terms of their self-report regarding their reasons or motivations for AOD use.

Tables 4-7 and 4-8 identify the reasons why adults in these groups use AOD. Again, note the variability in motivating factors among the groups. Note that job stress, marital and family problems, social settings, addiction, and depression are relatively prominent among adults. Tables 4-9 and 4-10 indicate that social events, restaurants, and home are among the places most associated with alcohol use. However, the patterns differ among the populations.

Although the limited incidence and prevalence data on Asians and Pacific Islanders tend to indicate that the rates for Asians and Pacific Islanders are relatively low, these data must be interpreted cautiously. The study by Barnes and Welte (1985) reported that the alcohol use rates for Asian American men was relatively high. In several of these studies, significant differences were found in rates among groups when gender was a variable. Furthermore, when the sample is "Asian American" and not specifically disaggregated by specific Asian and Pacific Islander subgroup, the results become a composite of data for several unidentified subgroups. Because the Asian and Pacific Islander population is so diverse, specific identification of the subgroup in a study is important. The studies by Kitano and Chi and by Murakami mentioned earlier both reported significant differences in the drinking patterns among specific Asian and Pacific Islander

Table 4-5. Reasons Cited for AOD Use among Asian Youths

				Ethnicity			
Problem	Chinese (n = 409)	Japanese (n = 416)	Korean (n = 399)	Filipino (n = 150)	Vietnamese (n = 322)	Chinese Vietnamese (n = 78)
Marital/family problem	84.4	81.7	90.0	86.7	62.1	65.4
Academic/school problem	63.8	72.6	72.4	64.0	28.3	39.7
Peer pressure	86.8	93.3	91.2	90.0	92.5	92.3
Curiosity	82.6	93.8	93.2	81.3	87.9	84.6
Low self-esteem	58.2	74.8	45.4	66.0	34.8	29.5
Loneliness	61.9	77.3	77.4	69.3	59.6	54.5
Other	21.3	17.1	25.6	8.7	19.6	12.8

Note: Values are given as percentages.
Source: Adapted from Sasao, T. (1991). Statewide Asian drug services needs assessment. Sacramento: California Department of Alcohol and Drug Programs.

Table 4-6. "Other" Reasons Cited for AOD Use among Asian Youths

Reasons	Ethnicity						Total
	Chinese	Japanese	Korean	Filipino	Vietnamese	Chinese Vietnamese	
Parental modeling	8	16	4	0	16	3	47
Easily available	11	15	14	4	11	2	57
Depression	13	2	10	0	2	0	27
Social/peer pressure	27	22	14	3	8	4	78
Stress	2	4	9	0	1	0	16
Ignorance	5	0	0	0	7	1	13
Addiction	1	0	4	0	6	1	12
Family problems	7	6	21	4	4	0	42
Immigration adjustment	1	0	11	0	2	0	14
Total	75	65	87	11	57	11	306

Note: Values are total number of respondents.

Source: Adapted from Sasao, T. (1991). Statewide Asian drug service needs assessment. Sacramento: California Department of Alcohol and Drug Programs.

subgroups. Zane and Kim (1994) stated that studies regarding Asians and Pacific Islanders must disaggregate the data to identify specific subgroups.

Suggested Prevention Strategies

The Statewide Asian Drug Service Needs Assessment (Sasao, 1991) provides grassroots community suggestions for prevention strategies. A series of community forums, similar to focus groups, was convened in California for each of six Asian and Pacific Islander groups. Part of the discussion in each of these forums addressed service use and program effectiveness issues, barriers to prevention and treatment, and program needs. The reports from the Chinese American community forums indicated that insufficient funding for community-based agencies was the most serious barrier to effective prevention and treatment services. The other major barriers included the denial of the existence of AOD problems and the stigma of seeking help. Family counseling was recommended to promote better parent–child communication and to teach alternative coping skills (rather than turning to drugs). Recreational, sports, and other positive social activities were recommended, as were bilingual and bicultural youth counselors, peer support systems as alternatives to gang involvement, antismoking education campaigns, health education, and the use of indigenous churches to help reach out to and educate the community.

The Japanese American community forums emphasized the need to overcome the stigma of seeking help to improve service use. Many Japanese American families keep AOD problems hidden. Another problem is the lack of funding to offer culturally sensitive services for prevention and treatment. The forums recommended information and education as an important way to fight AOD abuse, including outreach services, training of bilingual and bicultural professionals, and family counseling. Training children and adults about the hazards of AOD was a top priority.

The Korean American community forums reported that a lack of funding for community-based, culturally competent programs was a major barrier. Because these types of programs are not available, Korean families are reluctant to seek services in existing mainstream programs. These forums also emphasized the critical need for family-oriented educational programs and recommended that prevention programs make parents aware of the types of messages they convey to their children to keep Korean youths off drugs. The forums also encouraged establishing more programs for both

Table 4-7. Reasons Cited for AOD Use among Asian Adults

	Ethnicity					
Problem	Chinese (n = 409)	Japanese (n = 416)	Korean (n = 399)	Filipino (n = 399)	Vietnamese (n = 322)	Chinese Vietnamese (n = 78)
Job stress	82.6	90.6	86.2	73.3	51.6	57.7
Marital/family problem	84.8	88.0	83.7	81.3	79.2	78.2
Financial/economic issues	71.4	79.8	68.7	76.7	57.0	61.5
Social settings	72.1	84.8	72.2	83.3	83.9	88.5
Discrimination	31.5	34.5	45.9	33.3	10.0	15.4
Other	23.7	22.0	24.7	10.0	22.7	6.7

Note: Values are given as percentages.

Source: Adapted from Sasao, T. (1991). *Statewide Asian drug services needs assessment.* Sacramento: California Department of Alcohol and Drug Programs.

Table 4-8. "Other" Reasons Cited for AOD Use among Asian Adults

Problem	Ethnicity						Total
	Chinese (n = 409)	Chinese Japanese (n = 416)	Korean (n = 399)	Filipino (n = 150)	Vietnamese (n = 322)	Vietnamese (n = 78)	
Poor spouse relations	1	0	1	0	0	0	2
Peer/social pressure	35	22	12	4	11	2	86
Stress	3	6	6	3	1	1	20
Depression	12	18	24	4	17	0	75
Addiction	4	17	31	0	26	3	81
Easily available	32	20	0	0	12	1	65
Immigration adjustment	0	0	5	0	7	1	13
Parental influence	0	0	0	0	2	0	2
Total	87	83	79	11	76	8	344

Note: Values are given as percentages.
Source: Adapted from Sasao, T. (1991). Statewide Asian drug services needs assessment. Sacramento: California Department of Alcohol and Drug Programs.

Table 4-9. Occasions and Locations for Personal Alcohol Use among Respondents

				Ethnicity		
Problem	Chinese (n = 169)	Japanese (n = 286)	Korean (n = 204)	Filipino (n = 69)	Vietnamese (n = 160)	Chinese Vietnamese (n = 32)
Business meetings	14.2	22.7	26.1	36.2	17.3	12.5
Social events	85.2	91.6	77.0	89.9	86.3	81.2
Home	59.8	51.7	58.8	40.6	60.6	65.6
Bars	23.7	37.4	39.7	33.3	22.5	15.6
Restaurants	65.7	71.7	51.5	37.7	47.5	46.9
Other	14.7	13.2	19.3	8.7	15.0	12.5
Currently abstaining	59.0	31.0	50.0	54.0	53.3	60.3

Note: Values are given as percentages.

Source: Adapted from Sasao, T. (1991). *Statewide Asian drug services needs assessment.* Sacramento: California Department of Alcohol and Drug Programs.

Table 4-10. "Other" Occasions and Locations for Personal Alcohol Use

	Ethnicity						
Occasions	Chinese	Chinese Japanese	Korean	Filipino	Vietnamese	Vietnamese	Total
Cultural events	12	17	10	3	20	3	65
With friends	5	4	6	1	5	0	21
Sports events	2	8	5	0	1	1	17
Picnic	2	0	5	0	0	0	7
Job stress	0	7	5	1	1	1	14
Depression	0	0	2	0	0	0	3
Addiction	0	1	0	0	1	1	3
Total	21	37	33	5	28	6	130

Notes: Values are total number of respondents. Respondents were allowed to indicate multiple "other" occasions.

Source: Adapted from Sasao, T. (1991). Statewide Asian drug services needs assessment. Sacramento: California Department of Alcohol and Drug Programs.

parents and children to promote both positive parent–child communication and mutual support in dealing with personal problems.

The Filipino American community forums cited the stigma of seeking help, the lack of bilingual and bicultural personnel in prevention and treatment programs, the lack of culturally sensitive services, the lack of community programs, and insufficient agency funding as major reasons for underuse of prevention and treatment services by Filipino Americans. It was emphasized that bilingual and bicultural staff are essential to the effectiveness of prevention and treatment programs. It was suggested that more organizational involvement and leadership within the Filipino community are necessary to address AOD problems. The forums also stated that political clout is vital to achieve the goals of implementing successful community-based programs. Drug education, outreach, and family involvement were also cited as important factors. Because many Filipinos are recent immigrants, they need more education on the hazards of AOD abuse to modify the attitudes and habits they acquired in their native country.

The Vietnamese American community forums reported that the lack of bilingual and bicultural staff in prevention and treatment programs, the lack of appropriate referral systems, the lack of community-based programs, and the stigma associated with seeking help were the major barriers to service use. In addition, many Vietnamese Americans were not aware of existing services in their communities. This lack of awareness is mostly because of the differences between public health systems in Southeast Asia and mainstream U.S. programs. For example, Vietnamese individuals who are recent immigrants might seek the help of native "fortune tellers" to solve mental health problems, rather than going to Western professional clinics. The forums suggested more community education and outreach efforts and making available more prevention and treatment services. Vietnamese children should be provided positive alternatives to being at home alone or with their peers on the streets while their parents are at work. Recreational programs should be provided in the community to help provide positive leisure activities and to help new immigrants adjust to mainstream American culture.

The Cambodian American community forums reported that the lack of bilingual and bicultural staff, the lack of community-based prevention and treatment programs, and the lack of established referral systems were all significant barriers to meeting the service needs of their community. Public health education campaigns were also suggested to educate recent immigrants.

The Laotian American community forum reported that the lack of bilingual and bicultural program staff, the lack of culturally sensitive services, the lack of community-based programs indigenous to the Laotian community, and insufficient agency funding were major barriers. Furthermore, educational programs for the Laotian community were recommended because the drug abuse laws in Laos are different from those in the United States.

The Hmong American community forum reported that the cost of treatment and transportation made many services inaccessible. Communication is difficult without bilingual and bicultural translators. There are insufficient bilingual and bicultural services, and it is estimated that a significant number of individuals are isolated and unable to access AOD prevention and treatment services. Educational programs with bilingual staff should be developed to educate and assist the Hmong community. This population needs public health education regarding AOD abuse. Mainstream services must have the language capability and provide the necessary transportation to meet the needs of the Hmong.

The Thai American community forum reported that the most significant barriers to service use were the lack of bilingual and bicultural personnel, the lack of culturally sensitive services, the lack of available information in the appropriate language, the lack of transportation, and the lack of conveniently located facilities. There is also an overall lack of public health education and information, family counseling and support groups, bilingual and bicultural agency staff, and links between community service programs and Buddhist temple programs. Currently no specialized AOD prevention programs exist that target the Thai American community.

The Asian Pacific Alcohol Peer Consultation and Training Project needs assessment (Hatanaka et al., 1991) provides additional suggestions regarding prevention strategies. This statewide alcohol needs assessment in California found that prevention strategies must include more and improved bilingual outreach and educational services, educational materials that include general information, and referral and health education materials. Outreach should be given to each of the six populations (that is, Chinese, Japanese, Korean, Pacific Islander, Filipino, and Southeast Asian), with an emphasis on reaching the indigenous, community-based social networks. Community leaders, churches, temples, and schools are often effective ways to reach the respective communities. Because of the desire to avoid "losing face," individual counseling for at-risk individuals can be more effective than group treatment approaches. Close family members should be included whenever possible in the treatment plan. Southeast Asian groups in particular emphasize the importance of including the immediate family in any prevention and treatment effort because the whole family assumes the shame and guilt of an individual member. It was suggested that the media be used as an outreach tool to these communities. The Japanese American respondents suggested health-focused media efforts to get the attention of both American-born and foreign-born Japanese audiences. It is presumed that the Japanese population is extremely health conscious and is interested in health-related issues such as AOD abuse. The Korean respondents emphasized a media approach that had a strong shock value to deter AOD abuse. For example, they suggested that true-to-life scenes of alcohol-related traffic crashes be shown on 30-second public service announcements.

Finally, there is a lack of bilingual and bicultural educational materials for Asian and Pacific Islander populations. Especially lacking are materials targeting recent immigrants, Pacific Islanders, and Southeast Asian groups. Specialized public health and community education is necessary to overcome the denial and stigma that are major barriers to alcohol abuse prevention and treatment. In addition, few bilingual and bicultural service providers are available for these populations.

National Asian Pacific American Families Against Substance Abuse (NAPAFASA) conducted a demonstration project to describe promising AOD prevention programs for Asian and Pacific Islander youths between 1990 and 1993. The project was funded by the Center for Substance Abuse Prevention under the Programs of National Significance demonstration program. Over the three years, 18 existing programs were selected, visited, and monitored to identify the elements that seem to be effective prevention strategies (NAPAFASA, 1993).

The participants gave each of the programs high ratings and would recommend the programs to their peers. The factors that appeared to make the programs successful in engaging Asian and Pacific Islander youths and preventing AOD abuse at least during the course of the program, were the following:

◆ The organizations that sponsored the programs were well known to the Asian and Pacific Islander populations; they had community credibility and were indigenous to the infrastructure of the communities in which they provided the services. In most cases, the organizations that provided the services had served the Asian and Pacific Islander populations for at least five or 10 years and in some cases as long as 20 years.

◆ The organizational management and the project staff were—in most cases—Asians and Pacific Islanders, most of whom were bilingual and bicultural.

◆ Although recruiting and maintaining parent participation was difficult, the parents of the youths and the adults in the community supported the agency and the programs.

◆ The community at large supported and recognized the organizations as making positive contributions to the Asian and Pacific Islander population as well as to the community at large.

◆ The youths involved in the programs were highly motivated and wanted to participate in these various programs. In one case, the youths were actually paid a stipend for being peer educators and counselors regarding AOD abuse and human immunodeficiency virus/acquired immunodeficiency syndrome. However, all other programs involved youths who were volunteers. Many youth leaders who were mentors, tutors, and counselors were also volunteers.

◆ An emphasis was placed on taking pride in one's culture, ethnicity, language, traditions, holidays, and ceremonies, as well as on enhancing self-esteem. Many activities involved cultural festivals; traditional ceremonies; ethnic foods; and drama, music, and artistic work that related to their cultures and history.

◆ All programs had a great deal of group activity. Group members were made to feel accepted, supported, needed, and part of an effort that was worthwhile. Many groups engaged in community service activities for which they were publicly recognized (for example, performances by the "Creative Images" group of the Asian American Drug Abuse Program, Los Angeles).

◆ Cultural norms, philosophy, religion, and culturally based values were supported and reinforced. As a result, immigrant youths were helped to adjust to mainstream American society. One program was sponsored by a Catholic parish that was indigenous to the local Asian and Pacific Islander community.

◆ AOD prevention was presented within the context of related health and social issues important to youth. Thus, the programs were relatively comprehensive in terms of addressing the issues and needs of youth. Most programs collaborated with the schools, parents, and other social institutions in the indigenous community.

A few research studies have been conducted on prevention strategies for Asian and Pacific Islander youths. Graham and colleagues (1990) reported on an evaluation of a program in Los Angeles. The large sample of seventh graders participating in Project SMART (Self-Management and Resistance Training) was studied. The study included Asian, African American, Hispanic, and white youths. The study tested the efficacy of the social skills and intended to affect management curricula for three cohort groups between 1982 and 1985. The aim of the Project SMART program was to prevent or reduce the use of cigarettes, alcohol, and marijuana. In short, the study found significant program effects for female youths, but not for male youths. A significant program effect for the "Asian" students was found (the specific Asian and Pacific Islander groups were not identified) as well as a marginal effect for Hispanics and a nonsignificant effect for African Americans. No apparent trend was found for program effects for white students.

Zane and Kim (1994) reported on the success of the Asian Youth Substance Abuse Project (AYSAP) in San Francisco. A consortium of seven community-based agencies collaborated to prevent high-risk youths from getting involved in AOD abuse. The consortium drew on social competence, empowerment, parenting skills, and community resource development strategies and its success was attributable to the intensive structure of the program. Filipino youths participating in a brief counseling program reported significant improvements in psychosocial functioning, self-esteem, and family support. Increases in interpersonal adjustment were also noted.

The AYSAP project identified some important aspects of a culturally responsive prevention strategy. First, it is critically important to link peer- and family-oriented prevention approaches into the natural support systems of specific Asian and Pacific Islander communities. It is also important to structure prevention interventions so that they complement this support system. For example, the Filipino community program provided AOD prevention and family empowerment interventions within a religious context at a Catholic parish. Self-disclosure in this spiritual setting made it easier for individuals to overcome the shame and stigma associated with revealing family problems and AOD abuse. Although a fatalistic view of life is dominant in Filipino culture, spiritual practices are seen as a culturally appropriate way of changing one's behavior. This prevention program capitalized on these beliefs to introduce alternative ways of dealing with family problems that often place youths at risk for abusing drugs.

Second, the key to empowering many Asian and Pacific Islander families involves providing immigrant parents with the skills and mastery they need to help their children adjust to American cultural norms and expectations.

For example, a prevention approach teaches parents their appropriate role in the American educational system and validates their responsibility as parents. Parents are encouraged to deal effectively with the educational system and to see themselves as cultural experts who can enrich their children's lives. Mass media campaigns targeting the specific population reinforced antidrug messages and challenged the idea that refugees and immigrants are better off when they become acculturated.

Third, the program developed innovative strategies to minimize shame and loss of face among Asian and Pacific Islander families. For example, a Japanese American community program adopted a graduated approach to handling intergenerational conflicts in Japanese families. In many Asian and Pacific Islander communities, intermediaries are often used to resolve interpersonal problems. These intermediaries (usually individuals with high status in the community) address personal problems without the same degree of loss of face that family members would have. This approach recognizes how difficult it is for Japanese and other Asian and Pacific Islander family members to confront one another. By recognizing this cultural factor, the project can develop a system using intermediaries (sometimes staff workers of the project) to bridge the communication gap and resolve problems.

Finally, personalized community education programs appear to be more effective than a generic mass media approach. For example, a door-to-door education campaign targeting the Vietnamese community was effective in disseminating information on the effects of drugs and treatment and support services available in the community.

Of course, more prevention research and evaluation studies should be done to identify the specific cultural variables and their relationship to AOD prevention for each specific Asian and Pacific Islander population (Cheung, 1989). Similarly, more research should be done to determine how cultural, physiological, and psychosocial variables interact to prevent AOD abuse.

Evaluation of Outcome Measures

There are many important research issues in terms of evaluation and measuring success for ethnic cultural groups such as Asian and Pacific Islanders (Cheung, 1989). Cheung emphasizes that ethnic and cultural variables with regard to AOD prevention should be researched to identify not only the differences in AOD patterns but also explain why the

differences occur. To do so, research must identify the incidence and prevalence among specific population groups (that is, the specific subpopulations within the Asian and Pacific Islander category), specific risk factors,
protective factors, and other prevention factors to determine how specific
aspects of ethnicity and culture interact to prevent AOD abuse. In addition, ethnicity at both the individual level and the collective level must be
analyzed to have a framework that will address AOD prevention and treatment issues in a comprehensive way.

Yen (1992) offers several suggestions regarding cultural competence for
evaluators working with Asian and Pacific Islander populations, including
analyzing issues such as age and gender, language and dialects, effects of
immigration or migration, class and cultural differences, and heterogeneity within the group. Mainstream research instruments should be used cautiously with Asian and Pacific Islander subjects. Because the meaning of
language is key to the reliability and validity of research instruments, it is
important to consider that Asian languages are context oriented. Thus,
certain questions may be difficult for Asian and Pacific Islander subjects
without additional descriptive, contextual material. Furthermore, the self-
disclosure of sensitive issues can be problematic because Asians and Pacific
Islanders are concerned about loss of face and may give invalid responses.
Gaining access to data and subjects is another potential problem for evaluation designs for Asian and Pacific Islander populations. Yen suggests that
the framing of the evaluation questions should involve representatives of
the community. Given that Asian and Pacific Islander populations—
particularly specific subgroups—may be relatively small in number, sampling techniques may not be possible or appropriate. The stereotyping of
results based on incomplete data can occur, leading to the "model minority" myth and misinterpretation. For example, what may be considered the
"underutilization" of mainstream American AOD abuse and treatment programs may lead to the assumption that Asians and Pacific Islanders have
no problems. This lack of utilization may be a result of the lack of access
and the inappropriateness of some programs for this population.

Kim and colleagues (1992) also discuss cultural competence for evaluators working with Asian and Pacific Islander populations. They suggest
that the process of evaluation can be empowering for Asian and Pacific
Islander communities. The white Anglo American mainstream culture is
different from that of Asians and Pacific Islanders. The authors also review some conceptual approaches to understanding evaluation and
research regarding the patterns of AOD use and abuse by Asians

and Pacific Islanders. These conceptual approaches include the cultural content approach, acculturation theory, orthogonal cultural identification theory, cultural conflict approaches, and alienation and identity conflict. Kim and colleagues (1992) also suggest a service success rate formula as a way to estimate the degree to which a program serves a particular target population. They suggest that a culturally competent prevention agency would conduct a needs assessment, provide training to enhance cultural competence of its staff and board members, provide a staffing pattern that has sufficient bilingual and bicultural staff and board, and examine the performance of the agency in terms of its relationship to Asian and Pacific Islander populations, culture, and community institutions.

Classroom Exercises

A classroom evaluation exercise should be experiential. Before the exercise, the class should be divided into small teams to go into the local community and identify Asian and Pacific Islander populations and service programs. Assuming a reasonable number of Asians and Pacific Islanders live in the local community, the teams should try to establish a relationship with community representatives to discuss real program evaluation issues. On the basis of these initial discussions, plans for a needs assessment (which may include etiological, epidemiological, and ethnographic data collection) should be developed as a classroom exercise. A second exercise can involve an existing service program. The class should develop a plan for community residents and student teams to evaluate an existing program. If possible, this program should be one that serves Asians and Pacific Islanders. Agency representatives can be interviewed to discuss their goals and objectives regarding services to Asians and Pacific Islanders, how their own goals and objectives are evaluated, and their level of success. Asian and Pacific Islander community representatives should also be interviewed to compare their perceptions of the agency's services with that of the agency representatives.

References

Adlaf, E., Smart, R., & Tan, S. (1989). Ethnicity and drug use. *International Journal of the Addictions, 24*, 1–18.

Agarwal, D., Eckey, R., Harada, S., & Goedde, H. (1984). Basis of adelhyde dehydrogenase deficiency in Orientals. *Alcohol, 1,* 111–118.

Ahern, F. (1989). Alcohol use and abuse among four ethnic groups in Hawaii: Native Hawaiians, Japanese, Filipinos, and whites. In National Institute on Alcohol Abuse and Alcoholism (Ed.), *Alcohol use among U.S. ethnic minorities* (Research Monograph 18, pp. 315–328). Washington, DC: U.S. Department of Health and Human Services.

Akutsu, P., Sue, S., Zane, N., & Nakamura, C. (1989). Ethnic differences in alcohol consumption among Asians and whites in the United States. *Journal of Studies in Alcohol, 50,* 261–267.

Asian, Inc. (1978). *Assessment of alcohol use service needs among Asian Americans in San Francisco.* Unpublished manuscript.

Austin, G. (1989, Winter). Substance abuse among minority youth. *Prevention Research Update 5.* Los Alamitos, CA: Western Center for Drug-Free Schools and Communities.

Austin, G. (1994). *ATOD use among Asian-American youth.* Unpublished manuscript.

Austin, G. (in press). Developing cultural competence in evaluation of substance abuse prevention for Asian and Pacific Islander communities. In *Cultural competence monograph 5.* Rockville, MD: Center for Substance Abuse Prevention.

Austin, G., & Gilbert, M. (1989, Spring). Substance abuse among Latino youth. *Prevention Research Update 3.* Los Alamitos, CA: Western Regional Center for Drug-Free Schools and Communities.

Bachman, J., Wallace, J., Kurth, C., Johnston, L., & O'Malley, P. (1991). *Drug use among black, white, Hispanic, Native American, and Asian American high school seniors (1976–1989).* Ann Arbor, MI: University of Michigan.

Barnes, G., & Welte, J. (1985). Patterns and predictors of alcohol use among 7th-12th grade students in New York State. *Journal of Studies on Alcohol, 47*(1), 53–62.

Barnes, G., Welte, J., & Dintcheff, B. (1993). Decline in alcohol use among 7th-through 12th-grade students in New York State, 1983–1990. *Alcoholism: Clinical and Experimental Research, 17*(4), 797–801.

Chan, A. (1986). Racial differences in alcohol sensitivity. *Alcohol and Alcoholism, 21,* 93–104.

Cheung, Y. (1989). Making sense of ethnicity and drug use. *Social Pharmacology, 3*(1–2), 55–82.

Chi, I., Lubben, J., & Kitano, H. (1989). Differences in drinking behavior among three Asian-American groups. *Journal of Studies on Alcohol, 50,* 15–23.

Ellickson, P., Hays, R., & Bell, R. (1992). Stepping through the drug use sequence. *Journal of Abnormal Psychology, 101*(3), 441–451.

Graham, J., Johnson, A., Hansen, B., Flay, B., & Gee, M. (1990). Drug use prevention programs, gender, and ethnicity. *Preventive Medicine, 19,* 305–313.

Hansen, W., Johnson, C., Flay, B., Graham, J., & Sobel, J. (1988). Affective and social influence approaches to the prevention of multiple substance abuse among seventh grade students. *Preventive Medicine, 17,* 135–154.

Hatanaka, H., Morales, R., & Kaseyama, N. (1991). *Asian Pacific alcohol peer consultation and training project.* Los Angeles: Special Services for Groups.

Inciardi, J. (1992). *The war on drugs II.* Mountain View, CA: Mayfield Publishing.

Johnson, B., & Nishi, S. (1976). Myths and realities of drug use by minorities. In P. Iiyama, S. Nishi, & B. Johnson (Eds.), *Drug use and abuse among U.S. minorities.* New York: Praeger.

Johnson, R., & Nagoshi, C. (1990). Asians, Asian-Americans, and alcohol. *Journal of Psychoactive Drugs, 22,* 45–52.

Kandel, D., Single, E., & Kessler, R. (1976). The epidemiology of drug use among New York State high school students. *American Journal of Public Health, 66*(1), 43–53.

Kim, S., McLead, J., & Shantzis, C. (1992). Cultural competence for evaluators working with Asian-American communities. In M. Orlandi (Ed.), *Cultural competence for evaluators.* Rockville, MD: Center for Substance Abuse Prevention.

Kitano, H., & Chi, I. (1985). Asian Americans and alcohol. In National Institute on Alcohol Abuse and Alcoholism (Ed.), *Alcohol use among U.S. ethnic minorities* (Research Monograph 18). Rockville, MD: NIAAA.

Kitano, H., & Chi, I. (1989). Asian-Americans and alcohol: The Chinese, Japanese, Koreans, and Filipinos in Los Angeles. In National Institute on Alcohol Abuse and Alcoholism (Ed.), *Alcohol use among U.S. ethnic minorities* (Research Monograph 18). Washington, DC: U.S. Department of Health and Human Services.

Kitano, H., Lubben, J., & Chi, I. (1988). Preventing Japanese-American drinking behavior. *International Journal of Addictions, 23,* 417–428.

Klatsky, A., Siegelaub, A., Landy, C., & Friedman, G. (1983). Racial patterns of alcoholic beverage use. *Alcoholism: Clinical and Experimental Research, 7,* 372–377.

Legge, C., & Sherlock, L. (1990–1991). Perception of alcohol use and misuse in three ethnic communities. *International Journal of Addictions, 25*(5a–6a), 629–653.

Maddahian, E., Newcomb, M., & Bentler, P. (1985). Single and multiple patterns of adolescence substance use. *Journal of Drug Education, 15,* 311–326.

Maddahian, E., Newcomb, M., & Bentler, P. (1986). Adolescents' substance use. *Advances in Alcohol and Substance Abuse, 5*(3), 63–78.

Marchand, L., Kolonel, L., & Yoshizawa, C. (1989). Alcohol consumption patterns among the five major ethnic groups in Hawaii: Correlations with incidence of esophageal and oropharyngeal cancer. In National Institute on Alcohol Abuse and Alcoholism (Ed.), *Alcohol use among U.S. ethnic minorities* (Research Monograph 18). Washington, DC: U.S. Department of Health and Human Services.

McLaughlin, P., Raymond, J., Murakami, S., & Gilbert, D. (1987). Drug use among Asian Americans in Hawaii. *Journal of Psychoactive Drugs, 19,* 85–94.

Morgan, M., Wingard, D., & Felice, M. (1984). Subcultural differences in alcohol use among youth. *Journal of Adolescent Health Care, 5,* 191–195.

Murakami, S. (1985). An epidemiological survey of alcohol, drug, and mental health problems in Hawaii. In National Institute on Alcohol Abuse and Alcoholism (Ed.), *Alcohol use among U.S. ethnic minorities* (Research Monograph 18). Rockville, MD: NIAAA.

Murase, K. (1977). Delivery of social services to Asian Americans. In R. Morris (Ed.), *Encyclopedia of social work*. Silver Spring, MD: National Association of Social Workers.

Musto, D. (1973). *The American disease*. New Haven, CT: Yale University Press.

Nakagawa, B., & Watanabe, R. (1973). *A study of the use of drugs among Asian American youths in Seattle*. Seattle, WA: Demonstration Project for Asian Americans.

Namkung, S. (1976). Asian-American drug addiction: The quiet problem. In P. Iiyama, S. Nishi, & B. Johnson (Eds.), *Drug use and abuse among U.S. minorities*. New York: Praeger.

National Asian Pacific American Families Against Substance Abuse. (1993). *Programs of national significance: Asian and Pacific Islander demonstration project*. Unpublished manuscript.

National Institute on Alcohol Abuse and Alcoholism. (1989). *Alcohol use among U.S. ethnic minorities* (Research Monograph 18). Washington, DC: U.S. Department of Health and Human Services.

National Institute on Alcohol Abuse and Alcoholism, & National Institute on Alcoholism in Japan. (1991). *Alcohol consumption patterns and related problems in the United States and Japan: Summary report of a joint United States-Japan alcohol epidemiological project*. Washington, DC: U.S. Government Printing Office.

O'Hare, W., & Felt, J. (1991). *Asian Americans: America's fastest growing minority group*. Washington, DC: Population Reference Bureau.

Phin, J., & Phillips, P. (1978). Drug treatment entry patterns and socioeconomic characteristics of Asian Americans, Native Americans, and Puerto Rico clients. In A. J. Schecter (Ed.), *Drug dependence and alcoholism. Vol. 2: Social Behavior Issues*. New York: Plenum Press.

Porter, M., Vieira, T., Kaplan, G., Heesh, V., & Colyar, A. (1973). Drug use in Anchorage. *Journal of the American Medical Association, 223*, 657–664.

Sasao, T. (1987). *Patterns of drug use and health related practices among Japanese Americans*. Unpublished manuscript.

Sasao, T. (1989, August). *Patterns of substance use and health practices among Japanese Americans in southern California*. Paper presented at the third annual meeting of the Asian-American Psychological Association, New Orleans, LA.

Sasao, T. (1991). *Statewide Asian drug service needs assessment*. Sacramento: California Department of Alcohol and Drug Programs.

Segal, B. (1992). Ethnicity and drug-taking behavior. *Drugs and Society, 6*, 269–312.

Skager, R., Fisher, D., & Maddahian, E. (1986). *A statewide survey of drug and alcohol use among California students in grades 7, 9, and 11*. Sacramento, CA: Office of the Attorney General, Crime Prevention Center.

Skager, R., Frith, S., & Maddahian, E. (1989). *Biennial survey of drug and alcohol use among California students in grades 7, 9, and 11*. Sacramento, CA: Office of the Attorney General, Crime Prevention Center.

Stimbu, J., Schoenfelt, L., & Sims, O. (1973). Drug use in college students as a function of racial classification and minority group status. *Research in Higher Education, 1*, 263–272.

Sue, S., & Morishima, J. (1982). *The mental health of Asian Americans.* San Francisco: Jossey-Bass.

Sue, S., & Nakamura, C. (1984). An integrative model of physiological and socio/psychological factors in alcohol consumption among Chinese and Japanese Americans. *Journal of Drug Issues, 14*(2), 349–364.

Sue, S., Zane, N., & Ito, J. (1979). Alcohol drinking patterns among Asian and white Americans. *Journal of Cross-Cultural Psychology, 10,* 41–56.

Takaki, R. (1989). *Strangers from a different shore.* New York: Penguin Books.

Trimble, J., Padilla, A., & Bell, C. (1987). *Drug abuse among ethnic minorities.* Rockville, MD: National Institute on Drug Abuse.

U.S. Bureau of the Census. (1991). *1990 Census.* Washington, DC: U.S. Government Printing Office.

Wilsnack, R., & Wilsnack, S. (1978). Sex roles and drinking among adolescent girls. *Journal on Studies on Alcohol, 39,* 1855–1874.

Wong, H. (1985). *Substance use and Chinese American youth.* Unpublished manuscript.

Yamamoto, J., Lee, C., Lin, K., & Cho, K. (1987). Alcohol abuse in Koreans. *American Journal of Social Psychiatry, 4,* 210–214.

Yee, B., & Thu, N. (1987). Correlates of drug use and abuse among Indochinese refugees. *Journal of Psychoactive Drugs, 19,* 77–83.

Yen, S. (1992). Cultural competence for evaluators working with Asian Pacific Island-American communities. In M. Orlandi (Ed.), *Cultural competence for evaluators.* Rockville, MD: Center for Substance Abuse Prevention.

Yu, E., & Liu, W. (1987). Alcohol use and abuse among Chinese-Americans: Epidemiological data. *Alcohol Health and Research World, 11*(2), 14–17.

Yu, E., Liu, W., Xia, Z., & Zhang, M. (1985). Alcohol use, abuse, and alcoholism among Chinese Americans: A review of the epidemiological data. In National Institute on Alcohol Abuse and Alcoholism (Ed.), *Alcohol use among U.S. ethnic minorities* (Research Monograph 18). Rockville, MD: NIAAA.

Yuen, S., & Johnson, R. (1986). *Mother-daughter comparisons in reported alcohol use.* Unpublished manuscript.

Zane, N., & Kim, J. (1994). Substance use and abuse. In N. Zane, D. Takenuchi, & K. Young (Eds.), *Confronting critical health issues of Asian and Pacific Islander Americans.* Thousand Oaks, CA: Sage Publications.

Zane, N., & Sasao, T. (1992). Research on drug abuse among Asian Pacific Americans. *Drugs and Society, 6,* 181–209.

Zane, N., Takeuchi, D., & Young, K. (Eds.). (1994). *Confronting critical health issues of Asian and Pacific Islander Americans.* Thousand Oaks, CA: Sage Publications.

Pacific Islanders

5

Noreen Mokuau

The persistence of alcohol and other drug (AOD) abuse in the United States affects the quality of life of many Americans. AOD abuse is a chronic problem that contributes to death, disease, and disability. Statistics from *Healthy People 2000: National Health Promotion and Disease Prevention Objectives* (U.S. Public Health Service, 1991) depict the magnitude of AOD abuse problems in this country:

◆ Approximately two-thirds of Americans drink occasionally and, of these, 18 million experience problems as a result of alcohol use.

The author extends a *mahalo* to **Karen Crocker, MSW** (University of Hawaii School of Social Work) and **JoAnn Tsark, MPH** (Rehabilitation Hospital of the Pacific) for their bibliographic assistance in the preparation of the manuscript. *Mahalo nui loa* also to the following people, who shared information with me about their important work with Pacific Islanders: **Timena Brown, MEd,** Fetu Ao; **Lana Kaʻopua, MSW, ACSW,** AIDS Education Project; **Alyson Kau, MSW, CSAC, NCACI,** Drug Addiction Services of Hawaii, Inc.; **Terry Kelly, MSW;** and **Maria Santiago,** Kamehameha Schools/ Bishop Estate, Native Hawaiian Safe and Drug Free Schools and Communities Program; **Dixie Padello, Shannon Kaaekuahiwi,** and **Barbara Apo, MA,** Na Wahine Makalapua; and **Kahu Tyrone Reinhardt, MA,** Papa Ola Lokahi.

◆ More than half of all fatal motor vehicle crashes among people ages 15 through 24 involve alcohol.
◆ Tobacco accounts for more than one of every six deaths in the United States.
◆ Smoking is responsible for 21 percent of all coronary heart disease deaths, 87 percent of lung cancer deaths, and 30 percent of all cancer deaths.
◆ An estimated 1 to 3 million Americans use cocaine regularly, and 900,000 use injectable drugs.
◆ Maternal drug use contributes to increasing numbers of drug-exposed babies, 375,000 cases per year.

These problems posed by AOD abuse are associated with other social problems, such as low income, low educational achievement, unemployment, poor housing, and violent crime.

The disturbing effects of AOD abuse in the United States are amplified for an ethnic and racial population such as Pacific Islanders. Although small population census size and the lack of a comprehensive national data set preclude accurate statistical projections for Pacific Islanders, an increasing amount of descriptive and preliminary data document high rates of AOD abuse among this population. This evidence suggests that Pacific Islanders experience problems related to alcohol, tobacco, marijuana, and cocaine. Newly emerging national statistics on the decline of alcohol, tobacco, and illicit drug use among the American population (*New York Times*, 1994; U.S. Public Health Service, 1991) may not accurately reflect the circumstances of Pacific Islanders and need to be cautiously interpreted.

Sociodemographic characteristics illustrate the vulnerability of this population to AOD abuse. Comprising approximately 0.1 percent (365,024) of the total U.S. population (249 million) (U.S. Bureau of the Census 1991e, 1993), Pacific Islanders are a relatively young population with low income and low educational attainment. The 1990 Census reports that the average age of Pacific Islanders is 25 years, compared with 33 years for the total U.S. population. The per capita income for Pacific Islanders ($10,342) was lower than for the total U.S. population ($14,143) because of larger family size; 17 percent of Pacific Islanders lived below the poverty line in 1990, with Samoans and Tongans having the highest poverty rates, 26 percent and 23 percent, respectively. Only 11 percent of Pacific Islanders completed college compared with 20 percent of the total U.S. population.

This chapter reviews the significance of AOD abuse in the Pacific Islander population, and encourages social workers to address AOD abuse among Pacific Islanders. It also seeks to provide information to enable social workers to address AOD abuse problems in a culturally responsive manner. This chapter aims to achieve the following:

◆ Provide a perspective that will enhance social workers' abilities to conceive and conduct culturally competent practice with Pacific Islanders who have AOD abuse problems.
◆ Present a body of knowledge, skills, and values that examines the etiology, characteristics, and prevention of AOD abuse among Pacific Islanders.
◆ Complement the National Association of Social Workers' Curriculum Modules on AOD abuse in bachelor's and master's of social work programs.

The major sections of this chapter include a population description, with an emphasis on history and cultural characteristics; an analysis of the extent of the problem; and suggested prevention strategies. Two classroom exercises, a bibliography, and recommended readings are included as additional curriculum resources.

Population Description

Pacific Islander Americans are a distinctive people from the islands in a geographical triangle known as Polynesia, Micronesia, and Melanesia. Hawaiians (211,014), Samoans (62,964), and Tongans (17,606) make up the largest Polynesian groups; Chamorros or Guamanians (49,345), the largest Micronesian group; and Fijians (7,195), the largest Melanesian group (U.S. Bureau of the Census, 1993). Other small groups of Pacific Islanders in the United States include Tahitians, Mariana Islanders, Marshall Islanders, and Palauans. Approximately 13 percent of Pacific Islanders are foreign born. Seventy-five percent of Pacific Islanders live in Hawaii and California. The largest group, Hawaiians, live in Hawaii and make up 13 percent (138,742) of the total state population of 1,108,229 (Asian/ Pacific Islander Data Consortium, 1992).

In addition to Pacific Islander Americans, Pacific Islanders reside in indigenous island homelands that are politically affiliated with the United States. There is great diversity among the Pacific Islanders residing in U.S.- associated jurisdictions such as American Samoa (46,773), Guam (133,152), the Federated States of Micronesia (101,108), the Republic of the Marshall Islands (46,020), the Commonwealth of the Northern Mariana Islands

(43,345), and the Republic of Palau (15,122) (University of Hawaii School of Public Health, 1991; U.S. Bureau of the Census 1991a, 1991b, 1991c, 1991d). The American public has little awareness of or information about these Pacific Islanders, who have low visibility and relatively small numbers, yet the influence of American culture on these islands is pervasive.

History

Historical insight into Pacific Islander groups provides background information relevant to understanding AOD abuse among this population and may inspire resolutions addressing addiction. Alcohol and other drug use among Pacific Islanders is interlocked with multiple psychosocial problems that have origins in cultural norms and patterns marked by historical events. Kim, McLeod, and Shantzis (1992) identify two models that are useful for explaining AOD abuse among Pacific Islanders: cultural content and cultural conflict (in Mokuau, in press b).

The cultural content model stipulates that variations in AOD abuse behaviors might be explained by the different cultural norms and patterns that govern a group. For example, before the arrival of westerners to Hawaii in 1778, evidence shows that 'awa (an addictive plant) drinking was acceptable and occurred among the chiefs and the priests for medicinal and religious purposes (Alama & Whitney, 1990). Excessive drinking of 'awa may have occurred, but the general population was not aware of it. Alama and Whitney state that the introduction of alcohol—particularly rum and gin—by sailors and merchants after 1778 met with some regulation, but generally alcohol became readily available as a recreational drink for all Hawaiians. They suggest that liquor began to merge with food into the cultural domain of hospitality. The growing acceptance of alcohol in the Hawaiian community perpetuated stereotypes of Hawaiian men as economically and politically marginal and Hawaiian women as sexually loose. The influence of history is reflected in patterns of drinking by many Hawaiian men in the 1990s, among whom drinking is typically associated with relaxation, food, and hospitality.

The cultural conflict model suggests that AOD abuse may be influenced by circumstances in immigration history. This model indicates that the experience of immigration can generate situational high-risk factors, such as family conflicts and generational gaps, and these factors may contribute to AOD abuse (Kim et al., 1992). An illustration of the cultural conflict model can be seen in the adjustment of Samoans to American culture. The migration of Samoans from American Samoa to the United States started in the 1950s. It is attributed to the transfer of naval personnel, increased educational and employment opportunities in the United States, and a concomitant decline in opportunities in American Samoa (Department of Mental Health, 1981). Moving to a different country can create adjustment difficulties, particularly when the value system of the host country is different from that of the original culture. For example, generational conflicts exist between older Samoans who wish to retain cultural traditions and younger Samoans who struggle to fit into American society. One traditional Samoan value, *fa'alavelave*, urges providing support (typically financial) to family members at important events such as christenings, birthdays, funerals, and church celebrations (Calkins, 1962; Franco, 1985). When Samoans immigrate to the United States, they may experience high unemployment and poverty, and younger Samoan families may find it difficult to send financial contributions to family members back in American Samoa as well as in the United States. Generational conflict may occur for those younger members who may not be able to embrace a tradition that their parents and elders cherish.

The cultural conflict model assumes a slightly different twist for Pacific Islanders residing in their own island homelands. Typically, conflict becomes evident when a population migrates to a host country and finds it necessary to change indigenous values to adapt to the host country. However, with Pacific Islanders in U.S.-associated jurisdictions, conflict occurs at home as the islanders adjust to Western norms and values. Residents of the host island nations find themselves adjusting to values and norms of American culture that are often divergent from their indigenous ways. For example, Chamorros who live in Guam and the Mariana Islands, Trukese who live in Truk, and Palauans who live in Palau experience a breakdown of indigenous cultures after Western contact (Hezel, 1985; Polloi, 1985; Untalan, 1991). Much of the "maladjustment" manifests itself in AOD-using behavior patterns (Marshall, 1979; Whitney & Hanipale, 1991).

Cultural Characteristics

In the same way that historical data provide information about the context of AOD abuse, cultural knowledge enhances understanding of a population's perceptions of life and preferred resolutions to problems. Specific populations such as Pacific Islanders may need targeted efforts in dealing with

AOD abuse, and such efforts require understanding cultural characteristics and themes.

Pacific Islanders are a heterogenous population. They may be indigenous to islands that are part of the United States, as are Hawaiians; or they may have immigrated to the United States from Pacific Islands as nationals (Samoans) or citizens (Chamorros/Guamanians) (U.S. Bureau of the Census, 1993); or they may reside in their Pacific homelands and be affiliated with the United States through territories (Samoans; Chamorros/Guamanians), commonwealths (Northern Mariana Islanders), or free association (Palauans) ("Independence for Palau," 1994). Twenty-five percent of Pacific Islanders speak a language other than English at home, with Tongans (72 percent) and Samoans (64 percent) having the highest proportion of non-English speakers and Hawaiians having the lowest (8 percent) (U.S. Bureau of the Census, 1993). English-language capability hints at acculturation level: Pacific Islanders who speak their native languages may be less acculturated than Pacific Islanders who use English as their first language. Hypothetically, lower levels of acculturation may be associated with less education and lower socioeconomic status.

There is broad variation in the degree to which individuals subscribe to cultural traditions; however, within the diversity of Pacific Islanders, some common cultural themes exist. One theme is the value of the collective, which is often manifested in the relationships of the spiritual world, community, and the family. "The subjective relationships that dominate the Polynesian psyche are with all nature, in its totality" (Handy, Craighill, & Pukui, 1977).

For example, dominant values and behavioral norms in traditional Samoan culture focus on the family, communal relationships, and the church (Mokuau & Chang, 1991). The well-being of the collective takes precedence over that of the individual, and values of reciprocity, cooperation, and interdependence bond the person with the greater power of relationships. In their traditional agrarian culture, Samoans work as a communal unit and subsist on foods provided by the land and sea, seeking to live in a manner harmonious with nature.

In traditional Hawaiian culture, the people place great emphasis on relationships as reflected in genealogy. *Wakea* (Father Sky) and *Papa* (Mother Earth) are "the first parents of human life on earth as they are of plant life that springs living from earth under the influence of sun and rain from heaven and of animal life that feeds upon it" (Beckwith, 1981). "Conceived in this way, the genealogy of the Land, the Gods, Chiefs, and people intertwine with one another, and with all the myriad aspects of the universe" (Kame'eleihiwa, 1992). It is believed that all things come from this one source. The holistic worldview is that spirits, nature, and people are all related and that the oneness of all things is "a part of natural consciousness" (Handy et al., 1977).

A second theme in Pacific Islanders' holistic worldview of relationships pertains to the resolution of problems. Cultural characteristics among Pacific Islanders suggest that problems are resolved through the interaction of relationships, whether the engaging parties are human-to-human, human-to-animal, or human-to-vegetable. In Hawaiian culture, the relationship of people and families to animals and plants was predicated on the belief that such natural phenomena were forms of primordial gods, historical migrants, or ancestors who became elevated to the rank of gods (Handy et al. 1977). Thus, in old Hawaii—as well as in modern times—it was not unusual to hear of a Hawaiian who "spoke" to animals and plants that were spiritually empowered. A Hawaiian man who is having difficulties with his daughter may consult with his family god, the lizard (*mo'o*), to learn ways to improve the relationship. In respecting the reciprocity of relationships, a Hawaiian may talk to plants and trees before picking flowers, asking permission before taking them, and always leaving an offering when taking something of significance—replenishing and nourishing the earth in return (Dudley, 1990). Thus, the centrality of spirituality is evident in Hawaiian culture.

Human-to-human forms of problem resolution in Hawaiian culture include traditions known as *kukakuka* (talking conference), *ho'oponopono* (family-centered approach), and *lomilomi* (massage). *Kukakuka* and *ho'oponopono* are the gathering of people to discuss an issue respectfully and completely to resolve it. These discussions have protocol and procedures that are always guided by spiritual beliefs. *Lomilomi* is a form of easing problems from the body through massage—again, with a belief that the process is guided by spirituality.

A third theme of cultural relevance for Pacific Islanders relates to self-empowerment. As indigenous peoples, Pacific Islanders are part of a larger movement of indigenous populations worldwide who are mobilizing to protect biological diversity, cultural survival, and indigenous homelands (Durning, 1993). The sovereign nation movement of Hawaiians is an assertion and renewal of Hawaiian independence and pride (Alexander, 1990; Blaisdell, 1992; Ka Mana O Ka' Aina, 1990), with a variety of models being proposed (Dudley & Agard, 1990; Ramirez, 1993). The Micronesian island of Palau demonstrates the efforts of Pacific peoples to gain independence. After 10 years of negotiation, recent discussions between the United States and Palau have resulted in a compact of "free association" ("Independence for Palau," 1994). Under the compact's terms, Palau will no longer be under trusteeship of the United States and will become an independent nation, with continued defense and support from the United States for 50 years. The compact provides for Palau's self-rule, determination of its future, and eventual total independence.

Extent of the Problem

An accurate assessment of the prevalence of AOD abuse among Pacific Islanders is impossible because of the current method of national statistical reporting. Many federal and state agencies present demographic and public health data for the category of "Asians and Pacific Islanders," combining two groups, Asian Americans and Pacific Islander Americans. Such reporting combines information on both groups and thereby prevents any reliable understanding of the extent of problems among either Asian Americans or Pacific Islander Americans. In those cases that identify the two populations separately, many statistical agencies neglect to present data on Pacific Islanders by different ethnicities such as Hawaiian, Samoan, and Guamanian or Chamorro. Despite the difficulties of statistical reporting, some information is available from the states of Hawaii and California, which have high Pacific Islander populations. Some information is also available on Pacific Island populations residing in their island homelands. However, this information is descriptive, often anecdotal, and tends to focus on specific groups, such as Hawaiians.

Hawaiians

Accumulated information indicates that Hawaiians in Hawaii experience serious problems with alcohol, tobacco, and illicit drugs. In a statewide survey focusing on health risk factors such as alcohol use and abuse, cigarette smoking, and drinking and driving, results indicate that Hawaiians consume alcohol and smoke cigarettes at higher rates than other populations in Hawaii (Department of Health, 1994). Populations compared included whites, Filipinos, Hawaiians, Japanese, and "other."

Alcohol

The survey showed that Hawaiians had the highest percentage of binge drinking (five or more drinks on an occasion, one or more times in a month) and chronic drinking (60 or more drinks during the past month). Other risk factors associated with drinking are smoking and driving under the influence (DUI) of alcohol. High rates of drinking persist, even though Hawaiians appear to recognize the problems attendant with alcohol consumption, such as "losing control," "fighting," "passing out," and "not remembering" (Kamehameha Schools/Bishop Estate, 1994).

Previous studies comparing Hawaiians with other ethnic groups in Hawaii confirm contemporary trends and draw special implications for health. Several studies revealed that alcohol consumption among Hawaiians and whites was higher than among Japanese, Chinese, and Filipinos (Ahern, 1989; Austin, Prendergast, & Lee, 1989; Marchand, Kolonel, & Yoshizawa, 1989; Schwitters, Johnson, Wilson, & McClearn, 1982). In one multicultural survey in Hawaii, Marchand and colleagues (1989) noted that alcohol consumption among Hawaiians was higher for men and the drink of choice was beer. The authors note that the incidence rate of esophageal cancer is much higher among Hawaiians than whites (whose drinks of choice were wine and spirits) and imply that beer may have a specific role in the etiology of this type of cancer.

Alcohol use among Hawaiian youths also is higher than among other ethnic groups. Hawaiian youths ranked the highest when alcohol consumption among all ethnic youths declined from 1987 to 1989, as well as when it showed a slight increase between 1989 and 1991 (State of Hawaii Department of Education, in Kamehameha Schools/Bishop Estate, 1993c). Although the legal age for drinking in Hawaii is 21, alcoholic beverages such as beer are accessible and readily available to youths.

Polynesian drinking has been linked with cultural considerations emphasizing affiliation, rest, and celebration. One particular phenomena relates to *pau hana* (after-work) drinking, an event in which people (typically men) gather at job sites, at each other's homes, or at bars to relax after a day's work. Drinking is always accompanied by food substantial enough for an entire meal (for example, raw fish, seaweed, rice, noodles, meat); typically, the men make informal food assignments. A sense of relaxation, camaraderie, and bonding exists.

In another cultural example, Hawaiian male youths and young adults in rural communities will spend weekends drinking beer with friends at beaches or parks. The highlight of getting together is to drink and "talk story."

Talk story is a cultural form of communication that "is very personal and nonconfrontive. . . . It is conducted within a storytelling context to preserve the integrity of relationships" (Paglinawan, 1983).

Smoking and Other Drugs

Hawaiians have the highest rate of "current regular" smokers in Hawaii, that is, those who have smoked 100 cigarettes and smoke regularly now (State of Hawaii Department of Health, 1992). Eighty-five percent of all lung cancer cases in Hawaii are caused by cigarette smoking (State of Hawaii Department of Health, 1992), and Hawaiians have the highest incidence and mortality rates for lung cancer in the state (Papa Ola Lokahi, 1992). Both men and women smoke heavily.

Three surveys indicate that Hawaiian adults and youths have higher rates of illicit drug use than other ethnic groups. McLaughlin, Raymond, Murakami, & Goebert (1987) found that Hawaiian and white adults use drugs such as barbiturates, marijuana, hashish, inhalants, LSD, PCP, amphetamines, cocaine, methadone, heroin, and painkillers at higher rates than Japanese, Chinese, and Filipino populations. Chandler and Kassebaum (1991) found that Hawaiians in the prison system use marijuana as the drug of choice, although the pattern of use more frequently indicated multiple drug use. Finally, in a survey of high school students in Hawaii, Anderson and Deck found that Hawaiian and white students had the highest levels of drug use (Austin et al., 1989).

Other Pacific Islanders

The extent of AOD abuse among other Pacific Islander populations in the United States is unknown. However, the limited data available suggest that the second largest Pacific Islander population in the country, Samoans, also experiences AOD problems. A statewide survey designed to track AOD abuse among multiethnic populations in Hawaii revealed that Samoans, Hawaiians, Portuguese, and Koreans were at high risk for abusing alcohol, marijuana, tobacco, and other drugs (Pleadwell 1992). Another report suggests that problems of AOD abuse, particularly use of marijuana and crack cocaine, are also evident among Samoans in California (Lindo 1989). In American Samoa, alcohol—primarily beer—is consumed in large quantities. One estimate suggests that in 1986 more than 100,000 gallons of beer were sold in the territory of American Samoa—nearly 22 gallons per capita (Keener, in Whitney & Hanipale, 1991).

Documentation indicates that drinking alcohol is a growing problem among certain Pacific Islander populations who live in their island homelands. For example, on several Micronesian islands (such as Truk, Yap, and Palau) drinking alcohol has been incorporated into community life. Defined as a substance that leads to temporary insanity, alcohol is acceptable among men, who can be wild and irresponsible, but is not acceptable among women, who need to care for the family and be responsible (Marshall, 1979):

> Drinking often and with abandon is highly valued among young men in Truk; not to drink is negatively valued . . . because abstinence indicates unwillingness to face risks, to play the game of death, to be macho.
>
> Women and alcohol are not allowed to mix in Truk . . . women are responsible first and foremost for home and hearth. They tend children, cook the food, wash the dishes and the laundry, gather firewood, and perform myriad other jobs of utmost importance to the basic maintenance of the family. . . . Were a woman to go out drinking . . . and become "irresponsible," what would become of all these essential duties?

Linkage of AOD Abuse with Crime and HIV/AIDS

The extent of AOD abuse problems among Pacific Islanders might be further illustrated by examining crime reports on substances and the incidence of acquired immune deficiency syndrome (AIDS). Research shows a strong association between crime and AOD abuse (Ichiho, DeLisio, Sakai, & Maritsugu, 1990), whether the crime is against people or property. Information on crime, related to specific substances, provides a picture of the involvement of Pacific Islanders with drugs. Some information exists about the link between AOD and AIDS (Mokuau, 1995a), and a study of AIDS among Pacific Islanders may be instructive in understanding related problems confronting this population.

Crime

In reviewing arrest records in Hawaii for adults by race and drug offense (two categories: manufacture/sale and possession), it was noted that Hawaiians and Samoans rank high in crimes related to substances (Crime Prevention Division, 1994). Reports on the sale and possession of illicit drugs, however, indicate slightly different patterns for Hawaiian and Samoan adults. When comparing 10 ethnic groups (white, black, American Indian, Chinese, Japanese, Filipino, Hawaiian, Korean, Samoan, other), Hawaiians rank second to whites for the manufacture, sale, and possession of opium or cocaine and marijuana. Samoans rank third for the manufacture, sale, and possession of opium or cocaine but rank seventh for the manufacture/sale and possession of marijuana. The greatest number of arrests in these categories for adults was for the possession of opium or cocaine.

The arrest records for youths by race and offenses show similar trends. White, Hawaiian, and Samoan youths manufacture and sell opium or cocaine at equally high levels; whites and Hawaiians have comparable arrest rates for the manufacture and sale of marijuana; and Hawaiians and whites have the highest arrest rates for the possession of marijuana. The greatest number of arrests in these categories for juveniles was for the possession of marijuana.

As might be expected, DUI offenses are also notable for these populations. Although more white adults and youths were arrested for drunk-driving offenses, Hawaiian adults and youths ranked second to whites. Samoan adults ranked sixth, and Samoan youths ranked third.

HIV/AIDS

The human immunodeficiency virus (HIV) and AIDS are newly emerging health problems in the Hawaiian community. In 1994, of the total AIDS cases in Hawaii (1,393), 326 were people of Asian and Pacific Islander ancestry; of those cases, 136 were Hawaiians and 7 were Samoans and Chamorros (Department of Health, 1994). AIDS statistics for Hawaiians and other Pacific Islanders may not generate immediate alarm; however, when combined with other information, there is cause for concern (Mokuau & Kau, 1992). For example, in addition to increasing rates of substance abuse, Pacific Islanders' high-risk factors for susceptibility to HIV may include high teenage pregnancy rates and low participation in health and education programs.

Suggested Prevention Strategies

Prevention efforts designed to be culturally competent are predicated on understanding AOD abuse in the context of the culture of the targeted group. General solutions cannot always be used to solve specific problems (U.S. Public Health Service, 1991), and prevention strategies should be devised that consider the uniqueness of the history, characteristics, and themes of a cultural group. The Center for Substance Abuse Prevention (1993) offers one definition of cultural competence: "Cultural competence refers to the set of academic and interpersonal skills that allow individuals to increase their understanding and appreciation of cultural differences and similarities within, among, and between groups."

It is proposed that the definition of cultural competence be expanded to move beyond "understanding" to "action." Cultural competence would, therefore, require an ability to respond actively to the needs of a group in a manner congruent with cultural history, characteristics, and themes.

Conceptual Frameworks

Conceptual frameworks organize information in a systematic and integrated manner. The importance of such frameworks is that they allow coherent examination and linkage of assessment and intervention information. For a description of all the conceptual frameworks pertinent to AOD abuse, the reader is referred to the Curriculum Modules on Alcohol and Other Drugs for bachelor's and master's of social work programs. However, a few models are identified here that may be especially pertinent for prevention strategies for Pacific Islanders. These conceptual frameworks are the ecological systems perspective, the biopsychosocial model, and the public health model.

The ecological systems perspective "presents the view that human needs and problems are generated by the transactions between people and their environments" (Germain & Gitterman, 1980). Examined from this perspective, AOD abuse problems are influenced by such factors as a person's interpersonal skills, relationship with the family and community, and social norms. Problems are resolved through establishing reciprocal relations between organisms and environments, such that human beings maintain a good fit with the environment (Germain & Gitterman, 1980).

The biopsychosocial model is the perspective that AOD abuse and prevention strategies for abuse are grounded in the interaction of the biological, psychological, and sociocultural aspects of functioning. Biological aspects emphasize the influence of genetic and physiological processes on AOD abuse. Psychological aspects focus on the influence of emotional and mental dependence on alcohol and other drugs. Sociocultural aspects highlight the influence of social and cultural norms as antecedents and consequences for AOD abuse.

The public health model considers problems deriving from a system made up of three components: the agent, the host, and the environment. The agent is a catalyst of the problem, such as alcohol or another drug. The host is the person affected by the problem, reflecting the personal traits that predispose one to AOD abuse. The environment is all other factors that contribute to AOD abuse susceptibility. Prevention efforts are directed toward all components of the system, with a collaborative and interdisciplinary focus. With highly vulnerable populations, both risk and protective factors are examined.

The significance of these three models to Pacific Islanders is that they emphasize the integrative view of the individual and the environment in understanding the etiology and prevention of AOD abuse. Specifically, these models emphasize the influence of the environment on the attitudes and behavioral patterns connected with AOD abuse, the importance of relationships in understanding the source and resolution of AOD abuse, and working with the strengths of a population to reduce AOD abuse prevalence. This viewpoint corresponds with cultural themes previously described, such as immigration, the collective, and contemporary actions for empowerment.

Primary and Secondary Prevention Strategies

The public health field identifies two levels of strategies to prevent problems and enhance functioning: primary and secondary. Primary prevention "refers to those scientific practices aimed at simultaneously preventing predictable physical, psychological, or sociocultural problems for individuals or populations at risk; maintaining or protecting current strengths, competencies, or levels of health; and promoting desired goals and the fulfillment or enhancement of human potentials" (Bloom, in Johnson, 1990, p. 347).

Secondary prevention refers to practices directed at people identified with problems to reduce prevalence and ensure that the problem does not become more severe and debilitating. Designing primary and secondary prevention strategies that are culturally responsive to Pacific Islanders requires several considerations, including the following:

◆ Service accessibility—Services must be accessible, community-based, and within a population's economic limits.
◆ Culturally valid content—The content of prevention materials must reflect Pacific Islander culture and must be developed with the participation of Pacific Islanders.
◆ Culturally valid delivery—Prevention materials in forums or classes must be presented by Pacific Islander leaders.

Education is the mainstay of prevention strategies. It is important to provide materials that inform a population about AOD abuse risks and that encourage behavioral and attitudinal change. Educational materials with appropriate cultural content and delivery need to be accessible.

Accessibility

Providing prevention services in high-density Pacific Islander communities enhances accessibility. One way to bring services in is to sponsor statewide or regional educational workshops or conferences on AOD abuse in communities with high-risk behaviors. In the past, many conferences focusing on problems confronting Hawaiians have been held in urban areas. For many Hawaiians, not only are the urban surroundings culturally inappropriate, but also the drive from rural communities (or the plane ride from other islands) makes the conference inaccessible.

Services can be located in organizations that are already a part of a network in high-density Pacific Islander communities. For example, in the Samoan community, the church is a focal place for communal gatherings. It could therefore serve as a natural resource for discussing and distributing materials on AOD abuse (E. Wilson, personal communication, August 4, 1994). In Samoan communities, accessibility to information on alcohol and other drugs is increased through television and radio media targeted to the Samoan population (T. Brown, personal communication, July 5, 1994). Such media programs are in the appropriate language, present information about the increasing rate of AOD abuse among Samoans, and identify services that render assistance.

The high rates of poverty and unemployment among Samoans and Tongans make it imperative that prevention services be of low cost or, preferably, at no cost. When competing expenses exist with limited financial resources, Pacific Islanders will probably use available resources on necessities such as food and shelter rather than on AOD abuse prevention materials. The costs for treating AOD abuse and for addressing AOD-related problems, such as crime and HIV/AIDS, far outweigh the expenses of prevention efforts. Money spent on educational materials helps to contain public costs by reducing the prevalence of these problems.

Content Validity

The usefulness of information contained in prevention materials will be increased if it reflects the cultural characteristics, norms, and values of the target population. Furthermore, information that is gender and age sensitive will also increase its usefulness. Although AOD abuse can occur among both men and women of Pacific Islander extraction, men appear to be at especially high risk. Problems of AOD use are also increasing among adolescents. Thus, education efforts need to continue to address the concerns of men and adolescents and, at the same time, promote information about the vulnerability of women.

The Kamehameha Schools/Bishop Estate Native Hawaiian Safe and Drug Free Schools and Community Program (NHSDFSCP) in Hawaii has devised several prevention strategies that respect and incorporate Hawaiian culture. Its educational materials are developed with the direct input of people of Hawaiian ancestry on staff and from Hawaiian communities (T. Kelly, personal communication, July 5, 1994). Educational tools—such as posters, videotapes, comic books, magnets, and message pins—promote a drug-free community. The following are examples of cultural relevance:

◆ Videotapes are age sensitive, using rap music for adolescents and Hawaiian chants for adults (Kamehameha Schools/Bishop Estate, 1990, 1993a, 1993b).

◆ The messages contained in the videotapes reflect actual stories and are presented by Hawaiian people in the context of family concerns (Kamehameha Schools/Bishop Estate, 1993a).

◆ A special comic book is gender sensitive and contains sections on issues relevant for male and female adolescents; it is presented in the nonstandard English used by this population (Kamehameha Schools/Bishop Estate, 1994).

◆ Magnets are distributed with drug-free messages in both Hawaiian and English in bright colors (for example, *He Hawai'i au; 'ai 'ole i ka la 'au 'ino*—Hawaiian and drug free).

One important aspect of prevention strategies for Pacific Islanders relates to the traditional worldview about relationships and the appreciation of spirituality. It is believed that "alcohol and drugs block the path to spirituality" (T. Reinhardt, personal communication, July 5, 1994); therefore, helping them abstain from using alcohol and other drugs means helping them reconnect with their spirituality. For many AOD abuse counselors, helping Pacific Islanders to reconnect is a strategy of prevention. The NHSDFSCP has developed a *lokahi* (harmony) wheel, an educational tool designed to illustrate different facets of a holistic worldview (spiritual/soul, friends/family, work/job, thinking/mind, feelings/emotions, physical/body). This tool helps AOD abuse counselors teach clients about the importance of culture and of looking at the influences of alcohol and other drug abuse on each facet of life. Although the "spiritual/soul" facet is presented as separate from the rest, it is more accurate to view spirituality as infusing all other facets of life (T. Kelly, personal communication, July 5, 1994). Spirituality is also pervasive in Samoan culture, in which the church exercises strong authority (T. Brown, personal communication, July 5, 1994). Thus, prevention strategies that encompass the perspective of the church and the value of spirituality may be beneficial to this population.

Content Delivery

Whereas the message of educational materials and the accessibility of their presentation are critical, so too is the messenger. At a minimum, educational information should be presented by someone who is compassionate toward and knowledgeable about Pacific Islanders. Such material should be presented by someone of the targeted population group, either alone or in collaboration with other professionals. For example, peer educators are trained to work with multiethnic youths in Hawaii on adolescent health risk issues (Cole, 1992). The underlying premise is that students will hear a message on AOD abuse more readily if it comes from peers who are accepted leaders in the school setting rather than from adults. In another example, the spokespeople on alcohol and other drug abuse videotapes are minority students from communities with high-density Pacific Islander populations (Kamehameha Schools/Bishop Estate, 1990). These students discuss the negative influences of alcohol and drugs on youths in Hawaii. The impact of these students is amplified because they speak of personal situations against the backdrop of community settings that others from that community recognize.

Tertiary Prevention

Tertiary prevention focuses on providing treatment to discourage continued AOD abuse among people identified with the problem. Treatment options for AOD abusers are varied and include detoxification programs, short- and long-term residential treatment programs, outpatient programs (such as methadone programs), group therapy, and fellowship programs such as Alcoholics Anonymous (Johnson, 1990). Culturally competent treatment of Pacific Islanders with AOD abuse problems starts by including cultural characteristics and themes in prevention services. Two programs, one residential and one outpatient, illustrate the incorporation of culturally relevant strategies for people who value the Hawaiian culture. Na Wahine Makalapua, a mother–infant residential facility for women who have abused alcohol or other drugs, has several features emphasizing Hawaiian culture (D. Padello, personal communication, March 8, 1994). One of those features is the participation of Hawaiian elders (*kupuna*) from the community who work with the mothers. These elders teach the mothers about Hawaiian culture, emphasize the importance of children (*keiki*), and encourage the mothers to make healthy choices regarding their well-being and that of their infants. The role of elders in Hawaiian culture has long been appreciated and is a primary vehicle for learning about the scope and depth of cultural identity (Mokuau & Browne, 1994).

In The Cornerstone, an intensive outpatient program, one aspect of treatment relates to cultural views of addiction (Drug Addiction Services of Hawaii, undated). This program seeks to teach clients about cultural perspectives as a means to encourage cultural identity and discourage culturally inappropriate acts of AOD abuse. Hawaiian clients make up more than 50 percent of the program's caseload (A. Kau, personal communication, July 5, 1994). In addition to working intensely with clients in groups, the program also works with families, recognizing the cultural importance of family collaboration in recovery from AOD abuse.

Conclusion

Designing culturally competent prevention strategies for AOD abuse among Pacific Islanders is complex and arduous, but it can be achieved. In addition to possessing an extensive knowledge of AOD abuse, professionals must have the knowledge, skills, and values necessary to empower culturally diverse people who are disenfranchised in American society. Prevention strategies must have a sound and systematic integration of information on AOD abuse within the context of culture. With Pacific Islander cultures, information must be incorporated on historical background, cultural characteristics, and cultural themes.

Prevention strategies for AOD abuse among Pacific Islanders can only be successful if they are concurrent with broader social efforts to eliminate oppression and promote equitable treatment for all people (Mokuau, 1995a). Problems existing for Pacific Islander peoples are multifaceted and inextricably linked to one another. Understanding AOD abuse among Pacific Islanders represents only a partial picture of the scope and magnitude of problems presently confronting this population. Thus, to address AOD abuse, through reduction or prevention, problems of health, mental health, crime, and domestic violence must be considered (Mokuau, 1990, 1995b).

This chapter represents only a beginning. Ongoing efforts are required to address the comprehensive needs of Pacific Islanders. Of critical importance to all efforts are the recognition and inclusion of cultural strengths in the resolutions of problems and the participation of these indigenous peoples in determining the course of their lives.

Classroom Exercises

Exercise 1: Case Study

A Hawaiian family, Mr. and Mrs. K., and their three children, L., M., and N., moved a year ago from Hawaii to another state. The move was prompted by family economics—Mr. K. had discovered better employment and residential prospects in another state. Mr. K. secured full-time employment as an automobile mechanic, and Mrs. K. is employed as an administrative assistant at an elder care nursing home. The two oldest children attend high school, and the youngest child attends elementary school.

The K. family purchased a modest three-bedroom home in a rural community. The community is predominantly white, although many Asian Americans and some Hawaiians live there. It is a middle-class community with some expression of diversity. Supermarkets carry some ethnic foods (for example, chow mein noodles, soybean curd), and certain community events during the year reflect cultural themes.

All members of the K. family were born and raised in Hawaii. Although they all miss the extended family network and the unique multicultural climate available to them in Hawaii, they seem to be adjusting to their new community, with the exception of L., the oldest child. L. is a 17-year-old male with strong convictions about being Hawaiian. L. was a student in a well-known hula school (*halau*) and had participated in activities in the sovereign nation movement. His progress in his previous school had been satisfactory. In his new environment, however, L. has not developed extracurricular activities and is not doing well in school. On two occasions when he was referred by teachers to the school counselor for disruptive behavior, the counselor noted alcohol on his breath.

Use the following questions as a beginning point for developing a culturally competent approach for L. and his family:

1. Would you work with L. only, with L. and his parents, or with his entire family?

   [Directions for discussion: In a traditionally oriented Hawaiian family, there is a need to respect the importance of the collective and, in this case, the family. The worker needs to consider the Hawaiian worldview that problems and resolutions are intertwined with relationships; thus, working with the entire family is important.]

2. What factors that influenced L.'s drinking behaviors would you assist the family in identifying?

   [Directions for discussion: Several factors could have contributed to L.'s drinking behaviors, and the family should be encouraged to discuss these areas: (a) leaving extended family and friends; (b) interrupting L.'s identity development as a Hawaiian by severing his participation in cultural activities; and (c) L.'s feeling of exclusion from the family—as the others meet the challenge of adjusting to a new environment, he feels left behind.]

3. Identify one or two prevention strategies to reconnect L. with his Hawaiian culture.

   [Directions for discussion: It appears that L., if not his entire family, strongly identifies with Hawaiian culture. In addition to information on AOD abuse, prevention strategies might consider ways to strengthen his self-concept and cultural identity. The family needs to brainstorm ideas to achieve that. For example, the sovereign nation movement is not restricted to the Hawaiian islands. Hawaiians in the other 49 states correspond with groups in Hawaii or form their own groups; L. should be encouraged to participate. Contact with family and friends in Hawaii must be pursued.]

Exercise 2

Test Questions

1. Distinguish between the cultural content and the cultural conflict models for explaining AOD abuse among Pacific Islanders.
2. Identify two characteristics that reflect the heterogeneity of Pacific Islander peoples.
3. Discuss the importance of relationships as part of the worldview of Pacific Islanders.

4. Which Pacific Islander population is noted for the highest rates of smoking and drinking alcohol?
5. What is the alcoholic beverage of choice among Pacific Islanders?
6. How are the biopsychosocial, ecological systems, and public health models relevant to understanding and treating AOD abuse among Pacific Islanders?
7. Identify three factors pertinent to designing primary and secondary prevention strategies for Pacific Islanders.
8. What are some ways to increase the responsiveness of tertiary prevention strategies for Pacific Islanders?

Test Answers

1. The cultural content model suggests that AOD abuse behaviors might be influenced by the different cultural norms and patterns that govern a group. History indicates that Pacific Islander groups consumed addictive beverages before the arrival of Westerners, increasingly so afterward. Alcohol and other drugs have become incorporated into the culture.

   The cultural conflict model suggests that AOD abuse is influenced by circumstances of immigration history. Stressors associated with immigration—such as family conflicts, employment difficulties, and educational adjustment—contribute to AOD abuse.
2. Heterogeneity is expressed in several characteristics:
   (a) place of residence (United States or Pacific Islands)
   (b) U.S. status (citizens, nationals)
   (c) languages spoken at home (English, Samoan, Tongan)
   (d) poverty rates (highest for Samoans and Tongans).

   Further reading will indicate that heterogeneity is also expressed in religion, cultural events, cultural arts, the influence of different Western cultures, and so on.
3. Relationships are a fundamental part of Pacific Islanders' worldview. In general, people, animals, and plants all come from the same source and thus are all related. Problems and solutions, therefore, derive from relationships.
4. Hawaiians.
5. Beer.
6. They are relevant because of their emphasis on integrating the individual and the environment. Specifically, the models emphasize the

influence of the environment on the attitudes and behavioral patterns of AOD abuse among people, the importance of relationships in understanding the source of and resolution of AOD abuse, and working with the strengths of a population to reduce AOD abuse prevalence.

7. Service accessibility, culturally valid content, culturally valid delivery.

8. As with primary and secondary prevention strategies, the cultural responsiveness of tertiary strategies can be enhanced by incorporating cultural values and traditions into them. For example, given the emphasis on relationships, having respected elders influence and "teach" people with AOD abuse may be useful. In another example, explaining to users how alcohol and other drugs prevent a true expression of culture (by inhibiting a spiritual pathway) may also be useful.

Recommended Readings

Ahern, F. M. (1989). Alcohol use and abuse among four ethnic groups in Hawaii: Native Hawaiians, Japanese, Filipinos and whites. In D. Spiegler, D. Tate, S. Aitken, & C. Christian (Eds.), *Alcohol use among U.S. ethnic minorities* (pp. 315–328). Rockville, MD: National Institute on Alcohol Abuse and Alcoholism.

This paper reviews published and unpublished reports on alcoholism in Hawaii from 1964 to 1984. Results indicate that within the variability of alcohol prevalence estimates, the accumulated evidence suggests that Hawaiians and whites have higher rates than other populations.

Kame'eleihiwa, L. (1992). *Native land and foreign desires: Pehea LaE Pono Ai?* Honolulu: Bishop Museum Press.

This book emphasizes the importance of history in understanding and working with Hawaiian people. It is about the 1848 Mahele, the land reform that converted communal properties to private ownership. Unlike other books on Hawaiian history, the book provides an account of historical events from the Hawaiian perspective. Noteworthy in this text is the use of the concept of *pono* (equilibrium) to explain how land conversion reflects changes in Hawaiian worldviews.

Marshall, M. (1979). *Weekend warriors: Alcohol in a Micronesian culture.* Palo Alto, CA: Mayfield Publishing.

This book describes drinking behavior and the cultural attitudes and values that surround it for people on the Micronesian island of Truk. It documents how drinking can become incorporated and embedded into a cultural system and how it generates other social and psychological problems. The book suggests that treatment programs cannot be developed until an adequate understanding of the problem exists.

Mokuau, N. (1995). Exploring the relationship of substance abuse and HIV/AIDS among Pacific Islanders. In O. Amuleru-Marshall (Ed.), *Substance abuse treatment in the era of AIDS: Vol. II.* Rockville, MD: Center for Substance Abuse Prevention.

This chapter focuses on substance abuse and HIV/AIDS among Pacific Islander peoples. Although data are limited on this population, emerging evidence indicates that some groups of Pacific Islanders are vulnerable to high-risk factors such as homosexual sex, injecting drugs, transmitting sexual diseases, and teenage pregnancies. Prescriptions for culturally competent prevention strategies are described.

Yee, B. W. K. (in press). Life-span development of Asian and Pacific Islanders. In B. Yee, N. Mokuau, & S. Kim (Eds.), *Cultural competence for professionals working with Asian and Pacific American communities: Theoretical and practical considerations.* Rockville, MD: Center for Substance Abuse Prevention.

This chapter uses the life-span perspective as a framework for viewing key variables that are critical to the evaluation of AOD abuse prevention programs for Asian and Pacific Islander peoples. It concludes with an examination of innovative strategies for evaluating programs, a discussion of culturally responsive strategies, and ideas for improving multicultural competence in the future.

References

Ahern, F. M. (1989). Alcohol use and abuse among four ethnic groups in Hawaii: Native Hawaiians, Japanese, Filipinos and whites. In D. Spiegler, D. Tate, S. Aitken, & C. Christian (Eds.), *Alcohol use among U.S. ethnic minorities* (pp. 315–328). Rockville, MD: National Institute on Alcohol Abuse and Alcoholism.

Alama, K., & Whitney, S. (1990). *Ka Wai Kau Mai O Maleka: Water from America—The intoxication of the Hawaiian people.* Unpublished manuscript.

Alexander, P. (1990, June). The complex case for sovereignty and its application to native Hawaiians (p. 19). *Ka Wai Ola O Oha.*

Asian/Pacific Islander Data Consortium. (1992). *Asian and Pacific Islander American profile series 1A: Hawaii.* San Francisco: The Consortium.

Austin, G. A.; Prendergast, M. L.; & Lee, H. (1989). *Substance abuse among Asian-American youth.* Portland, OR: Western Center Drug-Free Schools and Communities.

Beckwith, M. W. (1981). *The Kumulipo: A Hawaiian creation chant.* Honolulu: University of Hawaii Press.

Blaisdell, K. (1992, November 22). Hawaiians: Right these wrongs. *Honolulu Star Bulletin and Advertiser,* p. B1.

Calkins, F. G. (1962). *My Samoan chief.* Honolulu: University of Hawaii Press.

Chandler, S. M., & Kassebaum, G. (1991). *Alcohol-drug use problems among Hawaii's adult prison inmates: A survey in eight correctional facilities—1990–91.* Honolulu: State of Hawaii Department of Public Safety.

Cole, S. (1992). Peer education programs. In *Proceedings: HIV/STD prevention, island style*. Honolulu: State of Hawaii Department of Health.

Crime Prevention Division. (1994). *Crime in Hawaii 1993*. Honolulu: State of Hawaii Department of the Attorney General.

Department of Health. (1994). *AIDS surveillance quarterly report*. Honolulu: State of Hawaii.

Department of Mental Health. (1981). *Samoans in America*. Oakland: State of California.

Drug Addiction Services of Hawaii. (undated). The Cornerstone: Intensive outpatient chemical dependency treatment program [Brochure]. Honolulu: DASH.

Dudley, M. K (1990). *Man, gods, and nature*. Honolulu: Na Kane O Ka Malo Press.

Dudley, M. K., & Agard, K. K. (1990). *A call for Hawaiian sovereignty*. Honolulu: Na Kane O Ka Malo Press.

Durning, A. T. (1993). In L. Brown (Ed.), *State of the world: 1993* (pp. 80–100). New York: Norton & Co.

Franco, R. (1985). *Samoan perceptions of work: Moving up and moving around*. Ann Arbor, MI: University Microfilms International, Dissertation Information Service.

Germain, C. B., & Gitterman, A. (1980). *The life model of social work practice*. New York: Columbia University Press.

Handy, E., Craighill, S., & Pukui, M. K. (1977). *The Polynesian family system in Ka'u Hawaii*. Rutland, VT: Charles E. Tuttle Company.

Health Promotion and Education Branch. (1992). *Hawaii's health risk behaviors 1990*. Honolulu: State of Hawaii Department of Health.

Hezel, F. X. (1985). Trukese suicide. In F. X. Hezel, D. H. Rubinstein, & G. M. White (Eds.), *Culture, youth and suicide in the Pacific: Papers from an East-West Center conference* (pp. 112–124). Honolulu: University of Hawaii Institute of Culture and Communication.

Ichiho, H., DeLisio, G., Sakai, T., & Moritsugu, S. (1990). The Hawaii State Department of Corrections substance abuse strategy. *Hawai'i Medical Journal, 49*, 200–204, 208.

Independence for Palau. (1994, July 21). *Honolulu Star Bulletin*, p. A16.

Johnson, H. W. (1990). *The social services: An introduction*. Itasca, IL: F.E. Peacock Publishers, Inc.

Ka Mana O Ka' Aina. (1990). What is sovereignty? A Bulletin of the Pro-Hawaiian Working Group. Honolulu: Author.

Kame'eleihiwa, L. (1992). *Native land and foreign desires: Pehea lae pono ai?* Honolulu: Bishop Museum Press.

Kamehameha Schools/Bishop Estate. (1990). *Drug-free TV music video*. Honolulu: Native Hawaiian Safe and Drug Free Schools and Communities Program, Kamehameha Schools/Bishop Estate (Videotape).

Kamehameha Schools/Bishop Estate. (1993a). *Let's start anew: E ho'omaka hou kakou*. Honolulu: Native Hawaiian Safe and Drug Free Schools and Communities Program, Kamehameha Schools/Bishop Estate (Videotape).

Kamehameha Schools/Bishop Estate. (1993b). *Nanakuli high.* Honolulu: Native Hawaiian Safe and Drug Free Schools and Communities Program, Kamehameha Schools/Bishop Estate (Videotape).

Kamehameha Schools/Bishop Estate. (1993c). *Native Hawaiian educational assessment: 1993.* Honolulu: Author.

Kamehameha Schools/Bishop Estate. (1994). *Alcohol perceptions of Native Hawaiians.* Honolulu: Native Hawaiian Safe and Drug Free Schools and Communities Program, Kamehameha Schools/Bishop Estate.

Kim, S., McLeod, J. H., & Shantzis, C. (1992). Cultural competence for evaluators working with Asian-American communities: Some practical considerations. In M. A. Orlandi, R. Weston, & L. G. Epstein (Eds.), *Cultural competence for evaluators: A guide for alcohol and other drug abuse prevention practitioners working with ethnic/racial communities* (pp. 203–260). Rockville, MD: Office for Substance Abuse Prevention.

Lindo, J. K. (1989). *Pacific Island resource.* California: Association of Asian/Pacific Community Health Organizations.

Marchand, L., Kolonel, L. N., & Yoshizawa, C. N. (1989). Alcohol consumption patterns among the five major ethnic groups in Hawai'i: Correlations with incidence of esophageal and oropharyngeal cancer. In D. Spiegler, D. Tate, S. Aitken, & C. Christian (Eds.), *Alcohol use among U.S. ethnic minorities* (pp. 355–371). Rockville, MD: National Institute on Alcohol Abuse and Alcoholism.

Marshall, M. (1979). *Weekend warriors: Alcohol in a Micronesian culture.* Palo Alto, CA: Mayfield Publishing Co.

McLaughlin, D. G., Raymond, J. S., Murakami, S. R., & Goebert, D. (1987). Drug use among Asian Americans in Hawaii. *Journal of Psychoactive Drugs, 19,* 85–94.

Mokuau, N. (1990). The impoverishment of native Hawaiians and the social work challenge. *Health and Social Work, 15,* 235–242.

Mokuau, N. (1995a). Exploring the relationship of substance abuse and HIV/AIDS among Pacific Islanders. In O. Amuleru-Marshall (Ed.), *Substance abuse treatment in the era of AIDS: Vol. II.* Rockville, MD: Center for Substance Abuse Prevention.

Mokuau, N. (1995b). Pacific Islanders. In R. L. Edwards (Ed.-in-Chief), *Encyclopedia of social work* (19th ed., Vol. 3, pp. 1795–1801). Washington, DC: National Association of Social Workers.

Mokuau, N. (in press). Substance abuse among Pacific Islanders: Cultural context and implications for prevention programs. In B. Yee, N. Mokuau, & S. Kim (Eds.), *Cultural competence for professionals working with Asian/Pacific American communities: Theoretical and practical considerations.* Rockville, MD: Center for Substance Abuse Prevention.

Mokuau, N., & Browne, C. (1994). Life themes of native Hawaiian female elders: Resources for cultural preservation. *Social Work, 39,* 43–49.

Mokuau, N., & Chang, N. (1991). Samoans. In N. Mokuau (Ed.), *Handbook of social services for Asian and Pacific Islanders* (pp. 155–169). Westport, CT: Greenwood Press.

Mokuau, N., & Kau, A. (1992). AIDS in the native Hawaiian community. *Journal of Multicultural Social Work, 2,* 43–49.

New York Times editors. (1994, July 21). Decline in illicit drug use stops. *Honolulu Star Bulletin,* pp. A1, A8.

Office for Substance Abuse Prevention. (1993). *Following specific guidelines will help you assess cultural competence in program design, application, and management.* Rockville, MD: U.S. Department of Health and Human Services.

Paglinawan, L. (1983). Ho'oponopono: A lecture. In E. V. Shook (Ed.), *Ho'oponopono* (pp. 4–20). Honolulu: University of Hawaii School of Social Work.

Papa Ola Lokahi. (1992). *Native Hawaiian health data book.* Honolulu: Author.

Pleadwell, B. A. (Ed.) (1992). Substance abuse report concerns health officials. *Hawaii Health Messenger* (p. 3). Honolulu: State of Hawaii Department of Health.

Polloi, A. H. (1985). Suicide in Palau. In F. X. Hezel, D. H. Rubinstein, & G. M. White (Eds.), *Culture, youth and suicide in the Pacific: Papers from an East-West Center conference* (pp. 125–138). Honolulu: University of Hawaii Institute of Culture and Communication.

Ramirez, T. (1993, January 13). Native Americans provide sovereign clues: They offer a model for a nation-within-a-nation. *Honolulu Star Bulletin,* pp. A1, A7.

Schwitters, S. Y., Johnson, R. C., Wilson, J. R., and McClearn, G. E. (1982). Ethnicity and alcohol. *Hawaii Medical Journal, 41,* 60–63.

U.S. Bureau of the Census. (1991a). *Census Bureau releases 1990 census population counts for American Samoa.* Washington, DC: U.S. Department of Commerce.

U.S. Bureau of the Census. (1991b). *Census Bureau releases 1990 census population counts for the Commonwealth of the Northern Mariana Islands.* Washington, DC: U.S. Department of Commerce.

U.S. Bureau of the Census. (1991c). *Census Bureau releases 1990 census population counts for Guam.* Washington, DC: U.S. Department of Commerce.

U.S. Bureau of the Census. (1991d). *Census Bureau releases 1990 census population counts for the Republic of Palau.* Washington, DC: U.S. Department of Commerce.

U.S. Bureau of the Census. (1991e). *Race and Hispanic origin.* Washington, DC: U.S. Department of Commerce.

U.S. Bureau of the Census. (1993). *We the American....Pacific Islanders.* Washington, DC: U.S. Department of Commerce.

U.S. Public Health Service. (1991). *Healthy people 2000: National health promotion and disease prevention objectives.* (DHHS Publication No. PHS 91-50212.) Washington, DC: U.S. Department of Health and Human Services.

University of Hawaii School of Public Health. (1991). *Pacific Island mental health and substance abuse: A supplement to a reevaluation of health services in U.S.-associated Pacific Island jurisdictions.* Honolulu: The University.

Untalan, F. F. (1991). Chamorros. In N. Mokuau (Ed.), *Handbook of social services for Asian and Pacific Islanders* (pp. 171–182). Westport, CT: Greenwood Press.

Whitney, S., & Hanipale, F. (1991). *Feeling strong: Themes in Samoan drinking and recovery.* Pago Pago, American Samoa: Unpublished manuscript.

Gay and Lesbian People 6

Karen A. Holmes
Robert H. Hodge

Alcohol and other drug (AOD) abuse among people who are gay or lesbian is a complex phenomenon. This chapter will provide the following: (1) an overview of the characteristics of gay and lesbian people placed within the historical context of oppression; (2) an overview of AOD abuse patterns among gay and lesbian people; (3) suggestions about AOD abuse prevention strategies; and (4) selected classroom exercises designed to increase understanding of the experience of gay and lesbian people.

The term "gay" has often been used in the literature to refer generally to both men and women. This chapter uses the terms *gay men* and *lesbian women* where *gay* and *lesbian* are adjectives rather than nouns. Being gay or lesbian is a part, but not the totality, of who individuals are. However, to be concise, the term *gay or lesbian people* is sometimes used. The authors acknowledge that there are no universally accepted terms to identify gay and lesbian people.

In a departure from NASW Press style, the term "lesbian women" is used in this chapter at the author's request. The term is used to signify the women's multidimensionality.

History and Characteristics of Gay and Lesbian People

Western thinking is predominantly dichotomous and linear. Something is either good or bad or strong or weak, as if a great yardstick in the mind contains only polar opposites. This is how sexual orientation has often been viewed, albeit erroneously: If one is not heterosexual, then one is homosexual. If one is not A, one must be Z. Sexual orientation, like most phenomena social workers address, is more appropriately viewed as a continuum. People who would define themselves as bisexual, for example, do not exist if sexual orientation is dichotomized into the polar opposites of gay and straight. Human sexual orientation may be viewed as more dynamic and fluid rather than exclusively static or fixed.

For the sake of clarity in this chapter, heterosexuals are defined as people whose affectional or erotic attractions are toward people of the other gender. People who are gay or lesbian have affectional or erotic attractions to people of the same gender (Gonsiorek & Weinrich, 1991). Sexual orientation may or may not shift over time. For most people, "human sexuality exists along a continuum as an interaction of biological, cultural, historical, and psychosocial influences" (Garnets & Kimmel, 1991, in Greene & Herek, 1994, p. 3). Sexual orientation—like all human sexuality—is more complex than what one "does in bed." Because of this complexity and for reasons discussed later, understanding of gay men and lesbian women is limited thus far.

Fasinger (1991) has referred to gay and lesbian people as the "hidden minority." That one line begins to capture the problems inherent in any discussion of homosexual people, gay people, gay men, or women who are lesbian. Any discussion of the characteristics of a group that remains at least to some degree invisible is fraught with generalization. Furthermore, gay and lesbian people are as different from one another as are "straight" men and women. Just as it is impossible to talk about the "straight community" as a singular, unidimensional entity, it is impossible to talk about the "gay community." Many gay communities exist. They may share some but not all characteristics with one another and with the larger society as well. Diversity according to race, ethnicity, cultural identity, age, class, politics, religion, and differential abilities also make generalizations problematic. Gay and lesbian people are no more clones of one another than heterosexual people are. With that caution, a brief historical overview of gay and lesbian people follows.

With the exception of the Bible, traditional history takes little note of the presence of gay men or lesbian women, although there can be little doubt that they have existed throughout society. Unfortunately, the Bible has been used as a tool to oppress gay and lesbian people.[1] The destruction of Sodom and Gomorrah (Genesis 19) is often used as evidence of God's condemnation of homosexual activity, yet biblical scholars have suggested that the "sin of Sodom" was the "violation of Hebraic standards of social justice, including the violation of the norm of hospitality to the stranger" (Nelson, 1985, p. 166). It is more than a little ironic that this story may be used to justify intolerance and inhospitality, if they are the qualities that the story condemns. Quotes from Leviticus are used to condemn homosexuality: "You shall not lie with a man as with a woman, it is an abomination" (18:22). Leviticus also says: "If a man commits adultery with the wife of his neighbor, both the adulterer and adultress shall be put to death" (20:10). If the first quote is to be accepted literally, it is interesting that the second is not (Griffin, Wirth, & Wirth, 1986). These and other passages from Leviticus were part of the holiness code of the Old Testament. Nelson (1985) notes that "selective literalists today frequently single out these [antihomosexual] texts, forget (or are unaware of) their historical context, and ignore the numerous other proscriptions in the same code, such as those against eating rare meat, having marital intercourse during menstruation, and wearing clothing of mixed fabrics" (p. 166).

Paul's words in Romans 1:26–27 are also often used to condemn homosexuality. Interestingly, in verses 29–31 Paul goes on to equally condemn various other things he considers improper, such as strife, deceit, gossip, arrogance, boasting, disobedience to parents—and most ironically, in the midst of this litany of condemnation, he condemns the sins of being unloving and unmerciful! In Romans 14:13 Paul exhorts, "Therefore let us not judge one another anymore." These seeming contradictions have not gone unnoticed and several noted biblical scholars including Boswell (1980), Scanzoni and Mollenkott (1978), and Spong (1991) have discussed translation errors from the ancient Greek and Hebrew that have been used to form the modern interpretations of these and other verses.

---

[1]The Bible actually says little about lesbian women, which is likely a reflection of the patriarchal societies of the times. However, even in recent literature and in the popular media, one typically hears about "gays" or specifically about gay men as if there are no gay, or lesbian, women. This may still reflect the essentially male-dominated structure of society in which women in general are less visible and women who are lesbian are almost invisible.

It is sad that selective or incomplete biblical interpretations have been used to justify prejudice, discrimination, and hatred toward gay and lesbian people. The New Testament contains no words from Jesus himself about homosexuality. However, many words came from Jesus about love and acceptance as well as about refraining from judging one another: "A new commandment I give to you, that you love one another, even as I have loved you, that you also love one another" (John 13:34). In verse 35, Jesus says, "By this all men will know that you are My disciples, if you have love for one another."

More recent historical works that address the extermination of millions of Jews in Nazi Germany seldom note the extermination of unknown numbers of gay and lesbian people. During the Nazi regime, from 1933 to 1945, Jews were identified by yellow stars, rounded up, forced into ghettos, and eventually put into labor camps until they died or were killed. People believed to be gay or lesbian were identified by pink triangles and they, along with the Jews, gypsies, Jehovah's Witnesses, and other so-called "undesirables" were also exterminated as part of the Nazi "final solution."

A contemporary history of gay and lesbian people has evolved since the late 1960s. On a fateful night in 1969, weary of continual harassment and police raids on gay bars in New York City, many gay men spontaneously took a stand. Subjected to yet another police raid, the gay bar patrons at Stonewall took to the streets in protest, an event that signaled the beginning of the gay liberation movement. Few history books include any mention of the Stonewall riot, and only a very few include an index citation for gay or lesbian rights. This contributes to and maintains the invisibility of gay and lesbian people. In the early 1970s, the women's liberation movement (also referred to as the "second wave of feminism," the "first wave" having culminated in the passage of the 19th Amendment to the U.S. Constitution) hit the United States. As part of the overall push for women's equality, many women who are lesbian saw an opportunity to gain their measure of equality. For many, the convergence of the two "liberation" movements heralded new opportunities to "come out" to parents, employers, or society at large and identify themselves as gay or lesbian people in search of equal treatment and full civil rights.

Changes were also occurring within the ranks of the mental health professions. Classical psychoanalytic theory, on which social workers had relied for many years, had originally viewed homosexuality as a pathological condition of arrested development. Up until the 1970s, homosexuality was classified as a mental disorder in the American Psychiatric Association's

(APA) *Diagnostic and Statistical Manual of Mental Disorders* (DSM) (APA, 1968). However, in 1973 the APA announced that homosexuality was no longer viewed as a mental disorder and the classification was removed from subsequent editions of the DSM. Various professional organizations, including the National Association of Social Workers (NASW) and the American Psychological Association, saw specialty groups develop from within their ranks. In 1977 NASW issued a public social policy statement on gay issues that affirmed "the right of all people to define and express their own sexuality," and vowed to "combat archaic laws . . . and other forms of discrimination which serve to impose something less than equal status upon the homosexually oriented members of the human family" (Hidalgo, Peterson, & Woodman, 1985, p. 1). In 1979 the NASW Task Force on Gay and Lesbian Issues was appointed, and in 1982 the National Committee on Lesbian and Gay Issues was created as a standing committee of NASW. The structure of the Council on Social Work Education (CSWE) includes a Commission on Gay/Lesbian Issues in social work education. The Association of Gay Psychologists was formed in 1973 and among its recommendations was the establishment of a task force on the status of lesbian psychologists. By 1980, this evolved into the Committee on Lesbian and Gay Concerns, and in 1984, Division 44, the Society for the Psychological Study of Lesbian and Gay Issues, was established formally within the APA (Greene & Herek, 1994).

Gay and lesbian people continue to advocate for equal civil rights in areas such as housing discrimination, child custody, and employment benefits (for example, coverage of life partners on health insurance plans). In reaction to this advocacy, a substantial backlash has occurred against gay and lesbian people, including what are now referred to as hate crimes. *Hate crimes* are acts of violence directed toward individuals specifically because they belong to a particular group, such as African Americans, Latinos, Jewish people, or gay and lesbian people. Motivated by prejudice and fear, hate crimes take many forms, including verbal assaults or threats, vandalism, arson, physical assault, and murder. The actual incidence of such hate crimes against gay and lesbian people is impossible to determine because many victims have not come out and are therefore unlikely to report their victimization unless forced to, as in the case of serious injury. In comparison with other stigmatized groups, hate crimes directed at gay men are especially prevalent and more violent (Herek, 1989).

Barnes and Ephross (1994) published results of a study on the impact of hate crimes, but with the exception of the introduction to their article, no mention is made of sexual orientation. Either no gay or lesbian people were included in their sample of 59 victims, or the interviewers did not explore sexual orientation. It would not be surprising if sexual orientation was ignored. In documenting hate crimes, the federal government has resisted including gay and lesbian people among those who are the targets of hate crimes. The Hate Crimes Statistics Act focuses on data collection about violence based on race and ethnicity, but not sexual orientation. Violence and the threat of violence have always been effective tools used for keeping women, people of color, and other minority groups "in their place." As with all hate crimes, acts of violence against gay and lesbian people serve to maintain the status quo by intimidating into silence those who attempt to deviate from the accepted social norm.

To avoid becoming the target of such hate crimes or simply to decrease the negative consequences of being gay or lesbian in a homophobic society, many gay and lesbian people "pass" as straight (that is, they allow others to assume that they are heterosexual). In the absence of visible differences, there is no way to identify someone as gay or lesbian, so "passing" is thought to be common. An obvious implication of this relative invisibility is that most of what is believed to be known about gay and lesbian people is actually applicable only to those who identify themselves as gay or lesbian. No one can say with certainty how many gay and lesbian people there are, although efforts have been made to determine this number. One of the first studies to address the question of numbers of gay or lesbian Americans was conducted by the Kinsey organization in the 1940s. Their data suggested that approximately 10 percent of the population was gay or lesbian, a figure that is still quoted with great frequency (Hidalgo et al., 1985). Other estimates have ranged from 4 percent to 17 percent (Gonsiorek & Weinrich, 1991), depending on which sampling methods and sources were used to gather the data.

Extent of the Problem

Determining the extent of AOD abuse problems among gay and lesbian people has been hampered by at least three factors. First, no one can say with certainty how many gay men and women who are lesbian there are. Second, alcoholism, other drug abuse, and addiction have only recently been highlighted as significant social problems, although they have wreaked havoc in society for years. Third, denial and secrecy commonly characterize alcoholism and other drug abuse in all populations. Therefore, we may or may not really know the incidence of AOD abuse in the general population, and we really do not know how many gay and lesbian people abuse alcohol or other drugs. Another factor that plays a role in this discussion is homophobia.

Homophobia is an intense, irrational fear of homosexuality and homosexuals (Weinberg, 1972). In contemporary usage, homophobia can refer to negative feelings toward gay and lesbian people. These feelings can include not only fear, but also disgust, contempt, and outright rage. It is no secret what this society thinks about homosexuals. "Homo," "queer," "faggot," and "dyke" are words that every child has likely heard, but they are most hurtful to those who—now or later—define themselves as gay or lesbian. In the United States, homophobia is focused more on gay men than lesbian women, which may be another reflection of a patriarchal social structure. Three of the four labels cited earlier are directed at men. This is likely another indication of the invisibility of lesbian women, although it may also suggest that women in general are just less important or threatening, even women who are lesbian.

Homophobia affects everyone in this society, but especially gay and lesbian people. It is impossible to be raised in a culture or society that condemns and rejects who you are without absorbing some degree of self-hatred. This self-hatred among gay and lesbian people is referred to as internalized homophobia. The manifestations of internalized homophobia are varied, but they include shame, which is highly related to AOD abuse.

Drug Abuse

Comparatively more research exists on the incidence of alcoholism among gay and lesbian people than on other types of drug abuse. Of the few studies to address the question of abuse of drugs other than alcohol among gay and lesbian people are those by Smith (1982) and by Ziebold and Mongeon (1982). They noted that among client populations it is unlikely that a separation exists between alcohol abuse and other drug abuse. This suggests, albeit tentatively, that where alcohol abuse is found, other forms of drug abuse are likely to be in evidence. This connection between alcohol use and other drug use may be particularly relevant to those who socialize in gay and lesbian bars.

A study of nitrite inhalant use (amyl nitrate) in the Baltimore–Washington, D.C., area (Lange et al., 1988) indicated that its use had remained fairly constant over a five-year period. However, among gay men in this study, levels of self-reported nitrite inhalant use had decreased. Sixty-nine percent of the gay men had tried nitrites at some time, but only 21 percent had used them in the previous six months. These findings are especially noteworthy because nitrite use has been linked with Kaposi's sarcoma, which is one of the manifestations of human immunodeficiency virus (HIV). This finding of decreased nitrite use by gay men may suggest that the massive HIV prevention efforts initiated by and directed to the gay male community early in the acquired immune deficiency syndrome (AIDS) epidemic have met with some success.

When AIDS initially garnered attention in the early 1980s, those afflicted first with the disease were primarily gay men, and many reported high and varied drug use patterns (Jaffe, Choi, Thomas, & Haverkos, 1983; Valdiseri, 1984). According to an observational study by Israelstam and Lambert (1984), marijuana and amyl nitrate were commonly used, and in the gay bar scene in many cities other recreational drugs were also prevalent. Noting that alcohol is the more pervasive problem, Israelstam (1986) also commented on the difficulties inherent in studying recreational use of drugs (other than alcohol). He states that use of illegal drugs is relatively more covert and that recreational drugs are numerous and taken for many reasons with varying consequences (p. 444). He suggests that interventions for alcohol abuse are also frequently applicable to the abuse of other drugs.

A considerable body of literature links drug abuse and risk-taking behavior in relation to HIV disease and AIDS among gay men. Leigh and Stall (1993) provide a comprehensive review of this literature, including three appendixes that categorize the focal variables of the various research studies. Their work was to "examine the evidence for and against the hypothesis that a causal relationship exists between alcohol and/or drug abuse and high-risk sexual behavior for HIV transmission" (p. 1035). Although they caution that methodological questions make conclusions difficult, they nonetheless state that "despite these difficulties, it is clear that there is a positive relationship between drug abuse and high-risk sex; what is less clear is the level at which this link exists" (p. 1038). In a related finding, the Centers for Disease Control and Prevention (CDC) reported in October 1993 that 11 percent of AIDS cases in the United States are linked to "men who have sex with men and inject drugs."

The CDC does not, however, maintain any HIV/AIDS statistics on the incidence of lesbian women who inject drugs. This fact and the literature discussed thus far illustrate again that women who are lesbian are virtually invisible. This lack of data makes it difficult to understand the issues that may be unique to this group. Some women who are lesbian may use or abuse drugs, but this use cannot be documented given the paucity of existing research literature. Commenting on the state of the knowledge about women who are lesbian and alcohol use, Anderson and Henderson (1985) state that "rigorous empirical research on any aspect of a drinking problem among lesbians appears to be nonexistent" (p. 518). As a result, we must advocate that research be developed and conducted to fill this void.

Alcohol Abuse

In general, it is believed that some 10 percent of the U.S. population suffers from alcohol dependency or alcoholism. The early research on alcohol abuse among gay and lesbian people suggests much higher percentages for these groups. A frequently cited study by Saghir and Robins (1973) indicated that 35 percent of women who are lesbian and 30 percent of gay men were dependent on alcohol, although the focus of their study was not on alcohol. Their sample consisted of 89 gay men and 57 lesbian women who were active in gay organizations in Chicago and San Francisco. In her proposal to the National Institute on Alcohol Abuse and Alcoholism, Fifield (1974) estimated that perhaps 100,000 (30.3 percent) of the women who are lesbian living in Los Angeles suffered from alcohol abuse. Fifield's pioneering research has been quoted heavily over the years, although her methodology was not rigorous. "She interviewed bartenders, soliciting their opinions on patterns of usage. . .and analyzed self-reports of alcohol users to determine high-risk and abusive drinking patterns. She also interviewed recovering gay alcoholics and users of gay social service organizations" (Saulnier, 1991, pp. 71–72). Lohrentz and colleagues (1978) indicated that among their sample of 145 gay men in two urban areas and two university towns in Kansas, 29 percent were abusing alcohol. Sandmaier (1979) published a 1972 study of alcohol use among African American women in a St. Louis housing project and found that 36 percent of the women who are lesbian in that study were either "heavy" or "problem" drinkers.

Overall estimates in the literature suggest that 18 percent to 38 percent of gay men and 27 percent to 35 percent of lesbians would meet diagnostic criteria of alcohol abuse or alcoholism (Hellman, Stanton, Lee, Tytun, & Vachon, 1989). However, the suggestion of a 30 percent to 35 percent alcoholism rate among gay and lesbian people is based on research only with those who have acknowledged their homosexuality. In addition, the small sample sizes and the lack of methodological rigor that characterize many noted studies tend to raise questions about the validity of these data. Anderson and Henderson (1985) have stated that "attempts to ascertain accurately the prevalence of either lesbianism or alcoholism continue to be severely handicapped by the large number of unacknowledged members of both populations. Denial, minimization, and secrecy about drinking behavior and problems of the alcoholic and her associates are a central feature of alcoholism" (p. 518).

Statistics that are applied to "the gay population" must be questioned. Were both gay and lesbian people included among the respondents? It is not uncommon to learn that findings based on research with gay men have been subsequently generalized to "the gay population" even though lesbian women were not included. (For years the Food and Drug Administration has conducted drug trials on male prison populations to decide whether a drug was safe to put on the market.) Did the sample include only "open" (self-identified) gay and lesbian people? If so, what—if anything—do we learn about those who choose to remain hidden? In the final analysis, we are left to speculate whether the incidence of AOD abuse is higher or lower in the total population of gay and lesbian people. Regardless of having imprecise data, AOD abuse problems are found among gay and lesbian people. Of particular importance to the present discussion is how AOD abuse among gay and lesbian people is identified, understood, and treated by social workers and how these AOD abuse problems can be prevented.

AOD Abuse Prevention among Gay and Lesbian People

Alcohol and other drug abuse prevention can be viewed on three levels: primary, secondary, and tertiary. The primary level is the ideal, whereby efforts are made to prevent people from ever starting to use AOD. The logic is that if one never uses drugs, one will never abuse, become dependent on, or addicted to them. Secondary prevention is directed at casual or experimental users to keep them from increasing their use or to assist them in becoming nonusers. This level can be viewed as early intervention or curbing an evolving problem before too much damage is done. Unfortunately, social workers are most often involved only on the tertiary level, the point at which intervention is needed because a full-blown problem of alcoholism, other drug abuse, or addiction exists. At each level, AOD abuse prevention strategies directed toward gay and lesbian people are complicated by the realities of being a gay or lesbian person in a homophobic society.

To create effective prevention strategies for gay and lesbian people, one must first understand the larger social context in general, then look at the more limited social contexts in which many gay and lesbian people are found. All people, regardless of sexual orientation, share certain basic needs. High in importance among these needs is a sense of connection with others. In sociological terms, Mead (1934) spoke of the importance of the "generalized other," wherein a person takes on the attitudes of the wider society regarding oneself. As we are seen and responded to by others in our environments, we become known to ourselves. When the environment is condemning, rejecting, and hostile, as it has historically been for gay and lesbian people, it is not surprising that alternative environments are created.

In major cities gay and lesbian communities exist, some of which are bounded by certain geographical areas and some that are less well defined but known from within. The center of these communities has often been the gay or lesbian bar. Within the confines of the bar, gay and lesbian people could be themselves and see themselves reflected in others like them. The bar is a critical point in considering the realities of oppressed groups. For example, whereas racial and ethnic minorities have historically found a safe haven within their respective communities, gay and lesbian people have not typically been accepted, even by their own families. It was necessary to create a sense of community. The bars provided this. Both in the past and now, the bars have often been the location for community-based fundraising activities, for political rallies, and for events of special significance to the community. When various facilities have refused to accommodate the needs of the gay or lesbian community, the community has turned to its own resources, including the bars. Unfortunately, bars also encourage alcohol consumption and, in all probability, the use of other drugs. What began as an attempt to meet a common human need for acceptance and social connection may well have had the unintended consequence of encouraging AOD abuse.

This has had especially dire consequences for gay men. For example, Linn and colleagues (1989) found that gay men who abuse alcohol are not likely to practice safe sex. This kind of risk-taking behavior contributes to the spread of sexually transmitted diseases, most notably HIV, which often results in AIDS. As noted earlier, Leigh and Stall (1993) concluded from their exhaustive examination of the literature that there is a positive relationship between drug abuse—including alcohol—and high-risk sex. However, a somewhat different conclusion was reached by Strumm and Hingson (1993), who noted conflicting findings relating alcohol use to risk-taking sexual behavior. Their review of the literature suggests that the correlation between alcohol use and sexual risk-taking is more closely associated with stability of relationships. They noted that adolescents in general and adults in unstable relationships showed a significantly higher incidence of sexual risk taking after using alcohol than did adults in stable relationships. They also note that this finding held for men regardless of their sexual orientation.

The unique role of the gay or lesbian bar must be understood and acknowledged in considering AOD abuse prevention. This is not to say that all people who are gay or lesbian spend time in bars, but many do, particularly those who are not otherwise openly gay or lesbian. For "closeted" gay and lesbian people, the gay bar may be the only place to find connection with others, a sense of belonging, and a feeling of being with others who are like them.

The role of the gay or lesbian bar is also important at the tertiary prevention level. A heterosexual person in treatment for alcoholism is told that his or her social habits will have to change: the after-work beer or happy hour is no longer possible, and long-time drinking buddies may have to be avoided. When the person in treatment is a gay man or lesbian woman whose only authentic (that is, openly gay or lesbian) social interaction has been at a gay bar, this approach essentially tells the client that he or she no longer has *any* social connection. Although the straight person can move to a new set of nondrinking friends whose hangout is not a bar, this may not be as easy for the gay or lesbian person to do. In both cases, but most especially for the gay or lesbian person, this is a huge loss that represents massive social and interpersonal isolation when vulnerability to relapse is especially acute.

Historically, particularly before the gay rights movement, this concern about the centrality of the bars would likely have been equally applicable to gay and lesbian people. More recently though, the lesbian bar has decreased in its importance as a social connection for lesbian women. Although it is unwise to try to generalize about gay or lesbian people, it may be safe to suggest that for many lesbian women who also identify themselves as feminists or political activists, there are now more opportunities for social interaction with like-minded, accepting people outside the bar scene. For some, particularly lesbian women in long-term committed relationships and those with children, the bar is simply not a significant part of their social lives. The demands of maintaining a relationship, nurturing children, and maintaining a job outside the home are likely to consume all available time and energy. However, the gay bars remain a focal part of the social scene for many single lesbian women and for many gay men. This suggests that different prevention strategies may be needed for each community.

The development of AOD abuse prevention strategies for any special population requires an understanding of that population. For all the reasons previously discussed in this chapter, this understanding has not been achieved for the population of gay and lesbian people. Some causal factors that underlie AOD abuse must be understood to plan effective prevention strategies. This, too, is lacking with respect to gay and lesbian people. The literature contains many articles that suggest causal factors, but none has been proven to hold much explanatory power over time. As Schilit and Gomberg (1991) have stated, "The literature is certainly not lacking in speculation about factors that may account for the high incidence of alcoholism among gay men and lesbians, but empirical research remains almost nonexistent" (p. 265). One segment of the literature has focused on psychoanalytic approaches. Small and Leach (1977) reviewed studies that focused on classic psychoanalytic theory in relation to establishing a causal link between homosexuality and alcoholism. They found none. Nardi (1982) has taken the position that psychoanalytic theory and research have suffered from using both sexist and oppressive concepts and methodologies, and this has resulted in false assumptions about the relationship between alcoholism and homosexuality.

A second focus in the literature has been social, cultural, and political explanations. Ziebold and Mongeon (1982) suggest that there is no evidence of a causal relationship between alcoholism and homosexuality. They also note that gay and lesbian people who abuse alcohol drink because they socialize primarily in gay bars and to "hide from the world and to escape from their feelings of being different" (p. 5). Also citing the role of the bars are Saghir and Robins (1973) and Diamond and Wilsnack (1978), who suggest that the gay and lesbian communities support drinking as a norm. Weathers (1976) also addresses this in relation to women who are lesbian: "While the relationship between drinking and socializing is a common thread running throughout American culture, the emphasis on this relationship is exacerbated in the lesbian subculture due to a lack of alcohol-free alternatives and limited social options . . . in the larger society" (p. 145). Many have identified homophobic attitudes emanating from the larger society as stressors that influence rates of AOD abuse in the gay and lesbian communities. Feelings of alienation and isolation (Burke, 1982) as well as self-hatred, fear of being different, and lowered self-esteem all result from society's homophobia. In Fifield's (1975) classic research on the gay community, she called alcohol abuse a manifestation of "oppression sickness," which affects groups with a history of systematic oppression. Nicoloff and Stiglitz (1987) discuss alcoholism and drug addiction among women who are lesbian as similar to alcoholism and drug addiction among other minority groups: "Addiction takes away the focus and power of minority individuals and communities, keeping them ineffective in the world. The job of the oppressor becomes easier when individuals engage in self-destructive behavior and render themselves powerless" (p. 286).

In the social work literature, Norton's (1978) dual perspective provides a useful framework for understanding the sociopolitical aspects of the experiences of gay and lesbian people. Although most often applied to racial or ethnic minorities, Norton stated that the dual perspective "can be applied to all people" (p. 82). The dual perspective comprises the sustaining system and the nurturing system. The sustaining system is the encompassing society in which instrumental needs such as goods, services, economic resources, and political power are addressed. It is from the larger sustaining system that status and power are conferred on specific individuals and groups. In general, the sustaining system does not value difference or diversity. The sustaining system might be called the white male system (Schaef, 1985) or, perhaps more accurately, the white heterosexual male system. According to Norton, the nurturing system exists within the sustaining system, and it comprises the immediate physical and social environment that provides a sense of culture, identity, and self.

Applying this framework to gay and lesbian people, both the sustaining and the nurturing systems have failed to provide adequately. The sustaining or dominant system's intolerance of difference has created an oppressive and hostile social environment for those who are different, that is, those who are not white, not heterosexual, not men. In addition, the vast majority of gay and lesbian people have been born into heterosexual families. As a focal part of the nurturing system, the family has often not only failed to nurture its gay sons and lesbian daughters, but also it has often rejected them. This is a different experience from that of racial and ethnic minorities who may have a nurturing system within the family. Without validation from either the sustaining system or the nurturing system, gay and lesbian people have had little choice but to create their own communities in an attempt to maintain a healthy sense of self.

Proposed Prevention Strategies

Social workers have a professional obligation to work toward the enhancement of human functioning at all levels of society. Whether we focus our efforts on micro or clinical practice or on organizing and advocating broader social change, we have many opportunities to enhance the social functioning of gay and lesbian people. Therefore, we have a role in preventing AOD abuse among special populations, including gay and lesbian people. We can inform ourselves of the issues unique to gay and lesbian people in general, especially as those issues relate to AOD abuse. We can advocate, both on a case-by-case basis (that is, on behalf of a particular client) and on a class basis (that is, on behalf of all gay and lesbian people), that gay and lesbian people be afforded the same quality service that would be afforded all clients.

The single most important strategy for preventing AOD abuse among gay and lesbian people is working toward the elimination of homophobia and heterosexism to facilitate the healthy integration of gay and lesbian people into the larger society.[2] Finnegan and Cook (1984) have alleged that "the central issues from which all other issues spring and without which gay and lesbian alcoholics would be just simple alcoholics is homophobia" (p. 86). They identify four institutional sources of homophobia: (1) certain organized religions, through established doctrine or selective interpretation of specific Biblical passages; (2) the medical and mental health profession, which pathologize homosexuality; (3) the law, either through repressive social controls or through "oppression by omission," whereby gay and lesbian people are excluded from equal protection; and (4) the media, through its frequently sensationalized treatment of gay or lesbian people and its failure to include any "healthy" images of people who are gay and lesbian.

Prevention strategies to eliminate religion-based homophobia include working within churches to educate people and to address questions of doctrine that have been used to support antigay positions. Media strategies with local newspapers include letters to the editor confronting antigay biases and editorial pieces providing alternative interpretations of Bible passages. Social work educators and practitioners who publish in professional journals can use examples of gay and lesbian people when referring to couples, families, adolescents, and older people, and, in all cases, when

---

[2]Heterosexism refers to the assumption that the world is "straight." The assumption of heterosexuality is reflected in religion, law, education, medicine, social services, and all social institutions.

discussing sexuality. Medical and mental health professionals, including social workers, must eliminate the assumption that all people are heterosexual through in-service training programs and revision of intake forms and hospital visitation policies, where "immediate family" is defined only as blood relatives or legal spouse.

One change in the law that could have the most far-reaching effects would be to legalize same-gender marriages. This legalization would provide societal sanction and support for gay and lesbian relationships, thereby helping to stabilize them. As discussed earlier, not being in a stable relationship correlates with higher rates of AOD abuse. If same-gender marriages were legal, partners would be seen as legitimate spouses in situations of illness, insurance benefits, parental and bereavement leave, company job transfers, work-related social functions, next-of-kin status, inheritance, property divisions, club memberships, and family discounts. Furthermore, where children may be involved, partners would be seen as legitimate stepparents at school functions and teacher conferences, as well as on medical and dental visits. Children of gay and lesbian couples would then have a way of referring to their other same-gender parent at school. Over time, in a country with mandatory schooling, everyone would become familiar with the idea of same-gender couples and parents as a normal variation in family structure. Other legal and legislative areas to address are providing legal protection from discrimination and challenging laws that criminalize sexual expression in same-gender couples.

Combating homophobia in the media can involve writing letters objecting to sponsors who deny endorsements and advertising contracts to openly gay or lesbian athletes. Positive letters can be sent to acknowledge sponsors who support programming that is sensitive to gay and lesbian people, showing gay and lesbian people along with their heterosexual counterparts. Letters of support can be written to major companies and organizations that lend their financial backing to gay and lesbian events (as VISA did in support of the Gay Games held in New York in 1994).

Unfortunately, even if external homophobia were eliminated magically at this moment, its legacy would remain. Homophobia is transmitted through social institutions, but it is internalized by individuals. Gay and lesbian people have, to varying degrees, internalized society's condemnation, denigration, and hatred. This internalization explains, in part, why so many remain "closeted," living lives that are inauthentic with respect to their true selves. The costs of such inauthenticity are incalculable, but they certainly include AOD abuse. A second prevention strategy would be to support people who are gay or lesbian to "come out" (both privately and perhaps publicly, if feasible) as a means of embracing their authentic selves. The decision to be completely open is not one to be taken lightly, however, because there are real potential negative consequences. Mothers who are lesbian often face a threat to child custody. Both gay and lesbian people face potential rejection from family and straight friends, as well as potential loss of jobs or promotions. The threat to profession and livelihood is perhaps greatest for gay or lesbian schoolteachers. These threats aside, the benefits of coming out in terms of one's mental health can be substantial.

Drawing on numerous sources, Finnegan and McNally (1987) have created a five-stage model of the coming-out process. What follows is an abbreviated overview of each stage. In stage 1, *pre-encounter,* individuals see themselves as part of the mainstream, essentially no different from others. If any inkling exists about one's sexual orientation being anything other than heterosexual, denial is used effectively to squelch it. If there are thoughts or feelings of possibly being "different," there may be some tentative exploration (for example, asking someone about "a friend" who has these "different" feelings), but this process is often shut down because it is too threatening. This is the stage of not knowing.

Stage 2, *encounter,* is characterized by the shattering—or at least chipping away—of denial. Something (or someone) happens, and the individual's sense of heterosexual identification is shaken. Some people in this stage describe themselves as bisexual, an identity that may be comparatively easier to accept. In this stage, some people will revert into powerful denial in an effort to cut off any further emotional discomfort. Others—surrounded by enough safety and support—will continue to question themselves, although perhaps tentatively.

For some, stage 3, *immersion and emersion,* is a time that is reminiscent of exciting childhood play or adolescence, with its excitement, peer bonding, and exploration. Having discovered other gay men or women who are lesbian in the world and having found that there is a community, the person who is coming out spends the first part of this stage—immersion—filtering everything through the newly acknowledged "gay lens." In the second part of this stage, emersion, an emergence of a more balanced awareness happens, that although "gay is good," not all of one's new experiences are positive.

Stage 4, *internalization,* results from acceptance of one's sexual orientation rather than simple acknowledgment or tolerance. This stage is often characterized by experiencing and working through feelings including guilt, rage, and grief. There may be guilt as a result of conflicts emanating from religious beliefs or guilt at not producing children in a family that values this greatly. There may be grief as a result of the losses that can occur, such as loss of family support or loss of heterosexual privilege and status. Accompanying these feelings may be rage at these same losses or rage directed at homophobia in general.

Finally, stage 5 is *synthesis and commitment*. The losses have been resolved, the guilt and grief have been worked through, and a positive sense of self has been achieved. In this stage, sexual orientation has been integrated as but one part of the total self, rather than as the totality of one's identity.

Conclusion

The contents of this chapter and the experiential exercises provide a foundation for understanding the unique issues of gay and lesbian people. This understanding will further efforts to prevent AOD abuse within this population. It is painfully evident, however, that heterosexist assumptions have colored most research efforts on AOD abuse. A relatively small body of research focuses on alcohol abuse among gay and lesbian people. Yet a much larger body of research on AOD abuse is generalized essentially to everyone, while failing to ask what percentage of the respondents might be gay or lesbian. It is time to develop research instruments that encourage gay and lesbian people to identify themselves, just as heterosexual respondents do with respect to marital status and family constellation. It is also time to focus on the unique issues of gay and lesbian people as they affect AOD abuse prevention. Progress has been made (although more should be done) toward developing strategies that are culturally sensitive and gender sensitive, yet the gay and lesbian communities have largely had to develop their own. It is time for gay and lesbian people to move from the margin of society toward the center, not displacing others, but taking their equal place among those entitled to quality social work services.

A recent editorial published in *Social Work* cites the poet Adrienne Rich, who artfully used the image of a mirror in which those omitted from consideration by society cannot see themselves reflected (Ewalt, 1994). Such is the experience of millions of gay and lesbian people, adolescents as well as adults—peering into the mirror and seeing only caricatures of oneself or gazing into the mirror only to see nothing. As Ewalt so poignantly says, "The well-being of this country may depend on whether people can look into the mirrors of one another and see themselves compassionately reflected" (p. 246).

Classroom Exercises

The following classroom exercises enhance understanding by providing experiential learning opportunities. The first is designed to increase overall sensitivity to the experience of gay and lesbian people. The second combines sensitivity to gay and lesbian people with content on alcoholism.

Trading Places

"Marooned" was developed for in-service training use by Diana Storms, a social worker in private practice.[3] It is a guided imagery fantasy that should be read aloud as students close their eyes and simply let themselves be led into the experience. The last part of the exercise includes many questions that are helpful in stimulating discussion about the potential effects—both personally and in the larger society—of being open rather than closeted, vocal rather than silent.

Instructions: Explain that the purpose of this guided imagery is to help students better understand the experience of gay and lesbian people. Note that it is designed for heterosexuals and that gay and lesbian people will not find anything new in it for them. Read the material aloud, then open up a discussion about the feelings evoked and the questions posed for consideration.

Marooned: Please, Scotty, Beam Me Up!

Imagine that you find yourself and your heterosexual spouse marooned permanently on a planet in a distant galaxy where homosexuality is the norm, and only 10 percent of the population are heterosexual. The 10 percent heterosexual minority, of which you are now a part, is considered by most of this planet's population to be strange and perverse, potential child molesters, a dangerous threat to the social order, psychologically disturbed, and morally corrupt and sinful. You know none of this to be true of you, yet this is how you are seen.

---

[3]"Marooned" has been reprinted here with permission of the author. Copies are available from Diana Storms, LMSW-ACP, 2472 Bolsover, Suite 250, Houston, TX 77005.

Heterosexual behavior is against the law on most of the planet. Most churches will not minister to heterosexuals nor, certainly, allow them positions of leadership. You will not be allowed any legally recognized marriage and will have no spousal rights. If your spouse is in intensive care, perhaps dying, you will not be considered a relative with any rights relative to your spouse. If your spouse's company is having a social function, you will not be invited. You will not be presumed to exist. Your spouse will be considered single. You may carefully edit what you say to coworkers about your weekends and evenings and, as a result, may be perceived as closed and unfriendly. You and your spouse will not be covered on the same medical insurance policy, so this insurance will cost you more. You will not be entitled to any family memberships or discount plans wherever these exist. You and your spouse cannot file joint tax returns, so you will pay higher taxes. If one of you has a job that transfers you, there will be no consideration about moving a spouse. You will be considered mobile because you have no marital or family obligations. If your spouse becomes seriously ill or incapacitated, you will be granted no extra time off to care for him or her. Should the disability be prolonged and your spouse unable to make decisions or sign papers, you will be unable to make any transactions on his or her behalf, unable to sell property to obtain needed money. If your spouse dies, no one will recognize, validate, or understand your grief.

If you have children, the courts of the land will consider you unfit to raise them. When your children go to school, they will never find any mention of or reference to their type of family. Only one of you will attend teacher conferences, open houses, and other school events, because there is no way to explain who the other parent is because no one is expected to have opposite-sex parents. One of you will be seen as a single parent; the other as a nonexistent parent, not seen at all. Your children will hear their peers call people they dislike by vile epithets that mean "heterosexual." When your children invite friends to your home, you and your spouse may make every effort to appear to be "just friends." Perhaps you will keep the doors closed and locked to the adult part of the house. If you have a small house, you will consider whether to sleep separately whenever your children's friends spend the night.

How would you choose to live in this society? Would you be careful and secretive about your life? Would you warn the children to keep your family life secret? Would you divorce your spouse and marry someone of the same sex to be more acceptable? Would you find others of this 10 percent minority and spend most of your time with them? Or would you stay isolated from other heterosexuals for fear of being labeled heterosexual yourself? How would you feel about your children turning out to be homosexual, like most of the rest of this world you find yourself in? Would you be afraid they would be ashamed of you or reject you? Would you be afraid their future homosexual spouses would reject you, perhaps limit your contact with your grandchildren? Would you therefore hide the nature of your relationship from your children? Would you scream bloody murder that the laws and attitudes are unfair? Would you protest that you are a perfectly reputable human being, not perverse, not sick, not sinful, not a bad influence on children and families? Or would you keep quiet, for fear of the repercussions to yourself, your spouse, your children, and your livelihood? Would you make yourself known, or would you hide? Which is better? How would you decide? What would you consider?

Dual Stigma

Finnegan and McNally (1987) have presented a two-part blackboard exercise that highlights what may be the central link between alcoholism and homosexuality: responses to stigmatized identity and oppression.

Instructions: Ask students to call out every negative myth and reaction they can think of to the word "drunks." Put the list on the board. The list is likely to be long and unpleasant, including terms such as weak, sick, mentally ill, immoral, sinful, promiscuous, disgusting, repulsive, dangerous, aggressive, threatening, irresponsible (p. 76). Ask which of these terms also apply to homosexual people. In all probability, many—if not all—the terms will be identified as having been used in relation to gay and lesbian people.

The second part of the exercise highlights the similarities between people with alcoholism and homosexual people's responses to stigma and oppression. Finnegan and McNally (1987) present this as an exercise used with alcohol service providers. However, as modified here, it does not necessarily require substantial knowledge of alcoholism to be effective.

Instructions: Put the following list on the board: denial, anxiety, fear, paranoia, hostility, anger, rage, arrogance, guilt, shame, self-pity, depression, fragmentation, isolation, alienation, confusion, low self-esteem. After describing these as typical psychological symptoms of alcoholism, illustrate how they are more fully understood as "responses to the oppressive, destructive effects of alcoholism" (Finnegan & McNally, p. 76). Then, drawing on the material in this chapter, review the list of "symptoms" again, this time noting how each is also a common response of gay and lesbian people to the destructive and oppressive effects of homophobia. Make certain it is clear that homosexuality is *not* a disease, "but homophobia is . . . a disease of society's attitudes, just like racism or sexism" (p. 76).

Recommended Readings

Gay and Lesbian People: General

Berzon, B. (Ed.). (1992). *Positively gay: New approaches to gay and lesbian Life.* Berkeley, CA: Celestial Arts.

Griffin, C. W., Wirth, M. J., & Wirth, A. G. (1986). *Beyond acceptance: Parents of lesbians and gays talk about their experiences.* Englewood Cliffs, NJ: Prentice-Hall.

Gay and Lesbian People: Alcohol and Other Substance Abuse

Berg, S., Finnegan, D., & McNally, E. (1987). *The NALGAP annotated bibliography: Resources on alcoholism, substance abuse, and lesbians/gay men.* Fort Wayne, IN: National Association of Lesbian and Gay Alcoholism Professionals.

References

American Psychiatric Association. (1968). *Diagnostic and statistical manual of mental disorders* (2nd edition). Washington, DC: Author.

Anderson, S. C., & Henderson, D. C. (1985). Working with lesbian alcoholics. *Social Work, 30,* 518–525.

Barnes, A., & Ephross, P. H. (1994). The impact of hate violence on victims: Emotional and behavioral responses to attacks. *Social Work, 39,* 247–251.

Boswell, J. (1980). *Christianity, social tolerance, and homosexuality.* Chicago: University of Chicago Press.

Burke, P. A. (1982, April). *Bar use and alienation in lesbian and heterosexual women alcoholics.* Paper presented at the Thirtieth National Alcoholism Forum, Washington, DC.

Centers for Disease Control and Prevention. (1993). *HIV/AIDS surveillance report,* 5–10. Atlanta: Author.

Diamond, D. L., & Wilsnack, S. C. (1978). Alcohol abuse among lesbians: A descriptive study. *Journal of Homosexuality, 4,* 123–142.

Ewalt, P. (1994). On not knowing. *Social Work, 39,* 245–246.

Fasinger, R. E. (1991). The hidden minority: Issues and challenges in working with lesbian women and gay men. *The Counseling Psychologist, 19,* 157–176.

Fifield, L. (1974). *Alcoholism and the gay community.* Washington, DC: National Institute on Alcohol Abuse and Alcoholism.

Fifield, L. (1975). *On my way to nowhere: Alienated, isolated drunk; gay alcohol abuse and an evaluation of alcoholism. An analysis of services for the Los Angeles gay community.* Los Angeles: Gay Community Services Center.

Finnegan, D. G., & Cook, D. (1984). Special issues affecting the treatment of gay male and lesbian alcoholics. *Alcohol Treatment Quarterly, 1*, 85–98.

Finnegan, D. G., & McNally, E. B. (1987). *Dual identities: Counseling chemically dependent gay men and lesbians.* Center City, MN: Hazelden Professional Publishing.

Garnets, L., & Kimmel, D. (1991). Lesbian and gay male dimensions in the psychological study of human diversity. In J. Goodchilds (Ed.), *Psychological perspectives on human diversity in America: Master lectures* (pp. 143–192). Washington, DC: American Psychological Association.

Gonsiorek, J. C., & Weinrich, J. (1991). The definition and scope of sexual orientation. In J. Gonsiorek & J. Weinrich (Eds.), *Homosexuality: Research implications for public policy* (pp. 1–12). Newbury Park, CA: Sage.

Greene, B., & Herek, G. M. (Eds.). (1994). *Lesbian and gay psychology: Theory, research, and clinical applications.* Thousand Oaks, CA: Sage.

Griffin, C. W., Wirth, M. J., & Wirth, A. G. (1986). *Beyond acceptance: Parents of lesbians and gays talk about their experiences.* Englewood Cliffs, NJ: Prentice-Hall.

Hellman, R. E., Stanton, M., Lee, J., Tytun, A., & Vachon, R. (1989). Treatment of homosexual alcoholics in government-funded agencies: Provider training and attitudes. *Hospital and Community Psychiatry, 40*, 1163–1168.

Herek, G. M. (1989). Hate crimes against lesbians and gay men. *American Psychologist, 44*, 948–955.

Hidalgo, H., Peterson, T. L., & Woodman, N. J. (Eds.). (1985). *Lesbian and gay issues: A resource manual for social workers.* Silver Spring, MD: National Association of Social Workers.

Israelstam, S. (1986). Alcohol and drug problems of gay males and lesbians: Therapy, counseling, and prevention issues. *Journal of Drug Issues, 16*, 443–461.

Israelstam, S., & Lambert, S. (1984). Gay bars. *Journal of Drug Issues, 14*, 637–653.

Jaffe, H. W., Choi, K., Thomas, P. A., & Haverkos, H. W. (1983). National case-control study of Kaposi's sarcoma and pneumocystis-carinii pneumonia in homosexual men. 1. Epidemiologic results. *Annals of Internal Medicine, 99*, 145–151.

Lange, W. R., Haertzen, C. A., Hickey, J. E., Snyder, F. R., Dax, E. M., & Jaffe, J. H. (1988). Nitrite inhalants: Patterns of abuse in Baltimore and Washington, DC. *American Journal of Drug Abuse, 14*, 29–39.

Leigh, B. C., & Stall, R. (1993). Substance abuse and risky sexual behavior for exposure to HIV. *American Psychologist, 48*, 1035–1045.

Linn, L., Spiegel, J. S., Mathews, W. C., Leake, B., Lien, R., & Brooks, S. (1989). Recent sexual behaviors among homosexual men seeking primary medical care. *Archives of Internal Medicine, 149*, 2685–2691.

Lohrentz, L. J., Connelly, J. C., Coyne, L., & Spare, K. E. (1978). Alcohol problems in several midwestern homosexual communities. *Journal of Studies on Alcohol, 39,* 1959–1963.

Mead, G. H. (1934). *Mind, self, and society.* Chicago: University of Chicago Press.

Nardi, P. M. (1982). Alcoholism and homosexuality: A theoretical perspective. In T. O. Ziebold & J. E. Mongeon (Eds.), *Alcoholism and homosexuality* (pp. 9–25). New York: Haworth Press.

Nelson, J. B. (1985). Religious and moral issues in working with homosexual clients. In J. C. Gonsiorek (Ed.), *A guide to psychotherapy with gay and lesbian clients* (pp. 163–175). New York: Harrington Park Press.

Nicoloff, L. K., & Stiglitz, E. A. (1987). Lesbian alcoholism: Etiology, treatment, and recovery. In The Boston Lesbian Psychologies Collective (Eds.), *Lesbian psychologies* (pp. 283–293). Chicago: University of Illinois Press.

Norton, D. G. (1978). *The dual perspective: Inclusion of ethnic minority content in the social work curriculum.* New York: Council on Social Work Education.

Saghir, M., & Robins, E. (1973). *Male and female homosexuality.* Baltimore: Williams & Wilkins.

Sandmaeir, M. (1979). *The invisible alcoholics: Women and alcohol abuse in America.* New York: McGraw-Hill.

Saulnier, C. (1991). Lesbian alcoholism: Development of a construct. *Affilia, 6,* 66–84.

Scanzoni, L., & Mollenkott, V. (1978). *Is the homosexual my neighbor? Another Christian view.* San Francisco: Harper & Row.

Schaef, A. W. (1985). *Women's reality: An emerging female system in a white male society.* San Francisco: Harper & Row.

Schilit, R., & Gomberg, E. (1991). *Drugs and behavior.* Thousand Oaks, CA: Sage.

Small, E. J., & Leach, B. (1977). Counseling homosexual alcoholics: Ten case histories. *Journal of Studies on Alcohol, 38,* 2077–2086.

Smith, T. M. (1982). Specific approaches and techniques in the treatment of gay male alcohol abusers. *Journal of Homosexuality, 7,* 53–69.

Spong, J. S. (1991). *Rescuing the Bible from fundamentalism.* San Francisco: Harper & Row.

Strumm, L., & Hingson, R. (1993). Alcohol use and risk for HIV infection. *Alcohol Health and Research World, 17,* 35–38.

Valdiseri, R. O. (1984). AIDS surveillance and health education: Use of previously described risk factors to identify high-risk homosexuals. *American Journal of Public Health, 74,* 259–260.

Weathers, B. (1976). *Alcoholism and the lesbian community.* Los Angeles: The Alcohol Center for Women.

Weinberg, G. (1972). *Society and the healthy homosexual.* New York: St. Martin's.

Ziebold, T. O., & Mongeon, J. E. (1982). *Alcoholism and homosexuality.* New York: Haworth Press.

Index

alcohol use by, 4–9
alcohol-related injury
  programs for, 17–18
characteristics of, 3
cigarette smoking by
  adolescent, 88
conclusions on alcohol abuse
  programs for, 22–23
fetal alcohol syndrome
  programs for, 18–19
overview of substance abuse by,
  1–2
primary prevention programs
  for, 14–17
school-based programs for, 14,
  15
tertiary prevention programs
  for, 9–12
Antabuse (disulfiram), 11
Anxiety drinking, 5–7
Asian Americans. *See also specific
  nationalities*
alcohol use by, 86–87, 89–96,
  98–109, 112, 113.
cigarette smoking by, 88, 90,
  92–96, 99–100, 102, 103
classroom exercise and, 121
cultural characteristics of,
  97–113
data on treatment of, 86
demographics of, 83, 96, 97
evaluation of outcome
  measures for, 119–121
historical background of,
  83–85
physiological flushing reaction
  among, 91
prevention strategies for, 109,
  114–119

substance abuse by, 85–89, 93, 94
substance abuse studies and,
  86–96, 110, 111
Asian Indians, 84–85. *See also*
  Asian Americans
Asian Pacific Alcohol Peer
  Consultation and Training
  Project, 115
Asian Youth Substance Abuse
  Project (AYSAP), 118

B

Bars, gay and lesbian, 163–165
Bicultural issues
  African Americans and, 70
  school-based programs and, 14
  staffing and, 47
Bilingual services, 47
Biochemical theories, 69
Booth, M. W., 47

C

Cambodian Americans. *See also*
  Asian Americans
alcohol use by, 103
cigarette smoking by, 103
community forums for, 114
Cancer, 135, 136
Casas, J. M., 45
Chamorros, 129, 131
Chinese Americans. *See also* Asian
  Americans
alcohol use by, 86–87, 89, 90,
  92, 99–100
cigarette smoking by, 99–100
community forums for, 109
substance abuse by adolescent,
  85, 92
treatment drug-addicted, 86

The Editors

Joanne Philleo, MSW, is training and development consultant, Bethesda, Maryland.

Frances Larry Brisbane, PhD, is dean, School of Social Welfare, State University of New York at Stony Brook.

Leonard G. Epstein, MSW, is senior coordinator for cultural competency initiatives, Health Resources and Services Administration, Bureau of Primary Health Care, Office of Minority and Women's Health, Bethesda, Maryland. He is the managing editor of the Cultural Competence Series.

The Contributors

Melvin Delgado, PhD, is professor of social work and chair of macro-practice sequence, School of Social Work, Boston University.

Muriel Gray, PhD, is associate professor, School of Social Work, University of Maryland at Baltimore.

Robert H. Hodge, LMSW-ACP, LCDC, was with Houston Therapies in Texas. He died in November 1995, after a year-long battle with brain cancer.

Karen A. Holmes, PhD, ACSW, LMSW-ACP, is dean and associate professor, Graduate School of Social Work, University of Houston.

Ford H. Kuramoto, DSW, is national director, National Asian Pacific American Families Against Substance Abuse.

Philip A. May, PhD, is director, Center on Alcoholism, Substance Abuse, and Addictions, University of New Mexico.

Noreen Mokuau, DSW, is professor, School of Social Work, University of Hawaii.

James R. Moran, PhD, is associate professor, Graduate School of Social Work, University of Denver.

Cover design by Naylor Design, Inc.

Interior design by Naylor Design, Inc.

Typeset by Patricia D. Wolf and Cynthia Hargett, Wolf Publications, Inc., in Janson and Univers

Printed by Graphic Communications, Inc., on 60# Windsor Offset